Possessed
By
Ghosts

Possessed
By
Ghosts

Exorcisms in the 21st Century

Wanda Pratnicka

CENTRUM Publishers

CENTRUM Publishers
P.O. Box 257
81-963 Gdynia
Poland

Translation: Jacek Laskowski, Great Britain

FIRST EDITION

Printed in Poland on acid-free paper

ISBN 83-918022-3-X

CONTENTS

Aknowledgments

Thank you, God, for creating me, leading me and inspiring me to write this book.

I would like to thank from the bottom of my heart my beloved Zbyszek Ploszczyca for the great amount of work he has put into the editing of this book. The initial text consisted of words, sentences, paragraphs, it was full of emotion and chaos. Zbyszek introduced order and harmony into it. Thank you Zbyszek.

I thank Ewa and Magdalena Olkulska very much for the designing the cover.

Also, from the bottom of my heart, I thank my children Tomek and Dorotka Kraska who were and are my best and dearest friends.

I acknowledge and send expressions of gratitude to all my patients who multiplied my knowledge and my experience.

FOREWORD

Why have such large numbers of souls not taken advantage of their right to pass through to the other side of death's curtain? Why are there so many souls suspended between heaven and earth? There are many reasons. The most important is the fact that they haven't come to believe in their own death. Little has changed for them. They overlooked the moment of death and judge that they live on. Often they are people closest to us. A father, mother, brother, sister, grandparent, friends, neighbors, colleagues from work or school. Will you meet with the same fate in the future?

When I ask a soul like that: "Do you know you're not alive?" the surprised answer I receive is: "No, I don't know." And straight after that: "What do you mean I'm not alive? What are you saying: of course I'm alive. How could you talk with me if I wasn't alive? After all, I can see, and hear, and feel!" So I repeat again: "No, you are not alive." Then they're angry and curse, others cry out: "God, why didn't anyone ever tell me life exists after death?" I hear this every day and that's why I decided to write this book.

I want to make you realize, dear reader, that what you know about death, how you think about it during your life and what you expect of it influences what happens to you after death, what fate awaits you. I wrote it for those who are brave and ready enough to prepare themselves and their nearest ones – now, when they have enough time – for a conscious and safe passage through to the other side of death's curtain. All of us, sooner or later, will have to confront this problem – in other words, to die. And we have certainly experienced situations where someone close to us departed. Souls which haven't passed through to the other side of death's curtain reckon they live on as before on earth, that nothing has changed for them. But does that mean that after their deaths nothing has changed for us who remain alive?

INTRODUCTION

For many years I really wanted to read the very book you're now holding in your hands, but I never found it. Unfortunately, till now no-one had written it. So I had to do it myself. I write it for you, dear reader, but also for myself. It contains answers to questions my patients asked me every day, but also answers to questions I asked myself. Although I've always had an intuitive knowledge of ghosts, I looked for confirmation of it in the external world.

Most often the mass media present cases of possession by ghosts in a sensationalist manner, in a very specific way. The TV viewer or newspaper reader will often learn that it's hopeless for the victim, that it's a question of fighting against windmills. Many will breathe a sigh of relief that they don't have to deal with it, but what about the people who have a serious problem with it? No-one will tell them what they should do in their predicament, or who to turn to. An awareness of the existence of ghosts and a knowledge about the subject in the way I present it is still very hazy in society at large.

I am addressing those who have tried everything, various ways and means to ease their distress and that of their near ones. Unfortunately, none of them worked or if they did then only for a snort while. I am also writing this for those who are only at the beginning, they sense that something that's not good is happening to them or their family, that there's something that's not the way it should be. I am writing for those, too, who are healthy and happy, there is nothing wrong with them or their near ones. They are the very people who could help in any number of tragedies which might be taking place within the neighbors' walls, help that unhappy family from the block, that hooligan, or that drug addict on the street where they live. Sometimes you can help with simple advice about what can be done in a given situation or just by informing people that something can be done. The people who read this book already know that something's possible; the others don't.

It's most often the case that the person who becomes possessed is not aware of their condition. By helping them we are, in fact, helping ourselves because we no longer have to listen to the arguments on the other side of the wall, or our neighborhood becomes more peaceful. In extreme cases we can prevent suicides, rapes or even crimes. It is, therefore, not just an individual, personal matter but one that most often affects us all.

What I'm involved in could be the panacea for very many misfortunes in our world. From all manner of psychiatric disturbances, deviations, dependencies including profound psychic illnesses requiring isolation through to chronic diseases reckoned to be incurable. The question of ghosts also applies to various everyday situations such as the wearing behavior of a member of the household, problems with school, with the family, problems at work or in business. They often lead to helplessness, solitude, isolation or to severe financial, health and social situations.

What is a frequent cause of a wide variety of diseases, misfortunes, major or minor disappointments? How can you deal with it, protect yourself, prevent it happening in the future? That's what this book is about.

It is also a reply to the endless questions posed by people who turn to me for help. They often believe that they're the only ones who have experienced these things, that they are exceptions. They ask themselves why they are have to suffer so. They think maybe they did something bad once and they're now being punished. Or maybe this is some curse at work, a spell or black magic?

What I want is that from now on they should not be alone during their fight with the unseen enemy. They're ashamed to tell anyone that they're experiencing something terrible, day and night, sometimes without a moment's rest. They don't understand what's happening to them nor why and added to that they have to conceal it from their closest friends at home and at work in case people start thinking they're mad, in case they lose their friends, their job, their spouse and sometimes everything together. The aim of this book is to make those affected, their families and their friends appreciate that what they're going through has already been experienced by a huge number of people and could also be experienced by you, dear reader, in the future. I want this book to reveal the reasons why things happen the way they do, so that what has been concealed, what has been forbidden for many centuries by the Church, can find an explanation.

Although nowadays the Church does acknowledge exorcisms, it does so only in extreme cases. It considers it to be the

activity of unclean powers or of Satan. Yet denying that something like ghosts doesn't exists because "it's safer not to know
about it", "it's nothing to do with me" or "it's just superstition,
who believes in garbage like that today?" doesn't alter the fact
that many people do suffer.

Till now these people couldn't find help because there
were very few people in the world who could help them. The
reason for this state of affairs is that these things weren't talked
about, pretending that the problem simply doesn't exist. A long
time ago giving this kind of help was threatened with burning at
the stake, hence knowing about ghosts wasn't popular. Now,
many centuries later, even those who are designated to help the
victims of ghosts don't know how to go about it. For more than
twenty years I have been a therapist, an exorcist. During this
time tens of thousands of people from Europe, America and the
furthest corners of the earth have approached me. So you see
this is a universal problem and not confined to just one person,
family or country.

To begin with I was surprised that I couldn't categorize
the people who turned to me into one social, intellectual, religious or cultural group. It doesn't matter what kind of family a
patient comes from - rich or poor. Their illiteracy or diploma
from the best college are of no significance. My patients come
from all walks of life - from housewives through workers, students all the way through to scientists, professors, lawyers and
politicians. I have been approached by priests and nuns though
one might think that they had professional guidance at home, at
hand. All my patients were similarly unhappy, lost, deprived of
hope for the future. They often emphasized that I was their last
straw, that they already tried literally everything. Doctors didn't
help, nor did medicines, nor did psychiatric and psychological
help. Equally futile had been the help of conventional and alter-

native medicine.

They have contacted me in various ways - by letter, telephone, personally. Often a family, friends, neighbors, workmates would come on someone's behalf.

Most frequently I help long-distance. It makes no difference to me if the patient is sitting opposite me or is at the other end of the world.

The aim of this book is to show where the source of many unexplained problems might be and maybe to help those who have lost all hope. I have a great amount of evidence to show that where other well-tried methods failed and where people spread their arms out helplessly, a miracle happened. A growth vanished, a disease regarded as incurable regressed, an addict of many years' standing became free of the habit, a business which was dying suddenly blossomed, etc. My help often did look like a miracle, but it was no miracle. Further on in the book I'll show through numerous examples that many people can find the solution to their problems themselves or by turning for advice to someone like me.

I help if it is necessary to do so, but most of all I show people how they can help themselves. I don't persuade them to turn their backs on doctors, medicines, hospitals, or to substitute them with something else. I merely point out that there are other reasons for our problems about which we didn't know till now. So it's worth taking it into account and to check, for example, before an operation whether that tumor is indeed caused by cancer or maybe by ghosts. But more about that later in the book.

Reading this book you'll come across repetitions which describe the same problem from different perspectives. Sometimes it's enough to read about something once and we instantly internalize it; other times we need to repeat something before we comprehend it. Repetitions are directed not only to your conscious and subconscious minds but also to the ghosts who are reading it along with the possessed person. I therefore ask you, dear reader, to be patient.

I also ask you to try and notice those passages which disturb you a lot, which make you angry or inspire some other strong feelings. This is a sign that precisely those bits of knowledge, those fragment of it, are what you need most.

ABOUT ME

I was born in Poland three years after the end of World War II. All around there was nothing but ruins, here and there were scattered houses in a very poor state threatening to collapse. It was rare for a family, even one with several children, to have a separate home. The children living in these hard conditions, spent most of their time on the street where they often came across a shell, a grenade, a bomb or a mine. Every day people used to tell of some unexploded bomb going off somewhere. The war continued to gather a plentiful harvest even though it had finished long ago. There were many wandering ghosts, from the war and those killed after its end. They were in a very pitiful state – their bodies torn and sometimes even in pieces. They were bemused, not knowing at all what had happened to them. They didn't know what they could do with themselves. The sight of such a ghost was terrifying for an adult, let alone a small girl like me.

I had parapsychic skills from birth. I could see and know what others couldn't see or know. That was not, however, a cause for joy. Whenever I tried to tell someone about it, they tried to prove to me that I was wrong, that I must have imagined it, that I was having hallucinations. This was done in various ways and if I was a bit too stubborn in support of my version, I was disciplined. After a while I stopped talking about it. I wanted very much to be like all the others. "There's probably something wrong with me," I used to think, "because if what I know or see were true then more people would see it."

There's a good example of this in the film "Sixth Sense". I suggest you see it, it's based on the truth.

Yet the more I wanted to hide something from the world, the more that something appeared of its own accord. For example: one November or December day, when I was about eight years old, I was traveling on the tram by myself. I was standing just behind the driver and I poked my head round the curtain. I adored traveling and watching like that. It was turning gray, the street was empty, not a single vehicle, the first snow was lightly falling. I was enchanted by the view, the tram was moving like on a carpet. Since they couldn't be seen I was wondering how the driver knew where the rails were . Suddenly I saw a woman standing on the track and I yelled with all my strength, almost into the driver's ear. The tram stopped almost instantly, the passengers fell on top of each other. I started to point to the track, that some woman there was trying to stop the tram. People rushed to the window, some of them got off, but the woman wasn't there. Maybe she withdrew quickly, I thought, but there should have been traces in the fresh snow. "But I saw her, she had a large scarf on her head, we nearly ran over her," I whimpered. I really got it then: I think everyone must have yelled at me – the driver, the conductor, the disgruntled passengers. For a lonely little girl it was quite a challenge. I cried, I was terrified, I couldn't understand: after all I saw her. Soon the tram moved off again and I saw the woman once more, glad that she was standing there but at the same time terrified that we were going to run her over. Unable to control myself I shouted out that there was a woman standing there. The driver slowed down but without stopping altogether. At that moment he noticed something lying on the track. He opened the door, ran out, followed by the conductor and other passengers, more and more rubbernecks. They ran up to the bundle lying on the track, picked it up – and inside it was a baby. It was cold but still alive. People wondered what would have happened if the tram had been traveling at its normal speed. A tragedy. "How could she see that?" they asked themselves. They carried me home on their shoulders, and that was my reward.

That is just one of the events I experienced. In some way I knew about things which were going to happen in advance – sometimes on the same day, and sometimes several days ahead. Several times I saved someone's life, or health, or possessions – a child's as well as an adult's.

When I told either of my parents about what I was feeling, or what I knew, they often didn't believe me. Even when my intimations proved real, my parents only looked at each other meaningfully but they didn't discuss the subject with me.

Since I couldn't find understanding in people close to me I wanted very much to find confirmation of my premonitions in other places. To begin with I thought the most appropriate place would be the church. I don't know to what extent that gave me inspiration but I ran there every spare moment I had. After a while I became almost a religious fanatic.

One day, at Easter, I categorically refused to go to church, which my parents found completely incomprehensible.

They knew I adored going there. I asked them, begged them, but all for nothing. My parents decided to break this whim of mine. I went, but all the way there I felt like someone going to the scaffold. During Mass I felt I could bear it no longer, and without saying anything to my parents I stood up and next moment I was running the length of the church. It was hard for them to tolerate that their daughter had affronted them in such a way.

We lived quite a distance from the church but I ran, or rather sped, towards the house not yet knowing why. I was completely breathless as I approached the house, when in the distance I noticed someone running down the banking straight in front of an oncoming car. I shout but the person doesn't hear, it's too late because the car hits him with all its force, runs over this person, and speeds even faster from the scene of the accident. I am alone, a ten year old little girl, a person run over by a car, and all around not a living soul. What can I do? How can I help? There is surely no help possible any longer; I run from door to door. At last an adult appeared and an ambulance was called.

It transpired that the victim of the accident was my favorite younger cousin. Virtually everything in him was broken, or rather crushed: his skull, jaw, arms, legs, spine. After several months' convalescence he was completely well again, so much so that there were no traces of the accident.

Writing about it now I wonder whether, if my parents had let me alone then and if I had run over to him in time, that accident could have been avoided. Or maybe my part was only to bring help. Even after this occurrence my parents did not change their attitude toward me.

And so I shut myself off within myself more and more, and there were more and more things I had to keep secret. In time I taught myself to push them away immediately, to forget about my flashes of enlightenment. Today I know that it's a gift but I only discovered that when I became an adult. To this day I regret that my parents didn't understand me, that I had to struggle with my world on my own. Today I am able to understand them. They simply wanted to shield me from everything, they didn't comprehend what was happening to me at those moments. In their view it was bad for me so, from their perspective, they chose the lesser evil. They regarded my abilities as eccentricities and they hoped very much that I would grow out of them.

I had a very low, in fact a non-existent, opinion of my own worth. It was lucky that, for all my strangeness, I was well-liked. I felt needed everywhere except at home. Subconsciously and perversely I kept telling myself that since my own mother didn't love me then the whole world could go right ahead and not love me. When I started my own family I felt the consequences of this kind of thinking very painfully. I suffered because I regarded myself as a victim but now I know that my surroundings were only showing what was inside me. The torturer exists only as long as there is a conscious victim. When the victim says: "Enough", the torturer changes into a lamb. It's a bit like we force the torturer to be cruel to us.

As soon as I understood that it was flawed thinking that caused my problems, I started battling against myself. Suddenly I saw that the world changed along with me like it was touched by a magician's wand. It was like I was newly-born. I was rejuvenated, better-looking, healthier, full of energy and zeal. I also saw that the many troubles I experienced in my life, instead of breaking me had made me stronger, even hardened me.

All my life people of various ages have looked to me for help, comfort, understanding and advice. I never sought them out, it was they who in some way found me by themselves. I didn't realize it at the time but in fact it was I who needed help myself, and yet there were all these people asking me to help them. That's not to say that my help in this time was ineffective: it was effective, very much so.

Whenever we are watchful we notice that the problem which we are working through with our patient is also our problem. Then we can bake two loaves in the same oven – help our patient and at the same time help ourselves.

After I worked through what I needed to work through at that time, my help took on a completely fresh dimension. More and more really   severe cases came to me, people who were sick and adrift, who had lost all hope for a better tomorrow. At the same time there were more and more successes, recoveries bordering on the miraculous. There were cases of people coming to me a couple of days before a very serious operation, or shortly before their deaths. They often said: "Mrs. Pratnicka, you are our last hope." I would ask: "Why so late?" I asked myself why so many people looked for help only when they were in great pain or when they were struck down by a serious illness. It transpired that lack of time was an important factor on the road to recovery. For then it's impossible to leave anything till tomorrow or even for another hour, the risk is too great for that. I, too, was greatly motivated by this: at such a time I would know precisely what the illness was and what its cause was.

There came a moment when I taught myself to see a sickness and its cause long before the appearance of any physical symptoms. This wasn't a case of a person standing in front of me while I photographed him like on an X-ray machine, though that, too, has happened to me. It came rather in the form of comprehension, and sometimes in pictorial form. It sometimes also happened that it was only after a patient's visit that I discovered the cause of the disease.

I would be very eager to take the cause off the person, to cure them. I didn't ask anyone for permission, I didn't even say anything to the person concerned, I simply helped them and that was that. At that time I used to think that the sickness had simply happened to them, that harm was being done to them and therefore they needed to be helped. My payment was the joy I felt at being able to help and that the person was better. It was only after some time that I understood that these people had become ill because their emotional problem had been waiting too long for a solution, that they were sick because they didn't want to face the problem. I grasped that instead of helping them I was, in some way, harming them since they weren't taking advantage of the opportunity their sickness was giving them.

From that time on I help only when the patient decides to help himself. Sometimes, however, there are exceptions and the following is probably one of those.

I had a couple of student friends, Kate and Barry, to whom I owed a great deal. She used to look after her grandmother, and he helped her with that. The grandmother had lost all memory and lived like a vegetable, knowing nothing about herself; this caused many difficulties. In addition, she often simply vanished from home. Even shutting her up in her room couldn't stop it. Somehow, only she knew how, she could undo the locks, leave the house and then the great search would begin.

One day, during an exam, Kate fell over in a very unlucky way and fell through a glass door. Huge chunks of glass pierced her body like knives. She was badly wounded. She was taken to hospital and for several hours she was sewn up, the doctors fighting for her life. It transpired that the reason for fainting was that she was in the early stages of pregnancy. Complications followed and she miscarried.

Throughout this tragedy, nobody remembered about the

grandmother. Barry found her at home, lying on the floor. She had fallen and broken a hip and both legs. The breaks were such that the bones were sticking out. Barry told me that no hospital would help her. She was just lying at home, left to her fate.

I had promised myself earlier that I wouldn't help just by myself and I wanted to keep my word. It wasn't easy in this case because this grandmother's tragedy kept returning to my thoughts like a boomerang. "Why only the grandmother?" I kept wondering. "After all, I don't even know her. Why not Kate, or both of them together, after all they've both been suffering." I realized that Kate was in good hands. Her family are all renowned doctors, plastic surgeons. Why did no-one want to help the grandmother since there were so many doctors in the family? After two days of torment I asked God what I should do.

I received permission to help and I prepared for a long-distance operation. I had done that many times before. Like a skilled surgeon I mended the bones, and healed the skin. When I saw that both legs and the hip were functioning, I decided to finish the operation. I received another instruction: to take care of the circulatory system, the veins and the arteries. I cleaned out the deposits, repaired what needed to be done and, satisfied with the result, I fell asleep. When I awoke no thought of the grandmother returned.

Two days later Barry rushed round and hadn't even come through the door before he was shouting: "What have you done? The whole hospital is in uproar!" This terrified me: I felt at fault not only in this instance but in all the previous ones, too. "I must have interfered with some higher order of the Divine Plan, it's true that the road to hell is paved with good intentions," I thought. But I was a little surprised since this time I hadn't done anything on my own but had asked for God's permission. I cried and cried, and Barry could do nothing to calm me down. Finally, it dawned on me what had really happened.

The last information I had was that the grandmother had had an accident and no hospital would take her onto their wards (now I know that God wanted me to think that because otherwise I wouldn't have undertaken an operation which taught me a great deal. It was a milestone on my path). It turned out that meanwhile the grandmother had been taken into a hospital, an operation had been carried out, and a hip replacement had been performed. So the two operations had overlapped in time. The effect was that not only did the grandmother stand on her own two feet straight away but she was chasing round the entire hospital waving the crutches which the nurses were stubbornly forcing under her arms and which she was refusing to use. She claimed she didn't need them. Nobody could restrain her.

There was a great commotion, doctors from all the wards came to see, the occurrence caused something of a sensation. Never before had a patient walked the day after such an operation. And what's more, there was no trace of the operation on her. According to their knowledge, after such an operation patients usually don't walk for months, or years, and in the case of elderly patients, even for the rest of their lives. The grandmother was given more and more tests to try to discover the causes of this extraordinary phenomenon. Doctors from all over Poland came, but the matter was kept a closely guarded secret because they could give no explanation. The doctors were slightly mistaken: the result of the operation could not, in this case, be the same as usual.

I begged Barry not to mention this occurrence to anyone, not even to Kate. I threatened I would deny everything. I thought that this subject would never come back to me, but it did, many times.

Kate often showed me her scars which looked like twisted ropes all over her body. Unaware of the fact that I knew it, she complained, her voice filled with reproach, that her grandmother had also been operated on but she hadn't even the smallest trace on her. Her body was now as smooth as a baby's bottom. She also claimed her grandmother had had nothing but benefits from it all: as soon as she was released from hospital her memory returned. Now it's she who looks after the house. She cleans, cooks, and reads books all day long, something she'd been unable to do at all before.

I was very pleased that I'd managed to restore her mind so that it could work properly. Her legs and her hip would have been mended by the doctors, though it would have taken longer. I believe that the grandmother was given a chance by God and, most importantly, she had used it. Unfortunately, not everyone wants to do that which examples in the rest of the book will confirm.

A few years later, at a celebration of a magnificent and famous healer's fifty years' work, many healers from all round the world were gathered. Towards the end of the celebrations we were joined by a man on crutches whom I didn't know. It turned out he was a healer with considerable achievements. The distinguished guest of honor asked him why he was in plaster. He told her that his leg hadn't healed for two years now. The guest of honor turned to me, through an interpreter, and said: "Please tell our colleague here about your case with the grandmother. How much time do bones need to heal even with the worst fractures?" I stood, flummoxed, because I didn't know which grandmother she was talking about. "That's what happens," she continued, "when we don't want to believe nor see the hand of God in things we do." And she started to tell him what I had done those years ago for Kate's grandmother.

I wondered how she knew all about it when even I couldn't remember the story. It was like she heard my question became she replied: "There is a place where all deeds are written down, both the praiseworthy ones and the ones we'd rather forget about. And there are people like Wanda here who want to forget about the good deeds."

This point of this story is to show that the impossible is possible. For you see, the next day I saw that man walking without crutches.

In everything I do I am led by God, a Higher Power, and Intelligence. That tells me what I should do at any given moment. That's why I don't wonder how I should help. It happens of its own accord. I know what to do, what questions to ask, what answer to give. I know much more about a patient than he knows about himself. I also have thousands of proofs to show that I do it well. I always wonder if the therapy I use doesn't disturb the Higher Order. That's why I'm always searching. I studied psychology, parapsychology, astrophysics, cybernetics and everything that might help me understand the meaning of everything I see and do.

I know that every human being is unique and that every one of us helps himself and others in their own way, known only to them.

I am often asked how I happened to concentrate on healing and why ghosts in particular. Many things came together to determine that. As long as I can remember people have turned to me with their problems. These were often things which had never been revealed, which the people themselves weren't conscious of. These people were sometimes people I knew, but most often they would be people I'd met by chance somewhere. I never questioned them about anything. They started talking of themselves about something which lay close to their hearts. A moment would come when I suddenly found the solution to their problem. Then someone else would come along and say: "You helped a friend of mine. Maybe you'll be able to help me." And in this way more and more people came to me.

After a time I noticed that after the resolution of some deep-seated mental problem, an illness which had been troubling the patient a long time would also recede. When it happened for the first time I was very surprised but I didn't connect the two facts together. Now I have several thousand such cases and I know for sure that sickness is closely tied to our fears, traumas, repressed emotions – anger, hatred etc. It also has other and very serious causes about which I'll write later.

The symptoms of an illness can be cured without delving more deeply into the causes that brought it on. That will however be only a superficial help and after a certain period the illness will return. It's like a dentist putting a filling on top of a tooth without cleaning it out first. Treatment can be carried out using conventional medicine, medication, operations, as well as alternative methods using natural ingredients. The latter way doesn't always require the patient to be present. The treatment can be administered just as well at long-distance as it can by being there. I have often been asked for that kind of help.

Once I really wanted to help a woman who lived in my neighborhood and who was suffering from profound and chronic depression. Her husband was working and the two tiny children looked after themselves since their mother was virtually unable to function, whether she was taking psychotropic drugs or not. There was a curious chill and dirtiness in their home even though it was kept more or less tidy. Then I saw something on her. It brought to mind a vortex of a gray mass enveloping her completely. Not knowing then what I know now, I tried to take it off her at a distance. It worked, and she felt like she'd been freed from tight knots. She suddenly started to live a normal life. After a short while, the "something" returned. I noticed that this shell round her was a living thing which was sucking the vital energy from the patient. Each time this "something" returned slightly smaller until it was completely cleansed. I didn't know then that this gray mass were ghosts. Maybe because it was a great number of them packed together in this vortex. Although I'd had contact with ghosts since childhood they'd always been there singly and never attached to the people possessed by them. Till then I'd assumed they simply wander around without doing any harm to anyone. That they can at most frighten someone when they show themselves. Nor did I know the reason why they are found here. That's how my adventure with ghosts began.

To begin with I only pulled them off patients without knowing what to do with them next. Later I taught myself to make direct contact with them. I discovered why they remain, what they expect, what they fear, and how to help them.

Today, I am a therapist for ghosts as well as people. Both the one and the other need the same care, understanding and the same doses of love.

At the very beginning I called myself an exorcist. I did so slightly out of contrariness and slightly because I wanted the object of my work to be recognized. The Church, however, would not have called me an exorcist since I didn't chase ghosts out of people, I didn't lay hands during the sacrament of exorcism the way that priests do. A church exorcist will perform exorcism by saying: "Leave, unclean ghost, in the name of Jesus Christ". I often wondered where this "unclean" ghost was supposed to go since it was damned and banished. Often, after such an event, the ghost will be guided by spite, a desire to cause harm just for its own sake. Thus the expelled ghost only sometimes really does leave. Most often, though, it continues to circle and, in time, returns. Sometimes it picks another human being to feed on.

I am a lay person and I help people and ghosts in my own way. For one and the other I am a therapist of souls. I help people to free themselves from ghosts, but also I help many ghosts to free themselves from people.

I help pass through to the other side (to so-called "Heaven", to the other side of death's curtain) those ghosts which are ready to now but were undecided immediately after death. I help those ghosts which don't know what to do with themselves to reach a decision. Sometimes it needs a long time to heal the wound which caused the ghost to decide to stay behind. When they comprehend it and forgive themselves and others, they leave unbidden.

One time I was conducting an exorcism and I must have been too serious because I suddenly heard the voice of my Spiritual Guides: "Exorcisms don't have to be so very serious". It was said in such a way that I burst out laughing. At that time I didn't yet know what it was really all about. Only later did I understand that going through into the next world is the greatest, the most beautiful celebration of reconciliation with God for all ghosts, and that an exorcism is a very important and joyful event.

Ghosts can sometimes be the reason why people are seriously ill and even die. It can also be the cause that things don't go right, that people argue and even kill one another because of ghosts.

Every case of possession has provided me with more knowledge. It has come from my patients and from the ghosts. I have seen what happens to patients when there is a ghost residing within them, and the change when that ghost leaves. This is most noticeable when the ghost returns for a time.

When a ghost resides within a person there are many consequences. Sometimes it may be a change only in the mental state, another time it may be in someone's state of health. It can be easily observed in problems with growths brought about by ghosts. When the ghost is within someone, the growth appears: and when it's not, the growth disappears. A truly spectacular phenomenon is when there is a complete change in the appearance of someone's face.

I have been provided with a lot of knowledge by ghosts which have remained on this side. Most frequently they carry over into their new existence the problems they had in their lives before death. Problems they couldn't deal with, or even ones they weren't aware of. Whatever they may be I help to resolve them sufficiently for the ghosts to go peacefully over to the other side. It comes easily to me because I have a lot of experience of solving the problems of living human beings.

When I started to escort the ghosts off I noticed that people became healthy, they dealt with their problems better, harmony and love started to reign in their families. So it is that I help the souls of the living as well as the dead.

THE ILLUSION OF DEATH

We fear many things in life: pain, old age, poverty, loneliness, the unknown, disasters, women fear birth, students fear
examinations, but for most people the greatest is probably the
fear of dying.

Death seems to be the most terrifying and is undoubtedly
the most unavoidable thing in the world. Why do we fear it so
much? Why is it such a painful event? Because we don't want
to leave this world. We cling on to our near ones: our husbands,
wives, parents, children, friends, lovers etc.

Those who continue in this life behave similarly: they are
afraid of being left alone and don't want to release the dying, departing soul. They both do so in the name of love but it has
nothing to do with love. It's not love that makes for this kind of
thinking but a crippling fear of what will become of us and how
we will be able to cope.

Others can be held back by their attachment to material

things, or careers, or power. Others again by their dependence on alcohol, drugs, food, sex, gambling.

We are also very afraid of death because we don't know what will happen to us, where we will go after leaving this world. We are not prepared for it. From our births on we are taught many things, women are even taught how to give birth, but no-one teaches us how to die, what death is and what happens to us after death. If we had learned about it during our lives we would recognize that dying is a very joyful, happy moment which we shouldn't be afraid of, which indeed we should look forward to cheerfully. Death and birth are one and the same. To be born on the Earth we have to die there on the other side. And the reverse is true: to be born there we have to die here but all that means is that we change one form of existence for another.

We all belong to God and we came to   the Earth not as a punishment, as some people and religions claim, but to learn in the earthly school. When we come to the world full of trust our lives run their course in harmony and love. If we come with rancor, fear and distrust then everything is filled with that whatever we do. We reproach God with having abandoned us and left us on our own, but this is not true at all. It is our erroneous thinking that causes us to live with bitterness, frustration, fear and dissatisfaction. This happens right till the moment we understand the basis of our erroneous reasoning. This can last one life or several.

When we understand that in fact God never did abandon us our lives start to change diametrically. We no longer need to cling on to the things we know and keep on fighting because we know that there is a profusion of everything, that God is abundance in every existence. After such a fulfilled life we return joyfully into the arms of our Father and death is nothing other than a return home. There is a good story on this subject.

A certain man found himself in heaven and together with God is watching his past life like on a three-dimensional film. After the screening he says to God: "Father, when things were going well for me on earth, I saw two sets of footprints on the path of my life. Yours and mine. But when things were going badly, I saw only one set of footprints. Why did you abandon me then, Father?" "Beloved son," is God's reply, "those were the moments when I was carrying you."

Our life on Earth can be compared to a huge school. When we come to this world we are like children who leave their parents to go to school, and our death is nothing other than our return home from school. When a child leaves home to go to school with joy, expecting to learn something, to meet friends with whom he'll have an adventure, his life's lessons are very harmonious. The child knows and trusts that everything will be fine regardless of the road it chooses since any road will lead to its aim. The child trusts that it has a sufficient amount of time and every opportunity. It also trusts that the school is safe and nothing bad can happen in it. It doesn't have to be fearful, to hurry, to take life too seriously because the fact is that every-thing is learning. The child knows that after lessons, waiting for it at home, are its beloved parents.

When a child leaves home for school with fear and dis-trust then it is in no state to learn much because it does very lit-tle other than wait till it gets home. It reproaches the parents for sending it to school. Its life is also filled with rebellion and en-mity. In everything it does it feels itself to be the victim of a cruel fate who has no influence on its own life into which it has been maneuvered. It has no desire either for learning or for life. The majority of us have this attitude to life. We are mad at God for sending us down here. We treat learning as a punishment instead of an opportunity for development. Remaining in a state of resistance we can learn very little and so we repeat the same lessons many times, rather like a student who has to repeat a class over and over.

The longer we go to school, the more we get used to it until at the end we start wanting to stay there for good. We forget that we came to Earth only to learn and that our life belongs in its entirety to God. It doesn't happen with everyone but it does with a great part of them. When those who have forgotten about it have to leave they go to God full of bitterness for having to leave all they have on the earth behind. It's like a student wanting to take home a toy it's playing with at school, not appreciating that at home it has everything it needs in abundance, more even and better than it needs. Death is our return home and that's why it can be full of joy, trust and love for, after all, we are returning to our true Parents.

I'd like to ask you, dear reader, if you have already ever thought about death and about what it will be like when you leave your physical body. What will happen with you then? What will you do? Where will you go? Are you afraid to think about it? Do you think you're young enough and healthy enough for it not to be worth worrying about in advance? Maybe you reckon that meditating about death is reserved for the old and the sick whereas you have many years to live before you get to that stage. Do you think only the old and the sick die? "True enough," you might say, "young people die, too, but in sudden accidents and I've always been lucky and I'm very careful so nothing like that will happen to me."

I'm not asking you this to frighten you. I only want to remind you that what you call death does exist and takes the old and the young alike and even small children, the sick but often also the healthy and strong. Avoiding thinking and talking about death is like running away from something that's chasing you, and when you no longer have any strength left to run away and you fall exhausted you suddenly realize that what you've been running away from is your own shadow. This isn't a metaphor because death accompanies life like a shadow from the moment we're born. Acceptance of death and ridding yourself completely of the fear of death will not only not shorten your life – it will positively prolong it.

You are surely aware that when you fear something you draw it upon yourself. If you're afraid of an accident then, after some time, you fall victim to it; you fear being mugged or burgled – you will certainly experience it. You fear death hysterically, you're afraid even to think about it, you pretend it doesn't apply to you – then you draw it to yourself like a huge magnet.

But now stop and consider, meditate a while. What does death signify for you? The end, or the beginning? When you rid yourself of the fear of death you will become fearless. Because the truth is that there is nothing more terrifying than that fear. Apart from death, what else could you possibly fear?

And now I'd like to tell you that you have nothing to fear because you never die. No, you haven't misread. You will never die. What we call death is merely the leaving of our physical body, it's like taking your clothes off. Just as we throw away the clothes that have worn out so we abandon our worn-out bodies. But that doesn't mean to say that you cease to exist. "Nonsense," you're thinking, "everything that is born must die, that's how it is and you can't help it." I want to console you. Nothing that is born dies, it just changes its form from one to another. From the heavy, coarse form that is our physical body to a very light form which is our body after death. Just as we possess a body, mind (not to be confused with brain) and soul in our lives, so after death we possess a body, mind and soul.

Don't ask me now how I know this. I will tell you in a later part of this book. For now accept as a certainty that you do not die.

Your body, mind and soul live eternally. How do you feel about this information? Are you pleased? Did you sigh with relief? Are you surprised? Or maybe you shouted that I'm writing nonsense. Maybe you're mad at yourself that you've been afraid all your life for no reason. Or maybe you don't want to give up that fear, after all you like being afraid so much. Or maybe you believe in death and nothing will convince you otherwise. Most likely you won't accept this knowledge immediately because you've believed in death for many, many years through many, many incarnations. You are not alone in thinking this way, very many people think like that. That's the way our parents thought, and our grandparents, and our great-grandparents and, following tradition, you probably think that way, too.

I'm writing this, dear reader, to make you realize that what you know about death, what you think about it during your life and what you expect of it bears on what will come to you after death, on how your fate will unfold in the future. Later in the book I'll give a considerable number of examples which confirm what I have written here.

And now I will describe a death, preferably a sudden one. A man is traveling in a vehicle and suddenly – crash, an accident. In the first moment the man is terrified, shocked; he thinks: "Oh, God, I'm dying." After a while he notices that no, he was mistaken. "Oh, what a relief," – for a moment he was thinking he'd died but no, he's still alive, what joy. The only thing is: how did he get out of that accident in one piece? It looked utterly hopeless, and yet he managed it. Suddenly he notices that there are people running about, shouting, administering first aid. They're shouting that he has died!? "Are you insane, can't you see I'm alive? I can hear, see, smell, I'm moving about even better than before. No, this is crazy, either I've gone mad or they have." So he tries to tell them that they're mistaken: "I am alive, I haven't died" – but they won't listen. Suddenly he notices that it's like he's slightly above them, slightly in the air. And what's that below him? "What's that? Is that butchered body in the great pool of blood me? How can that be? I mean, I have my own body, I'm not in pain, I feel so light, free, strangely happy." The body is taken into an ambulance. "One moment, what about me?" He goes with them to the hospital. The family has already been informed. Everyone despairs, wrings their hands. He chokes just at the sight of this grieving. "I must tell them quickly not to worry, after all there is no death, I am still alive." "What's this, they don't hear me, my wife's as if looking straight through me. What, she too? Even though we always understood each other so well, even without words."

Most ghosts relate their deaths more or less in that way. These people, or rather souls, experience real shock, they are alone, no-one sees them, no-one hears them, they are ignored. The same thing is described by those who experienced clinical death and who were revived from it. You'll say that the shock is the result of the person not expecting an accident, let alone death. But even when death is preceded by a long illness and waited for eagerly, it is described in the same or a similar way.

Those who didn't have the knowledge that life continues after death are usually hugely astounded by the fact. Their first reaction is a desire to tell those closest to them so that they'll know and not be surprised by it sometime. They try various ways to draw attention to themselves, most often without success. Some resolve to return to their bodies even just for a moment in order to tell. In the next chapter I'll describe examples of these events which I witnessed.

THE SOUL'S DECISION

It's important to understand that it's the soul itself that chooses when and how it is to die. It can change the decision even at the moment of death and revive. The way it happens most often is that when the soul has worked through all the lessons it came to Earth to learn, it decides to leave its earthly body. Every death, even one which seems to be the most accidental or one caused by a long illness, is the soul's decision. The soul not only doesn't die but, after the death of the body, is aware of everything that's happening around it.

My mother suffered from cancer. She was bed-ridden for almost a year, and suffered greatly. When I found out about her approaching death I was pregnant and shortly after her death I gave birth to my little daughter. Death and birth at virtually the same moment? Astonishing. We both had a considerable amount of time to get accustomed to the thought of her dying. When she was no longer able to get out of bed, while she was being fed she suddenly choked and lost consciousness. I was terrified, feeling full of guilt. How could I have been so careless? "God," I cried, "I've contributed to the death of my own mother, if not for me she might have lived at least a couple of days longer." I don't rightly remember what I did then, how I resuscitated her, I lost all sense of time. Eventually, she opened her eyes. How immense was my astonishment when the first words I heard from her then were: "I came back because you were in such a terrible state you wouldn't have been able to cope, but remember I'll die when you're not near me." Instead of being pleased that my mother was alive I stood dumb-struck, with my mouth open. How was it possible for a dying woman to influence what was happening to her at the moment of her death? And that it wasn't I who had saved my mother but that she had come back herself? "Open the door for Suzy," my mother said a few moments after regaining consciousness. "She's been standing outside this last hour and a half." "What Suzy? What are you talking about, mother?" I thought. As if she'd heard me, my mother retorted: "Pull yourself together, girl; have you suddenly forgotten Suzy?" I realized that she was probably talking about a friend of hers. I thought she was hallucinating but so as not to upset her I walked over to the door. There I was astounded to see the exhausted Suzy. As she came in, she said: "I don't know what's going on here with you, but I've been standing here an hour and a half and I haven't the strength to come in or to go away. I can't even feel my legs." I was bewildered. How could my unconscious mother have known what was happening the other side of the door. As if this wasn't enough, my mother said: "... and those people in the accident will all survive, they'll regain consciousness after two weeks, tell their families, there's no need for them to worry..." What people? What accident? For months mother had been treated with psychotropic drugs which often made her delirious but now she was speaking in a rational voice not brooking any denial, like before. "There, look," she indicated the window. We looked out and there, at the intersection, beneath the wheels of a tram, were two crushed motor-cars. It was a horrible sight, there was nothing to be done, and here was my mother saying they weren't to worry because everyone will survive? She went on to say a lot of other things, for instance about what was happening at the neighbors' where she'd never been and so on. It's hard to credit it, but everything she said that day was confirmed. Two weeks later she died. Today, my daughter is twenty-two years old.

It seems like a short period, but there has been a huge breakthrough in society's consciousness since then. That was in the days of socialist Poland when things like that weren't talked or written about. There were no publications available here about near-death experiences. To prove what ignorance of the subject there was in that time I can give the example of my family and friends. During that incident with my mother there were seven people present but not one of them believed her. There was quite simply no mention of the subject again, as if the event had not even taken place.

Fate decreed, however, that I did believe it because shortly after my mother's death, when I was in my house out of town, I met an acquaintance. She was much affected by how her mother had just been through a clinical death and she was telling me about it. She was shaken. "It's so embarrassing, so embarrassing, Wanda," she muttered. "If only you knew what she's blathering about. If this goes on much further I'm going to have to move out of the village because they'll all be pointing at us and I'll probably have to send mother to a lunatic asylum." She was in such a state that if, at that moment, I hadn't heard her out she would have had a heart attack or gone mad herself. I can't abide people who gossip. It seems to me to be a huge waste of time and I never let myself be stopped by women wanting to chat. This time, however, I was so intrigued that I instantly invited her to my place. She talked chaotically, but I resolved to be patient and I listened. I asked to meet her mother who rejoiced that at last someone was taking an interest in her experiences. She talked about everything she'd been through and her account almost exactly repeated what my mother had talked about. I stood up in defense of this woman and authoritatively stated that there was no reason to mock her or lock her up in a lunatic asylum. "She's not making it up, she's talking about what happened to her during her clinical death," I said. And to prove it I recounted my mother's story. They listened to me, but did they believe me? People still pointed at the woman for a long time after, until in time the matter faded. Many times after that I listened to her accounts with bated breath. She spoke with great passion.

From that time on I've met many people who have survived clinical death and seen what it's like on the other side. They understood that life continues after death and that, in fact, nothing changed. They even had their own bodies, and they remember that. They came back because they wanted to. They saw from the other side that they'd left some unfinished business, and they wanted to close it. Sometimes their near ones were in despair and they felt sorry for their families. Every one of them mentions a different reason but the fact is that they revived by themselves because they decided to. They are euphoric because they have discovered something extraordinary, something that's changed them and the whole of their lives up to that moment. They recall how, when they were outside their bodies, they wanted to tell their near ones that they were still living but that nobody heard them. On their return they have the opportunity to share what they've been through. They want others to benefit from their experience but often their nearest and dearest won't listen or won't believe them.

At the moment there are many books being published on the subject, many doctors describe the near-death experiences of their patients, interviews are broadcast on the radio and on television. Despite all this people in everyday life continue to meet with incomprehension, disbelief, and they're sometimes looked on, just like in the old days, as madmen, sometimes as blasphemers.

DEATH AND THEN WHAT?

Before coming into the world, as souls we make a plan for our upcoming life. The plan organizes the options for us so we go through life's lessons in the most effective way. It contains the smallest details of our future existence, e.g. the places where we will be living, the people we'll be taking our lessons with, our appearance at various ages, or emergency options – for ending our life, in case our plan is too ambitious.

At the moment of our birth, at a conscious level we forget about the plan, but at deeper levels the soul remembers everything. The soul also decides when and how it will end its incarnation. Even at the moment of death it has a choice, either to stay in its physical body and try to resolve its problem, or to die. Death doesn't come of its own volition. It is the soul that makes the decision when to die, where to go, which direction to take. It has free will and nobody can make the decision for it.

When the soul decides to depart and a person dies, the

consciousness realizes with surprise that it is still alive. It still possesses an energetic body even though the physical body is mourned over and buried in the earth. This fact may remain unnoticed by the consciousness. It sees itself just as it did during life – it sees, it hears, it feels the heat, the cold, it feels thirst.

On leaving the body, the soul notices around itself loving souls which died earlier and which are now waiting to greet it and lead it on a further journey. Also waiting are our spiritual guides whom we love. We recognize them easily. At this critical moment no soul is left to its own devices, no soul is deprived of help. There is a magnificent, ceremonial atmosphere full of joyful anticipation before the start of a great journey. Now the soul, free of earthly matters, assisted by loving beings slowly moves in the direction of the Light radiating love and happiness. It feels safe because it knows that it is loved and expected. Souls which were exhausted by sickness at the moment of death, or were unconscious or semi-conscious because, for example, they were given powerful painkillers, receive special help now. It can be compared with the medical help one gets here on Earth. Its purpose is to restore strength to the soul to enable it to continue its journey.

I described what the passing through the curtain of death towards "Heaven" looks like. Unfortunately, few decide to take it. Only those pass through who trusted, who were aware of themselves, their lives and the matter of death while they were still alive on Earth. They were honest with themselves, their near ones, and God. Those are certainly all the souls which are internally mature, in harmony during their lives, reconciled with themselves and the world. Those who during their earthly existence were righteous, sincere, warm people. While they were still alive they already knew what was going to happen to them when they died. They didn't need to be special. Many of them on Earth lived the life of ordinary human beings. They lived through the same emotions as everyone else, had various things on their conscience, experienced high and low points, successes and failures. Sometimes, like everyone else, they did something which God might not have liked, or didn't do something which, in their view, God demanded from them. It could be one or many constantly repeated misdemeanors. Those are the so-called sins the Church talks about. Many souls who went through to the Light had many faults and bad emotions. Sometimes they would be jealous, cunning, lazy, they cheated. Sometimes they stole, betrayed, manipulated others to gain some advantage, they gossiped, criticized, slandered, ridiculed, ate meat on Fridays, sometimes they lost control of themselves and started arguments etc. Of course, not all of the sins I've mentioned appeared at once or in one person.

It is, however, human to stray or to have sins on one's conscience. What we call a sin is, in fact, a lesson which we have to learn on Earth. A person has to learn that every deed has specific consequences. In the east they call it karma. Jesus described it as: "What you sow that shall you reap." I would describe it like this. When we do, speak, think well then we receive goodness, when we do, think, speak ill, then we receive evil. Every soul has been on the earth many times and what it has fully learned, one hundred per cent, comprises its conscience. Conscience is nothing other than the memory of all we have learned. We remember, for instance, that it's forbidden to steal because in another life we stole something and for that we were publicly flogged or our finger, or hand, was cut off, or maybe we lost our life. Now, when we are presented with an opportunity to steal something our conscience tells us that it's better not to do that or things could turn out badly for us. A person who listens to their conscience is calm because they know they're doing good. One who acts contrary to their conscience will have to endure various consequences of their action. Even without them the conscience will manifest itself in the form of a sense of guilt. That's when we say: "my conscience is troubling me". However, it speaks only when we have already gone through the lesson in question.

The case is different when it comes to a lesson that someone hasn't gone through yet – for here their conscience cannot tell them what to do. For instance: let us assume that a soul has never in any of its incarnations gone through the question of treachery. Then opportunities for treachery will appear time and again during its life. The thing is we have to experience what it means to betray and to take all its consequences, or to be betrayed and feel all the pain that comes with that.

At such a moment it's good to rely on intuition, or take advantage of the wisdom of the family or the neighborhood where we are living. There is no guarantee, however, that we will listen and behave appropriately. Whatever we do will be good for us even if we do act inappropriately. For it will become one of the lessons of the education for which we have come to Earth.

Depending on whether our subconscious classifies our deed as good and appropriate or bad and unworthy, it will create the consequences of our behavior for us. If it judges that we have committed a fault then, with the help of a sense of guilt, it will create a punishment for us. So you see we punish ourselves. Naturally, consciously we may not be aware of that. The greater the transgression in the subconscious's judgment, the greater the punishment. It can even manifest itself in the form of a serious illness, an accident, a misfortune, or imprisonment.

Who establishes whether a given deed demands a big or a small punishment? We establish it ourselves, our subconscious does. We are subject to its judgment. If, however, we remain aware of its functioning at every moment of our lives then nothing can threaten us because we'll know what it aims to do and we'll be able to negotiate everything with it and, consequently, change things. If we refuse to be aware of our subconscious (and this applies to the majority of people) then we are liable to suffer terrible consequences as a result. What for one person is a perfectly normal action can, for another, be a serious transgression. That's why one person steals, cheats, betrays and gets away with it while another punishes themselves just for thinking about it. To help you better understand how this works I'll give two examples from life.

There was an elderly man called John who suffered from heart trouble nearly all his life. He had had two heart attacks and he was close to having another one. I was called to help. It was his family who decided it whereas he was neither willing nor unwilling to use me. Nevertheless, he felt sufficiently poorly to undertake therapy, though without any enthusiasm. At a certain moment he started to tell me about how he can see himself as a small boy who is hitting his friend in the leg, and so hard that the other boy falls over and cannot stand up. He concluded later that the leg was broken because he saw the same boy with his leg wrapped in bandages. After the end of the session, John asserted that since he cannot remember the incident it's most certainly a figment of his imagination. I was of a different opinion, I'd had many sessions like this and I could distinguish when a story was true and when it wasn't. I asked if his friend was still alive. He said he was, that he lived close by but that they didn't talk to another. I asked the family to help organize a meeting of the two men after all those years. I'll describe in detail how the meeting went because it's quite significant. "You know, Francis, I'd really like to apologize to you for that leg," said John. "What do you mean, John? What leg are you talking about?" his old schoolmate answered. "You know, Fran, when I hit it with a stick and broke it." "John, I have never had a broken leg, you must have got me confused with someone else." "No, Francis, it was definitely you. I recollect it exactly, like it happened just a moment ago." "Honestly, it wasn't me." "So why did you never speak to me?" "It's my impression that it's you who didn't speak to me. When I addressed you, you always turned away from me." They argued like this for quite a bit longer. I said it wasn't important what happened half a century ago, what was important was now – that they should forgive each other. They did so willingly and spent the whole evening talking, remembering their youthful times. Two or three days after this meeting the doctor caring for John phoned to say that there was a place free at the clinic. He claimed that the patient's condition was serious and asked John to take himself to the hospital as soon as possible. John opposed it since he was feeling better but his excuses were in vain.

On the ward they gave him tests, then more tests and more tests. They kept doing them because they thought there'd been a mistake. They showed that the patient was completely cured. There was no third heart attack and the X-rays showed no trace of the two previous ones. The doctors didn't want to believe it, but the patient was in the care of the consultant right from the beginning. And there were earlier X-rays which showed unequivocally the heart attacks he'd suffered. From that time this elderly man looks a dozen years younger and has managed to visit half the world. Now, from time to time, he tells his friends about a man who ruined his life by punishing himself for something which most probably never happened.

Let us consider what would have happened if John hadn't cured that fragment of his life and had died. Most probably he would have considered himself a sinner, unworthy of going on the journey to "Heaven" and would have stayed, like others similar to him, in the world of ghosts leading the life of a stray soul. We also proved that people involved in the same occurrence remember it differently. We punish ourselves while the other person hasn't the slightest notion about the happening.

Another example is the case of Caroline whose mother had repeated from earliest childhood: "Don't let boys kiss you because they only want one thing." This sentence embedded itself very deep in the daughter's psyche. It left a trace in the girl's subconscious which was heavy with consequences. At fourteen, Caroline went to a friend's birthday party where she was given a glass of champagne. Being so young, even such a small amount of alcohol had an effect. The friend's parents arranged for her to be escorted home by a boy who was slightly older than her. When they were outside her house the boy not only tried to kiss her but he put his hand up her skirt and touched her vagina. She broke away and ran home as fast as she could.

When she grew up she married. She remembered her mother's warning only too well and her marriage was, for both of them, a nightmare. After a few years the most extreme form of cancer appeared on her pubic symphysis. The date of the operation was set but the doctors' prognosis was very pessimistic. Caroline wanted very much to live and a few days before the operation she came to me. Neither of us harbored any delusions but I tried. During therapy we reached the cause though Caroline didn't remember it at all. It transpired that her subconscious had judged the incident with the boy to be such an offense against her mother and herself that she punished herself by creating a tumor in her organism. Imagine, furthermore, that the tumor was the shape and size of a man's hand. It was with considerable difficulty that we tried to persuade her subconscious to forgive her that incident. It didn't want to do it. It considered that she was a very naughty girl because she almost let herself be kissed by that boy. It was even worse with the hand which found itself up her skirt. The crisis passed when she forgave herself and her mother. Later, she also forgave the boy.

She went to the hospital but the operation wasn't performed because the doctors noticed that the cancer had started to recede until in time it went away completely. Just like in the first case I described the real troubles would have started if Caroline hadn't recognized her problem. She was a hair's breadth away from death. Until that moment she had, throughout most of her life, subconsciously felt she was evil, unclean, because she hadn't listened to her mother. Her mother had warned her so assiduously and what had she done? Not only had she nearly let herself be kissed, there was also that hand up her skirt. An offense like that could not be excused, it needed to be punished and in no uncertain terms. And that's what happened. Her life was a great torment.

If she'd died she would have swollen the ranks of stray souls because, being a sinner, she wouldn't have dared to go to the Light. After working through that incident Caroline not only healed her body, she healed her soul, too.

Getting to the cause of such problems is usually hard. Hidden deep in our subconscious it has a great influence on us. As soon as we understand how our subconscious interpreted a given occurrence everything returns to normal. We feel then like we have been born anew. Into a dark corner of our consciousness a little light has penetrated and healed everything. What had seemed so terrible to the subconscious now, when it's understood and forgiven, withdraws. It can well be that we have in the course of our lives done many other, worse things than what is troubling us. But in those situations we were aware of our subconscious's reactions. They have no effect on us if the emotion with which the subconscious reacts to a given incident reaches our consciousness. Such sudden examples of healing are not isolated instances. I could multiply them but I fear there wouldn't be enough pages in this book. Besides, this book is on a different subject.

The incidents I involve myself in are, in the main, very similar. This is how they work: a long time ago we did something which our subconscious has judged to be bad, demanding punishment. It punished itself, therefore, by creating an illness, an accident or other misfortune whose quality and severity depends on how it classified the incident. The greater (subjectively) the transgression, the greater the punishment. When, years later, we discover its cause it can seem to us to be trivial, insubstantial, or even ridiculous but the moment it arose it seemed to the subconscious to be a substantial transgression against our value system.

So it is that only those souls will allow themselves to go to "Heaven" which, at the moment of death, had settled accounts with their own lives and have a clear conscience. Though they committed sins during their lives, they were able to forgive themselves and others. Deep down in their souls they knew that even the worst sins were only lessons that needed to be worked through. They parted without rancor from their loved ones, their families, their possessions, their work. Separating themselves from earthly matters allowed them to go straight ahead without looking back, regretting nothing they left behind. They believed in a loving and forgiving God. Even in their lifetimes they decided what they would do when they died without leaving anything to chance.

WHY DO SOULS STAY BEHIND?

Unfortunately, most souls that have left their physical bodies don't pass straight through death's curtain to the other side. Worse still, the number of souls left suspended between Heaven and Earth, souls which for a variety of reasons declined to go to God, is constantly increasing. There are many reasons for this and I shall talk about each of them in turn.

The most important factor is that after death, these souls either don't know or don't believe that they died. For them nothing has changed. They missed their own deaths and they think they're still alive. They are unaware of the fact that they could go to the Light. They assume that they are alive and therefore belong to the Earth. Even if they suffered a serious illness they think that they're now well again. If they were old or incapacitated they suddenly feel rejuvenated or at least that they were given vitality and energy (this happens only during the first moments after leaving the body). They continue to see the physical world and think they can function in it. They don't see the other souls which are in the same situation as them.

The number of these souls co-existing side by side is enormous but more often than not they don't see or hear each other for a very long time. Every moment confirms their belief that they're living as before. They note that they exist which convinces them that nothing has changed. These are legions of lost souls continuing to live an illusion, a pretend life. Very often these are people very close to us: our father, mother, brother, sister, beloved granny, granddad, friends, neighbors, colleagues from school or work. When I ask one of these wandering souls: "Do you know you're dead?" they usually respond with astonishment. "I don't know. Am I dead?" These moments are often a great shock to them. How could they know? Nobody had warned them that life after death is so very real. I have heard it thousands of times, I hear it virtually every day. Unfortunately, there's a great deal of ignorance concerning this matter.

One of the reasons I decided to write this book was that I wanted to communicate this knowledge and to help us understand things which are of such importance to us all. My task is to help readers prepare themselves and their loved ones for passing through death's curtain to the other side. We shall all, sooner or later, have to face up to the issue of our own deaths.

In Eastern cultures talking about death, about what awaits us afterward, is perfectly normal, an everyday thing. Even small children take part. This attitude means that death does not come as a surprise. This awareness protects the dying as well as those who remain in this life. It would be useful to have this custom introduced into Western culture. There would be far fewer solitary, wandering ghosts not knowing what to do with themselves, finding no help from anywhere in what is to them an incomprehensible situation.

If we can't talk about it on an everyday basis then the most appropriate moment to broach the subject is during a serious illness. It is very important to persuade the patient to discuss what he or she intends to do if he or she dies. As a rule we're afraid to talk about death with the sick. First of all because we don't want to frighten them, we figure it's not appropriate, we worry about what the patients will think of us. Maybe we're waiting for a legacy and we want to be on the best possible terms with them. We could be afraid the patient would think we want them dead. But when are they supposed to put their affairs in order if not when they're sick?

I'm not talking here about diseases like colds or flu, but about illnesses they may not survive. Talking about it doesn't necessarily mean that the patient will die right away. I'm talking about discussions that lead to answering questions like: what "would happen", "if" they died. If they are about to die then, at the deepest levels of their subconscious, patients know as much regardless of how much their near ones and their doctors deceive them by telling them something different. Talking about death is as important to the dying person as it is to those remaining in life, and I shall say more about this later.

The main reason why souls disregard their own deaths is the fact that so little in their existence changes after death. If they knew that then it would be easier for them to understand it, to notice it; they would know how to confront their new state, they would avoid any astonishment. Those who didn't believe in a life after death before they died are in an even worse situation. Even if they recognize that they died they simply don't know what they can do with themselves from now on. It's hard to believe in one's own death even for ghosts who were sick for a long time or who were very old.

Given that, imagine what must happen to souls who have

met with a sudden and unexpected death. There is a huge popu-
lation of wandering ghosts on this side of death's curtain whom
death took at the best moments of their lives. They had never
thought about death before. They were young, fit, and suddenly
they're not alive any more. A sudden accident, a lack of warning symptoms, no moment for reflection. I'm talking here about
sudden car or air accidents, climbing mishaps etc.

Such souls simply can't accept they're no longer alive.
There was only a tiny moment between their lives and their
deaths, a blink of eye, and they didn't catch it. If they'd known
about life after death then they might have had a chance of
working out that they're no longer alive. They simply don't believe the situation they find themselves in regardless of who or
what explains it to them. For many of them, death meant the
end of everything, not further life.

Some souls are severely confused long before their
deaths. When they come through death they're incapable of rec-
ognizing their true states. These tend to be the incurably sick
who have been treated with powerful pain killers, as well as
drug addicts and alcoholics. The mind of a sick person receiving painkillers is comparable to the mind of a drug addict. Even
long after death they're incapable of being themselves. Even
when they recover their senses they still lack knowledge about
life after death. I'll describe the consequences of this ignorance
later in the book.

The next reason why souls don't go to the Light is that
they're afraid of being punished for what they did. Sometimes
their sins are minor, but during their lives they believed in a
cruel, vengeful and punitive God. Now they feel unworthy of
receiving forgiveness. Even though waiting for them at the
moment of death there is a magnificent escort consisting of their
spiritual guides and dear ones who died before them as well as

the loving Light, they turn away and refuse to go further. They do not believe that God could forgive them their sins. This comes from the fact that they were unable to forgive them themselves.

You could compare the moment of death with a train bound for Heaven which only those with a valid ticket can get on. Anyone who thinks they're worthy of entering Heaven gets a free ticket. Everyone else stays behind in the station concourse. The train departs leaving a crowd of ghosts in the concourse who simply don't know what to do with themselves. They could have left, they were invited onto the train, but they refused. They were very frightened of punishment. The offense they accuse themselves of and which, because they felt it had to be punished, stopped them traveling could quite literally be anything. A broken promise, an unpaid loan, eating meat on a Friday, not fasting before Mass on a Sunday, various kinds of cheating, corruption, all the way to the most terrible sins like robberies, crimes, rapes, murders. They feared punishment and wanted to avoid it. There are as many ghosts as there are varieties of fear of punishment.

And so the concourse between Heaven and Earth is full of ghosts who have both minor infringements and great sins on their consciences. They don't believe that if only they could forgive themselves their sins then God would forgive them too. "Why is that so?" you'll ask. It's because God gave us free will. If we wish to feel guilty and constantly to punish ourselves for our deeds then we can. God will do nothing against our will. However, if we freed ourselves from the sense of guilt for sins committed, then in that same second we would have the chance to pass through to the Light. Ghosts don't have this knowledge and so give up, claiming that it's too late for them. They anticipated severe punishment in the shape of purgatory or hell. They wanted to avoid it at any price and that's why they stayed on this side of death's curtain. They don't realize that they have brought about the very thing they feared so much because by remaining they create what has in fact become their purgatory or hell.

How is it that some souls which have even serious sins on their consciences are able to forgive themselves and pass through to the Light? It all depends on whether the soul loved itself, others, and God. If during their life a person's heart was filled only with despair, sorrow, hopelessness, then there was no room in it for love. Love is the substance that illuminates the darkness in a person's heart. It gives great strength. A person who loves himself won't harm himself or anyone else. People like that are also loved by those around them. And they also believe that God loves them and like a good father forgives his children. These people can forgive themselves and others.

People who don't love themselves aren't able to love anyone else. They despise everything and everyone including themselves. They also hate God. They feel they are bad people, they see only evil all around them and they do evil things. They think that because they're bad then their Father is bad, too, and someone like that doesn't forgive. They don't want to and can't believe that anything could be different, that God is love which can forgive everything. How can they believe in love if they don't know what it is? Love is God. But they don't believe in God. A world without love and without God not only appears to be but is cruel. Living in a cruel reality a person will become cruel to himself and to others. He doesn't forgive, doesn't empathize, he applies the principle of "an eye for an eye, a tooth for a tooth", he moves in a vicious circle where love is equated with weakness. What a paradox. The thing that is the greatest strength in a world of goodness is regarded a weakness in this circle.

This circle has to be broken sometime, and death is an excellent opportunity for it. That is the time to forgive oneself, others, even God. Those who remain in life have the chance to forgive us. God also forgives us. Even when a person is no longer among us we can still forgive them: it is never too late for that. In this way we help not only the dying person but above all ourselves. I'll describe why this helps us later in the book.

The next very large group of abiding ghosts are the souls who during life did not believe in God and therefore had no-one to go to after death. They thought that life finishes in the grave, after which all that awaits is the abyss, nothingness. Other souls believed very deeply in God but thought they would lie in their graves till the day of the "Last Judgment" and only then would they rise up from the dead and go to "Heaven". They have, therefore, become victims of what they believed in or specifically of what their religion told them to believe in. They now feel deceived, not knowing what to do with themselves. Should they wait for the Judgment? For punishment? But where? In the grave? They live on, so they can't wait in abeyance. They've ascertained all this only after death when it is a little too late. You'll ask: "Too late to do what?" To go to the Light. It was at the moment of physical death that they should have decided where they would go.

This group also includes people who, in their lifetimes, were very foresighted and planned exactly what their lives after death would be, calculating that they would lie in their graves till the Last Judgment. These are all those who, during their lives, built vaults and showy monuments for themselves and their near ones, who planned what they'd be dressed in for their coffins so they would look their best in them. They wondered how many people would come to their funerals, what they'd say about them in the funeral orations etc.

All of them need energy for existence, just as people need air. So they circulate round the cemetery and steal energy from the people visiting there. This may sound like a joke, but it's no joking matter. It's about them that those stories about dead people coming out of graves are told. The members of this group identify themselves strongly with their bodies whereas human beings are not the same as their bodies.

This is how very many ghosts have stopped their journey. It comes as a great shock when they realize after death what's really happened to them. They continue not to know what to do with themselves because the moment of passing through to the other side of death's curtain is long gone. They therefore have no way out other than to draw energy from people or to permeate into someone permanently.

Probably the largest group of souls remaining in the world of ghosts after death are all those who during their lives were so attached to earthly matters that they're incapable of freeing themselves from them. These matters can be material or non-material. It can be a house, a car or other possessions. Everyone has surely heard of haunted houses and the ghosts that terrorize them. Others loved to eat, drink, take drugs, indulge in sex or gamble to excess. Others again were too fond of making decisions for their near and dear ones, butting into everything so now they find it too hard to surrender their authority.

Another reason for ghosts to remain is a desire to put right the errors they made during their lives so far. They think that by staying on this side they will have an opportunity to mend what they did badly.

There are also ghosts who cannot leave in peace because a curse has been put on them, black arts have been used against them. Another sizable group is comprised of those who committed suicide.

Some souls find it hard to leave the Earth because they've left someone who, in their opinion, should be looked after; these might be a parent of a small child, or a solicitous child with elderly and lonely parents and so on.

The souls described above remain on the Earth because that is the decision they took. There is, however, a large number of souls who would dearly like to pass through to the other side, to "Heaven", but are prevented from doing so by the despair of their dear ones. These souls are torn between their own good and the good of those they left. They may even be aware that it would be better for everyone if they did leave, but the living won't let them. We must remember, therefore, even during mourning and despite our sorrow, to think of those who have a right to leave. We do so in order not to harm ourselves or them. I know how difficult that is since I went through it myself. But my mother was able to demand that I do not detain her. How many souls do that? Very few.

What is astonishing is that, after death, a person finds himself in the very world he believed in during his life and which has become real. So, if a person believed in "Heaven" he goes to "Heaven". But if he didn't feel worthy enough or if he was afraid of punishment for his misdeeds, then he makes hell for himself and his nearest ones a reality.

WHEN SOULS STAY BEHIND

When a soul turns away from the Light and doesn't want to pass through to the other side of death's curtain, no-one tries to dissuade it from that course. God gave us free will and the soul can always, even at the moment of death, take advantage of it. Up until then the soul had help from all around, enough energy and an aim, it knew where to go. From the moment it shuts itself off from the chance to enter "Heaven" it starts to wonder what to do next. Most often it returns to its near ones, its family or to people with whom it was directly involved during its life. That's where it feels safest. It can also return to its home, to the hospital where it lay, to friends, to the cemetery, to its grave, to the church if it used to like being there, to its estate, to the bar where it can drink alcohol at will or shoot up with drugs.

Most of the souls which died in an accident stay in the place where it happened, constantly re-creating it. What has to be done then is to awaken the soul, make it realize that it is no longer alive.

THE MOMENT A PERSON DIES

Before coming into the world every soul makes a plan which it aims to accomplish during its upcoming life. Sometimes it completes this lessons easily and with joy. Sometimes, however, the lessons are very difficult or even impossible to discharge in the course of just one lifetime. It could be that the soul didn't take the advice of its spiritual guides who tried to persuade it to choose a more realistically achievable plan rather than an over-ambitious one. A lot also depends on the degree of the soul's development and on how quickly it wants to learn its lessons. An all-embracing love rules on the other side, everything is straightforward and easy to achieve, every moment is filled with great enthusiasm and a soul may feel it can deal with everything. It does not appreciate that being on Earth it will have a completely different state of consciousness.

When a person come to this world they forget about everything that happened before their birth. The soul still knows 'everything, but the conscious mind does not remember it.

Every soul has its own mission (lessons) to complete on Earth. These lessons are done in the company of other souls which are also learning at every moment. And so a soul whose exercise is, for example, to be a victim will find on its road a torturer or a tyrant, a manipulator will find people they can manipulate, a ruler will find subjects, a teacher will find pupils and so on. Of course, everything also works in reverse: a pupil will find a teacher, a tyrant will find a victim, and so on. When, for instance, the role of the victim has completed its exercise then the victim will stop wanting to play it. It notices that there is no torturer in its space any more. If, at the same time, the torturer has completed his lesson then he stops being a torturer. But if not, he will look for another victim. This is perfectly reflected in the saying: "As long as there's a torturer, there will be a victim. If there is no victim then there is no torturer." For one person a lesson that has to be done may turn out to be easy, but for another it may be very hard and they may need to do it over several incarnations. The purpose of playing a role is to make a person aware that they are the role's creators, and to remind them who they are – children of God. They have to understand that they are learning sympathy and love towards themselves, too, as well as faith in God and in themselves. It also teaches them how to forgive tyrants and forgive themselves, e.g. that we didn't stand up in our own defense, that we allowed ourselves to be hurt (mentally as well) etc.

If a person doesn't realize what a lesson is supposed to teach them and sets about their role too seriously, then their life turns into a nightmare. When it feels trapped with no way out then the soul may well decide to choose death. This happens, however, at a very specific, previously determined time. Before birth the soul establishes several times – opportunities to withdraw from doing its lessons. Most often it's not just one moment of death but several – at various intervals and various ages.

I'm not, of course, talking about the simple giving up on plans at a moment when difficulties arise which sometimes lead to suicide. We must realize that suicides are most frequently caused by the presence of ghosts. Passing through to the Light at a previously established time never happens through suicide.

Sometimes someone ignores their intuition and makes decisions in their life which take them away from the plan chosen by their soul. It can happen that they struggle blindly against life and end up at a dead end from which they can see no way out. They can then exploit one of the deadlines for ending their lives established before they came to the world. They can, but they don't have to.

They choose the kind of death that suits them best. It can be an accident or a peaceful death during a minor operation, but it can also happen (though this isn't always the case) that, having a huge sense of guilt, death is preceded by a long and serious illness, like it was expiating its sins. Nothing happens by chance, everything is planned precisely. Sometimes a soul thinks that it can no longer cope and subconsciously prepares itself for death, and then suddenly help comes along from outside, a person receives added motivation and, quite literally, revives. It can happen when a soul is doing a certain lesson with other souls which support it through their own progress.

Death usually follows when a soul has finished all the lessons for a given life, or when we aren't capable of accomplishing the over-ambitious aim we set out to achieve. To a soul this is no big deal, it will simply return to the source, rest and, full of fresh strength, will return to earth to finish its task with the same or other souls. In such a context there is nothing terrible about death.

When someone from our circle dies our subconscious thoughts usually become preoccupied with our own death. It seems terrible to us when we are afraid of it. We have to realize that it is we who give it this dimension. Every soul knows perfectly well when it will die and how much time it has till the end of its mission. Our fear is totally baseless. We have to realize that as long as we fear death we only half-live our lives. In such a life there won't be enough energy to achieve our real aims. Fear will crop our wings and how can we live without wings? We won't fly high enough because we're afraid of falling.

How different things are when we get used to the essence of death and we stop being afraid not only of death but of everything else, too, because if we don't fear death then we know we don't have to be afraid of anything at all. Then we can, along with our plans, take off way beyond mediocrity. We know for certain that we will achieve them. We'll do everything easily, lightly, and with pleasure; we'll always have enough time and energy. Whatever we put our hands to will be as easy as ABC.

When a soul finally decides to leave then there is no way of detaining it. It's good to arouse it so it can achieve its life's plan, but not to detain it. We are capable of detaining a soul that's decided to leave but neither it nor we will have any benefit from that. I know of many instances where it's turned into a curse for everyone concerned. We don't take into account the soul's decision, and the soul might have completely different plans from ours.

When we fight for the life of a dying person we most often do it for ourselves, to satisfy our egoistic aims. For various reasons we're afraid of being left alone in the world. Many people ask for my help to keep a person alive. Sometimes they're cases of a long and painful illness, comas, clinical death, in other words when a person is more unconscious than conscious.

They say: "Wanda, please help. It's such a shame, such a young man, he could live such a life if not for this illness." They're desperate and would do everything to detain this soul.

When I make contact with the soul and ask what its reaction to all this is, it nearly always replies that it wants very much to leave but sorrow for their nearest and dearest ensnares it like a chain and won't let them go. Some souls are very resolved. They rebel and tear off those chains, but many souls fail to do so. Sometimes a soul will ask me to intervene with its family, to explain and persuade them to let it go. Talking to the soul's nearest and dearest I sometimes find myself fiercely resisted, most often by families where there is a lack of love. Where the dying soul is loved their near ones always agree to its departure. Then the soul departs immediately without waiting for any goodbyes, like it was afraid that the family will change its mind.

A friend of mine, a diplomat, was visiting one of the countries in Europe. He was invited to dinner in the house of a prominent person. During the visit there he noticed that the host's daughter was behaving rather oddly. He called me to ask what I thought of it and wondered if I could help. He said she was young, very beautiful girl but the doctors couldn't find any disease in her. I checked it out and what I saw surprised not only him but me, also. It turned out that, in fact, she was no longer alive. She was functioning only because her soul didn't have the conscience to leave because it was so sorry for her parents. This information intrigued my friend and he talked about it a lot to the girl's parents. When an opportunity arose he also asked the girl about various things in her life, her interests etc. She replied politely but without any enthusiasm. He was mad at me for leading him astray. He thought that for some reason I didn't want to help him. It just so happened that two weeks later we were sitting together with some other people when the telephone rang with the news that the girl had fallen over as she was fainting and since then was in hospital in a coma. Even greater appeals for my help were made. Once again I told him the girl was no longer alive. Her soul asked me to persuade her parents to let her depart. I agreed, though it seemed like it was going to be a hard thing to do. I repeated to them exactly what she'd asked me to do. At first they wouldn't hear of it, they wanted to keep her with them by force, just like most parents in their situation do. After two weeks, however, they agreed to her departure. At that moment the doctors confirmed her death.

The question of a family's sorrow is, of course, a kind of challenge for the soul (it's the next lesson to be gone through). Every one of us has free will and is the master of their world. If a family's sorrow influences a soul then it means that deep inside the soul identifies with that sorrow. If it was able to say: "From this moment I belong to God and nothing will stop me!" then there's no power that could have any influence on it. it's worth bearing that in mind. Who knows, it may be that after our death we may find ourselves in the situation of a soul which wants to leave but cannot.

If a soul hasn't yet achieved its plan or if there is even the slightest shadow of hope that it could achieve it, then the soul will not depart. A person might be hopelessly sick and medicine might not give them any chance of recovery, but if they are meant to stay then they will be miraculously healed.

We often try to save young people. We think they could live longer, that they have so much to do, but this can be faulty reasoning. Age has no significance for the soul. Sometimes a soul comes to the world just to finish off some lesson and it needs only a few years of life. That's why young people, too, die.

There are cases where a soul which loves us wants to

help us learn some lesson, e.g. love. It sacrifices itself for us by coming to the world so as to die straight after birth or at a very young age. Maybe we'll learn to love and our hearts will open up only when something dear to us is taken away? If the soul had stayed, maybe we wouldn't have learned our lesson, our heart would have closed up again or never opened up. That's why medicine quite often turns out to be completely helpless in saving young children. Doctors and parents alike needlessly blame themselves. Some children die even without being ill, they simply depart. They didn't come to the world to live and that's why they leave as soon as they've performed their task. When we restrain a soul like that by force then we must realize that it has no plan for this life or reason to stay here on Earth.

It's a different thing altogether with children who die during pregnancy. Sometimes they're not ready to come, and sometimes we're not ready to receive them. So they turn back off the road.

There are children who need to do their lessons through illness. Even if they are ill for a long time and severely ill, too, they can recover completely. That's why every childhood cancer is almost completely curable.

When someone knows what awaits them after death they are less afraid because they have a fuller overview of what's going to happen to them. Unfortunately, the majority of those dying do not prepare themselves for this, oh so important, moment. Thinking about death as we live seems too terrifying. Usually we put that off for when we're old. Often we are then too old or too sick and frail to find enough strength to do it. It can happen that long before death we are given anesthetic drugs and we're not conscious of ourselves.

Death has to be prepared for in good time, starting from our earliest years so as to become accustomed to it. Only then will we be able to live our lives fully relaxed and to die without fear. Life won't then be so terrifying, nor death so hard. Nothing restrains a person who is ready for death at any moment of life. It means they can live virtually eternally, i.e. for as long as they desire. A person will attract to themselves the thing they fear. If they fear death so much, if they run away from even considering it, then death will let them know about itself at the least expected moment. Then the person will be completely bewildered, won't know what's happening to them nor what they are to do next.

Those who remain alive should make every effort to help the dying person to pass through the other side of death's curtain. That is the moment when the soul can be confused by almost anything. It can judge that it hasn't died at all, that it imagined it all, since what it sees and feels really contradicts its conception of death. Despite our sorrow and pain we should confirm the soul's conviction that it has died. We should burn a considerable number of candles until the time when we have the inner feeling that we are able to stop. It's always an individual matter. When we sense the presence of a dead person we should always address them by name. "Andy," – we should say his name just like we said it when he was alive so he knows it's about him and not someone else – "you're no longer alive, look here are your remains. Your body is now lifeless, go to God, to the Light, don't be afraid, don't stay here, go." In such situations nearly every one of us prays for the soul of the departed but that's not enough. Many souls don't recognize that it's their death, their funeral, their body. We have to keep telling them afresh until we succeed. If a lot of time has passed since the moment of death then a different kind of help is needed, and I refer you to the chapter "How to help them".

If we're dealing with a sudden accident then we need to

redouble our help since passing through to the world of ghosts is associated with a shock. It is, therefore, very hard for the soul to notice it.

It can happen that someone in our midst is unable to reconcile themselves with a death. Instead of asking the soul to go to the Light they detain it. Our duty is then to ensure that they don't do this even when our hearts are also suffering from despair.

You'll ask: what harm can we do to the dead by despairing at their death? The moment of death is an instant in which the greatest calm should reign. It is the time when the dead person must confront a new experience, leave everything with which their lives were linked and decide what to do next. It is impossible at such a moment not to have sorrow in the heart or not to cry. One must cry but mustn't detain the dead person at one's side. If we do that then we harm not only the dead person but above all ourselves. I will describe the consequences of a ghost remaining on this side of death's curtain very fully soon.

HOW IT INFLUENCES US?

From now on I shall refer to the souls which have refused to pass through to the other side of death's curtain as
ghosts. After some time following the death of the body the
ghost notices that it's beginning to be short of energy and it
doesn't really know where to get it from. If it were in touch with
other ghosts then it would probably realize how it should pro-
ceed but at the beginning it doesn't notice its companions and is
left to itself. It becomes weaker and weaker, more and more
apathetic, it finds it ever harder to think. The self-preservation
instinct kicks in. There are many places on Earth where ghosts
can draw energy. They may be water sources or tectonic faults.
Some ghosts find these places. They do not realize that, on the
other side of death's curtain, they could lead magnificent, carefree lives filled with love. When the chance arose they didn't
have enough courage to believe in a forgiving God. They were-
n't able to forgive themselves and, fearing punishment, they did-

n't pass through to the other side of death's curtain. At that moment they didn't know how they could do it and therefore for them the door was bolted. Sometimes they are looked for by their nearest and dearest, souls which died earlier and now find themselves on the other side of death's curtain. It can happen that they love the lost ghost so much they decide to resign from life in "Paradise". They lower their vibrations and come through the curtain to set off with help. Sometimes the searching can last a very long time, or they can be quite fruitless. That's because this is an unnatural process. Sometimes ghosts are helped by the intervention of prayer from people on Earth and then one of the spiritual guides will come to help and lead the ghost to the other side. Exorcism, too, can help. I have met many ghosts who spent several hundred years suspended between Heaven and Earth, and some of those were from previous millennia. Usually such ghosts can be helped only accidentally, when other ghosts are being led through.

Many ghosts don't know what source to use to recharge their energy and they resolve to steal it. Some of them sees nothing wrong in it, others feel bad judging that they're doing something reprehensible. Those will be the ones who most often don't hook up to a specific person but draw their energy bit by bit from various people. They will frequently attend large gatherings of people. All ghosts who haven't passed through to the other side of death's curtain must find a source of energy in order to function. They could ask God for it but they either don't want to or don't have the courage to. They prefer to steal it from an animal, a human being, or a plant.

To make it easier to understand how it looks I'll try to illustrate it by comparing it to deep-sea diving. At the very beginning we feel perfect, we look at the beauty of nature and we decide to stay under water for ever. We don't stop to think that this isn't a natural environment for us. We see only what we want to see. We think: "It's so wonderful here, whereas up there there's nothing nice to look forward to, maybe even punishment, there's nothing to think about – we're staying". We're on our own, free at last, happy, but what's this? Slowly we notice that we're running out of air. We didn't anticipate that. We wanted to trick nature but nature is far more intelligent than we think. We notice that the boat we came on has long gone. Where can we get air from? We're afraid we might die at any moment. We notice a fish swimming by and we wonder if we couldn't perhaps "siphon off" some of its oxygen. It works, we feel relief, we can breathe again. When we continue trying to draw air from it, we don't know how but we pervade it. We know that we haven't turned into a fish but through its mediation we can at least function for a while, admire the sights, but above all avoid the unpleasantness of punishment.

A ghost which has decided not to pass through to the other side of death's curtain will most often return to its family which it has recently left. Grief reigns in their home, everyone is shattered, broken, resigned. The mourners will often give anything to be able to put the clock back so that the beloved soul could be back among them, alive. Behaving this way we ensure that the soul cannot depart. As we cry we are begging along with the whole family: "Stay, don't go. How will we be able to live without you?" This is a very egoistic attitude to life and shows a lack of understanding of the essence of death. You'll say that you did it because the loss hurt you so much, that despair overpowered you. That you were beside yourselves, that you weren't yourselves, that you were in no state to think of anything else. I understand you perfectly. I, too, after the death of my mother, was incapable of living for six months. If it hadn't been for her attitude and her demand that on no account must I detain her on this world I probably wouldn't have allowed her to depart to the other side of death's curtain. You probably recall how I described her clinical death. She returned and chided me that she wasn't able to die because I didn't want to let her go. I gave up because I loved her so much. I released her but I continued to suffer greatly. I was in such deep mourning that if it hadn't been for my newly-born daughter and my six-year old son, the world would have stopped having any meaning for me. All that mattered were my little ones and how to look after them. Apart from that I was incapable of anything else and I don't really remember what was happening to me or around me.

I'm not persuading you not to grieve. Grief has to be experienced as intensively as possible. It's very important for our mental health. We have been left alone, unhappy, often lost and with a mass of problems which, before now, we might not have had to deal with. We should give ourselves as much time as we need. It's a time when we must think only of ourselves and of those who are in the same situation as us. I do however appeal vehemently that you allow the dead person to depart even when we feel that that's contrary to us, when literally everything within rebels against doing so.

When a ghost which did not pass through to the other side of death's curtain returns to its family and the family desires its return then there is not the slightest difficulty with energy. It simply hooks up to the members of the household and draws the energy from them. The mourners are usually so broken by their misfortune that to begin with they don't notice that the ghost has permeated one of them. When they do notice it's often too late for a response. Luckily, this applies only to adults. The majority of children come to the world under special protection which comes from God. Unfortunately there are instances where ghosts steal the energy, and occasionally, the body of a small child. I deal with a considerable part of such cases in the chapter about homosexuality and mental illnesses ("Autism").

A person in a normal state of mind will not allow anyone to take their energy, let alone allow themselves to be pervaded. Ghosts sense this and they seek out people who will allow them to suck from them like leeches for ever. They steal energy from weak people, sick people, old people, people in a state of alcoholic or narcotic dependence, tired people, sleep-deprived people, anxious, depressed or frightened people. In other words people who are already short of energy themselves. That's because they're not in a condition to sense the ghost's activity and to respond to it appropriately. A person like that most often doesn't suspect that they have a companion who shares the daily portion of energy that God gives them. They lose their health and their strength without knowing why. Acting like this ghosts can cause a body's exhaustion which can lead to serious illness and sometimes even death. Often ghosts stay outside a person but sometimes they may unwittingly enter inside. It's like a ghost walking close to a secret entrance and, by accident, leaning against the door which opens and the ghost accidentally falls inside. That's how a person can become possessed by a ghost which never planned it and never wanted it.

There are ghosts which have knowingly stayed in this world and which need a body. Hooking up to someone in order to draw off their energy isn't enough for them. They demand a body that can function in the world of humans. Therefore they seek out a victim whom they can rob. From the moment they possess someone that person has inside them, apart from their own spirit the ghost of another human being. It's not at all rare for there to be not just a few but dozens of ghosts inside one person. It's often the case that they know nothing about one another. Most likely the person they've possessed knows nothing about it, either. The person's near ones will notice sooner but when they tell them about it the person simply won't believe it. There can be more than a hundred of them in one person. The Holy Bible calls such a number "legion".

When one ghost hooks up to a healthy and strong person it can at first not be noticed. Although the person will feel a fall in energy levels, they'll probably put it down to the weather or overwork. When several ghosts hook up things present themselves differently. The person becomes apathetic, sluggish, doesn't want to do anything, is touchy. Sometimes they might start being ill. But to begin with they don't notice that there's something amiss with them.

Ghosts prefer to draw their energy from healthy, strong people, or to function in such bodies. How is it possible, many will ask, for a ghost to pervade the body of a human being? It often happens when we lose consciousness, e.g. when we undergo an operation and are given an anesthetic. Another opportunity for ghosts is when we lose consciousness even for a few seconds, by hitting our heads or during shock after an accident. All alcoholic libations provide ghosts with excellent opportunities. Young people are using drugs more and more often and thereby opening themselves wide to being permeated by ghosts. Even moments of a tiny change of consciousness during the smoking of a cigarette enables ghosts to gain possession. Sometimes we are sick, resigned and unconsciously we allow a ghost to enter our body. During mourning we are practically helpless if we descend into despair for the departed and open up to the other side. At such times we can be possessed by a mass of ghosts. When we play at spiritual seances, particularly if we're ignorant about it, it can happen that ghosts can come into the bodies and the minds of the participants permanently. You have to know how to lead the summoned ghosts back but the majority of people organizing these seances don't know that. It's easy to be possessed when we do tarot readings without knowing much about it or when we meditate in the wrong way. Ghosts frequently hook up to people or permeate them when they lose control of their emotions and show a tendency to identify with negative energies like anger, hatred etc.

A ghost usually hooks up to a person because it seems that it's the only way to get access to energy. It's similar when it pervades the body of a human. It may know that it's doing something evil but it believes that it wouldn't be able to exist or to function the way it would like to without doing it. It's more to do with the instinct for self-preservation, the instinct to survive than it is with the ghost's malevolence, as many believe.

At the beginning when it has just permeated a person, the ghost will feel uneasy, like anyone finding themselves in a new situation. It doesn't yet know how to behave, how much it can do, it simply tests the water. Much depends on what kind of ghost permeates what kind of person. A ghost seeks out the people who function at similar vibrations to its own. If, during its life, it was an aggressive madman then it will look for a person with similar tendencies. This works on the principle of "Like attracts like". That way a cunning person will be more cunning after being permeated by a ghost, and a jealous person will be more jealous, etc. Every trait will be more intensified. That's why it's so hard at the beginning to realize that there's something amiss. If, for instance, someone becomes very agitated about the behavior of a colleague at work they might put their over-reaction down to the circumstances – in this case the colleague – rather than to a ghost. When a person is permeated by a ghost functioning at different vibrations things may be altered. None of their shortcomings will be intensified but instead others will appear which weren't there at all before. A common feature of people possessed by ghosts is, on the one hand, an increased sensitivity, argumentativeness, occasional attacks of fury at completely unexpected moments and, on the other, sluggishness, lack of enthusiasm for anything, tearfulness. Mood swings develop, from huge stimulation to huge seeing the black side of things. A person who, till this time, was mentally and physically strong now doesn't really know what to do with themselves. It is as oppressive to them as it is to the people closest to them.

THE DEATH OF A LOVED ONE

When someone really close to us dies, someone we were strongly tied to emotionally, to whom our whole lives were tied it's like we suddenly don't have enough air and the ground beneath our feet has collapsed. The knot could be so strong that we can't imagine how to live without this person. Their departure takes away all our desire to live or do anything. It makes no difference if that death was sudden or preceded by a long illness. You might assume that if death was preceded by a long illness, there is more chance to prepare yourself for it at least in a small way. Observing it from a distance, this may appear so, but it is not the case. When death comes it strikes as like a bolt of lightning. I've been through it myself and I know what it's like. When someone suffers for a long time, the most we can hope for is a sense of relief that death has brought an end to their suffering.

It can happen that death comes suddenly, without any

warning. That makes us very confused, like we've been thrown into a different reality, one that is paralyzing us. Some people despair so violently that everyone around them experiences their suffering, while others remain unmoved, as if they couldn't care, showing no emotions on the outside. Others again might curse the world or God. And though there are many ways of experiencing grief, there is one shared characteristic: the great pain felt by those who remain alive. Every death is a great shock, but the death of young people who love one another is even harder to endure. Often the whole family suffers as a result. Everyone sympathizes with the misfortune, they soothe one another, comfort each other. It's good to have support at a difficult moment. It's essential to support people as often and as well as possible. Everyone must live through their grief as intensely and for as long as they want and need to. That is the best way to the recovery of mental health and to saying goodbye to the beloved person. But it must be remembered that one should say goodbye as soon as possible so that the beloved soul can pass through to the other side of death's curtain.

I'd like all those of you who have been left behind to realize that, despite your suffering, you are very lucky indeed. I'd like you to appreciate in your hour of grief the enormous good fortune you had to love and be loved, that you have experienced something truly magnificent that thousands, millions even, of people never experience. Look at yourselves not from the standpoint of the present loss but from the standpoint of what you have gained thanks to love. Despite appearances, true love is a great rarity. What we usually call love is merely an enchantment or an attachment which, sooner or later, passes leaving behind a very gray reality. Real love never ends; indeed, it develops more and more with the passing of time. No situation, no space, not even death can part it. Know that after passing to the other side of the curtain of death the beloved soul will always love you and will remember you, and when you die will be waiting to greet you when you come.

Often, however, we don't want to remember this at the moment of death. Our thoughts are crammed only with the sense of loss and nothing else. We don't take into account the great harm we are doing not only to ourselves but to the beloved, departing soul. We want to keep it at our sides for as long as possible. This is a very egotistical attitude which, sooner or later, will turn against us. This applies to all people who love each other and are forced to part through death. It makes no appreciable difference whether it's a pair of lovers, a parent and a child, or two close friends. All partings hurt equally. Unfortunately we simply don't comprehend the consequences of our behavior. We don't know that through our great sorrow and despair we tie our beloved soul with great virtual chains thereby doing a great wrong - without mentioning the wrong we do ourselves. Grief and despair will not allow it to leave even though it has the right and the energy to do so, and at the appropriate time, too. Our attachment to the beautiful moments spent together becomes the cause of misfortune, the soul's and ours. We don't take into account that it's very hard as it is for the departing soul to leave everything it loved, the person it lived for, the things it was involved with. It is torn, it simply doesn't know what it is to do. It would like to depart because it feels that it should; but it would like to stay because it misses life. That's why it's important not to add to the departing soul's predicament our own grief and despair. Every soul is given the appropriate time for its departure. If we don't let it go then that time passes and the soul is no longer able to depart under its own power. When, after some time, we grow accustomed to our loss we become more willing to bid farewell to the soul but by then it is incapable of leaving. The time accorded to it for that has passed.

What also happens is that's it's not we who hold back the soul but that it's the soul itself that decides to stay. But whereas in such circumstances we have no influence, we create the former situation ourselves. Unfortunately both cases sometimes create tragic results which are revealed to us in the very near future.

When a mutually loving couple is separated by a sudden, unexpected death, they find it hard to be reconciled to it. That's why it's quite normal, after the funeral, to recall our beloved tenderly, often thinking back to moments spent together. We recollect every kiss, every tender touch and every ecstasy of our love. Our imagination starts to create ever newer pictures and there is no end to our recollections. This kind of fantasizing brings us succor, our hearts seem to be lighter somehow. This is, however, a very crucial period during which we have to be very wary. To begin with we are very pleased to feel our beloved's presence so intensely it's like they were alive. We start to sense his touch, his caresses more and more tactilely. It makes us feel good. We don't notice that we are going further and further in what we're doing. There comes a moment when we feel as if we were making physical love. Soon this becomes part of the normal state of things and we start having sex with the ghost. This state of affairs can even go on till the end of our lives, but the moment we try to stop is when the problems begin.

What kind of problem? Weeks pass, then months and maybe years and what at the beginning gave us joy and contentment is no longer enough. We no longer want to live in solitude among ghosts. We want to be with people, with the living. We've come to know someone with whom we feel good, we have someone to talk with, go for a walk with, go to the movies with, or a party. We want to forget the past, or at least enough to make it possible to be with the living. Usually, however, we fail in this because the bond with the beloved ghost continues. Very often it won't let us have contact with other people. It will drive away anyone who comes towards us or is close to us. It has grown used to our commitment and it doesn't want to share us with anyone. It arranges things (this happens very often) so that people shy away from us: our family, work colleagues, even passers-by in the street. So we start to wonder what's wrong with us. It doesn't even enter our heads that anyone who comes close to us is, quite simply, pushed away by the ghost.

We are left completely alone. It can sometimes happen that we become attached for a short time to someone who is strong enough to resist the ghost. Then we can be happy: at last we are not alone, at last we have someone. We make a new relationship confident that there is a glorious future ahead of us. We can still remember what love is, how to love and be loved. We have a magnificent partner. Unfortunately, there is something amiss right from the start of the new relationship. We wonder what the reason for that might be. Maybe it's come too soon after the death? Maybe everything in the house reminds us of the dead person? Our new partner, out of love for us and respect for the ghost of the dead person, may bear patiently all that goes on in the hope that, with time, the situation will become normal and that we will be able to live together happily. We do not realize, however, that there are three of us in the relationship and not, as we think, just two. Neither our partner nor we associate the problems that arise, one after another, with the ghost. Sometimes our partner will sense someone's presence. They feel as if, day and night, someone was constantly watching them. And whereas we ourselves regard it as normal, having grown accustomed to it long ago, it may seem extraordinarily suspicious to our partner. We wait, we deceive ourselves that everything will be well, that somehow everything will sort itself out, but day after day things get worse. Sometimes we have constant headaches, we almost can't sleep at night, we wake several times a night. At work we're hardly alive, we constantly make mistakes, our colleagues keep away from us. We think: "If things go on like this, I'll lose my job".

Writing this I had in mind a young couple, but the same situation can arise in relationships at any age, even in the relationship between a parent and a child. Since we have detained a departing soul, the soul now demands from us our exclusive attention. The whole of our being is drawn to the living, but the ghost doesn't want to let us do that.

How then should two people who love one another take leave of each other? Should they not experience grief at all? Experience it, as I wrote earlier, in the most appropriate way for us - yes, but at the same time in such a way that we do not impinge on the peace of the departing soul. Let the soul know that we love it very much, that we miss it at this moment, but because we love it so much we are letting it depart. This is a very difficult time, for the dying person as much as for us. It is too late to think about it at the moment it affects us. That's why it's so important to consider death before we experience it. At these burdensome moments we should be aware that we all belong to God and that, at the moment of death, we are returning to Him. When we understand this or even start to think this way things will be much easier. Death is nothing other than a return from the school which is our earthly life back home, into the arms of a loving God. We come to Earth to learn something (Love), and when we have completed our lessons we return home. When we try to keep a departing soul by our sides it's like detaining a classmate from school without taking into account that we will see each other at home shortly.

People living in various personal relationships should talk to each other when they're alive about the fact that one of them will die sometime. In many families this is a taboo subject. Nobody dares to mention the death of a family member until it happens. Unfortunately, after it happens is too late for such conversations. If, while still alive, a person reconciles himself with death, he becomes strong and knows what to do with himself. Both as the person departing and as the person remaining. Then death won't surprise us that much and won't shatter us as much. I have seen a loving couple saying goodbye to each other as if they were parting for literally a moment. They both knew that they would meet again soon. The one who is departing has completed everything, but the one staying still has something to learn. Most probably it would have been impossible for them to learn it at all if they had stayed together. There was no regret or despair in this farewell, only great love and some sadness.

Death on Earth is birth on the other side of death's curtain. Though to many it may seem painful, if we prepare for it then it shows itself to be a blessing and stops causing pain.

During sessions of hypnosis my patients have sometimes gone through their previous incarnations and the periods between them. They often said: "I never expected death to be so simple and life to have such great sense from a wider point of view". Death is terrifying only when we fear it. Our dread stems most often from the fact that we know nothing about it. Sometimes the very thought of death shatters us. We can't imagine that one can talk about like it was something completely straightforward. That's why it's so important to learn to express our views on the subject, tie up all our affairs on Earth and assure our partners that we will wait for them on the other side of death's curtain.

The dying person should take care of their spouse's future and free them from their vows. Many people need permission for a new relationship so they don't have to live for many long years in solitude or feeling that they're betraying the beloved soul. The fact that the person remaining alive might fall in love with someone else doesn't mean that they'll forget about the first spouse or will love them any the less. A person who loves with true love does so with all their heart and in their heart there is room for more than one person. Such a person is also loved because love returns to the sender like a boomerang. You may not know where it will come from, but what is certain is that it will come back multiplied. A loving mother loves all of her children the same regardless of how many she has. A loving person is never alone, they have friends, the whole Universe supports them.

A person who allows their heart to close up through despair, grief and loneliness is embittered. They cannot love anyone and they are a burden to those around them. They never give, they merely take and demand. A jealous, insidious, revengeful person is most often alone and is afraid of everything - old age, disease, poverty. It's worth thinking about this when there are still the two of us here.

It can happen that we are so terrified of death that we can't talk about it even when it is high time to do so, for instance during a long and serious illness. We could pretend that it's not appropriate, that one shouldn't frighten the sick person, that if we do so they might discover that they are dying. We might even believe that doing so might hasten their death. All this masquerade is totally unnecessary. The sick person's soul already knows that the end of its incarnation is approaching. This knowledge should be allowed to get through to the sick person's consciousness. A sick person who is afraid of death and refuses to acknowledge it is like an ostrich which has buried its head in the sand hoping that no-one will notice it. But this will not save them from having to confront their problem. At this moment they have the chance to prepare gradually for death among people who wish them well. Later they will be taken by surprise and will be left to face death one on one. In a situation like that death will surprise both the person who is dying and the one who is staying with life.

So what happens is that both sides can cause harm that lasts for many years, sometimes to the end of their lives. The soul that is taken by surprise may not want to depart at all. After all, we have all deceived it saying it was only ill. We didn't mention that it was dying. It may succumb to the delusion that it continues to live, so it stays among the living as a ghost. It can happen that, pierced by pain, we don't want to let the soul depart. Such behavior has nothing to do with love or common sense. We don't appreciate that the place for a dead person is on the other side of death's curtain. Both sides will suffer if the soul does not get there. I'll write about this in more detail later in this book.

RAPES

I have written about couples who, during their lives, were happy together, loved each other. When they were separated by death, the strength of their bond caused the ghost of the dead partner not to pass through to the other side of death's curtain. To begin with a person will have sex with the ghost voluntarily, intentionally, and it will give joy and consolation. It can happen that, after some time, a person gets to know a living person and stops wanting to have sex with the ghost. In most cases, the ghost will not want to allow this. We can start sensing pressure to cohabit with it though we don't want to at all. The fact that we have a living partner is something the ghost doesn't like in the least. It may start wanting to take by force something which, hitherto, it had been given quite freely. It can also hinder or make impossible any closeness for the living person. What happens, too, is that the ghost starts to rape both living lovers, one first, then the other, thus revenging itself for being betrayed.

When it can't cope itself, it summons help from its companions (other ghosts). Most often, ghosts perform their acts of rape at the moment that the two living lovers are about to make love. This is a tragedy for many couples. Even if the partners separate, the ghost is still capable of raping both of them independently for a long time afterwards. I know of cases when a couple couldn't even come close and fought against ghosts for many years. When they came to me and I escorted the vexatious ghosts away they no longer had troubles of this nature. I have written about couple who were very close during their lives, but similar things happen in every kind of relationship.

You have to be very cautious if the ghost of a person whom you knew closely starts to visit you after death, especially if the basis of your relationship was sex. This can even apply to long forgotten liaisons. It can happen that the ghost is an old friend from school, from work, or an acquaintance from the block where you lived. It can be someone you didn't even find attractive and you might not have been involved with them at all. It's quite possible that you were the object of their sighs, their arousal. Many people come to me with this problem. They are always very keen that no-one should find out about it. It's often a spouse whose partner knows nothing about it. What transpires from conversations or letters is that to a large extent they could have avoided their misfortune but they didn't react as they should have done in time.

These stories all began in a rather similar way. The person who comes to me for help was at some time very powerfully aroused sexually and had no-one to unload this arousal with. The stimulation for this arousal could have been a meeting with a friend, a film they saw, a memory etc. At exactly that moment, the ghost arrived and fulfilled our need. When it started to appear again we didn't know exactly what we should do. It may be that we acquiesce to these visits but only at night or when we want to have sex. Most often, though, this later turns into a kind of obsession. The ghost wants to make love regardless of the circumstances or the time of day. That's when it stops pleasing us, but we don't really know how we can break away.

Here's how such an incident is described by a sixteen year old girl. In her neighborhood a handsome, charming middle-aged man died. Every time she saw him he used to be with a different girl. She longed to be in the place of these girls. Unfortunately, when he was living he didn't even smile at her. After he died, she often thought about him. One evening she was lying in bed when suddenly he appeared in the corner of her room like he was alive. She regarded herself as an unattractive person so when she saw him the sight of him pleased her. In the blink of an eye he was lying on top of her and started to make love to her. She was terrified because she had never had sex with a man before. She was always afraid that her parents will hear what was happening and fly into her room. In the morning she thought about the night visit a lot. That's how her "adventure" with the ghost began. The man started coming to her every night, then several times a night, until finally he started to rape her whenever he had the urge to, even during school lessons or in front of her parents at home. Then she used to roll into a ball and pretend that she had terrible stomach pains. Her parents and her teachers realized that there was something terribly wrong with her. She became lethargic, lost interest in everything, stopped learning. Then they turned to me for help. The girl begged me not to tell anyone. She was aware that if she hadn't let the ghost have sex with her that first time then she wouldn't have laid herself open to all that had happened to her later. She also understood that it was an error to brood about the dead.

There are many marriages which have stopped being a couple long ago. They stay together only because of the children, joint property, or out of habit. There's been no love there for a long time, if there ever was any. Many such couples no longer have sex. There can be many reasons for that, e.g. hurt feelings in one partner, the dying-out of passion, frigidity. Sometimes one of the pair wants to have sex while the other, out of spite maybe, constantly refuses. Sometimes it takes the form of manipulating the partner in the form of: do what I want you to and you'll get sex otherwise I'll continue to refuse it. When one of the partners in a couple like that dies and doesn't pass through to the Light, there can arise in them a thirst for revenge or a desire to satisfy their unquenched lust. The ghost will want to take by force what till then it couldn't get. Sometimes the partner will resist even then. In which case the ghost will have to leave. It can then start to seek out a different object which will not be so resistant. Rapes usually come when a ghost desires sex but imagines it can never get it voluntarily. Only in rare cases does taking someone by force bring the ghost any great pleasure.

A man once asked me: "Is it possible for the ghost raping someone to be an old man, and the person they're raping an old woman?" I said, but of course it is. After death ghosts often acquire strength and have more energy than they did when they were living, which cannot be said of the partner who remains on Earth. "Very well, you passed my test," said the man. "I asked this question in many parishes, monasteries, even in the Vatican, and they all sent me away with nothing thinking I was a madman." He started to tell me: "My parents never lived in harmony. My father liked a drink and he usually couldn't resist a skirt. When he died he was nearly ninety years old. I'm sad to say that when he died we all breathed a sigh of relief. Unfortunately, from the moment he died I noticed something unnerving about my mother's behavior. At first I thought she was taking my father's death badly. After all, they did spend a long time together. When I asked her she waved me away saying it was worse than that, that I couldn't even imagine. She didn't want to explain anything to me, but soon the situation clarified itself. Since I didn't want to leave her on her own in the state she was in, I resolved she would move in with me. I went to bed early because I had a heavy day at work. Through my sleep I could hear muffled moaning sounds coming from my mother's room. I leapt to my feet, ran to her room and saw her defending herself against someone who was invisible to me and seemed to be raping her. My mother is eighty-six years old and so I assumed that all that sort of stuff was behind her. I stood as if I was rooted to the ground, not knowing what to do. Involuntarily I shouted out: 'Leave her, you bastard!'. My mother started to calm down. She burst into tears and said this had been happening since my father's death. He had frequently raised his hand to her. Whenever I stood up in her defense, he would leave her in peace, just like now. I deduced that it must be him. He took fright at my voice, just as he did when he was living. After a while I came to the conclusion that apart from him there must be others, because my mother defended herself from all sides. She was at the end of her strength, almost lifeless. A doctor friend of ours, who also witnessed an attack, sent her to hospital and fortified her with medicines. My mother won't be able to keep going much longer. Can you help her?" he asked me.

    I escorted the ghosts to the other side: there were indeed many of them. For a while there was relief, but after a few days I received a call that his mother was worse again. This lasted several weeks before we realized that his mother had entered into an arrangement with her husband's ghost. She let him have normal sex but when he sometimes fancied something a bit stronger and summoned other ghosts to an orgy then she turned to me for help. I protested. It turned out that she thought that since he was her husband she had to put up with him even after death. When she said "No!" categorically, he left albeit unconsoled, but he never came back.

You don't even realize how many people are raped by ghosts day in day out, and every night. The ghost-rapist can be our life's partner or a complete stranger. It can be one ghost or a whole multitude. The victim of the rape can be anyone. Sometimes it can be a close friend who doesn't have the courage to talk about it. One might think it was just about a person's imagination, that it's not really happening. That's the conclusion usually reached by those people to whom the afflicted person complains. The person might do it once or twice but when the next successive attempt to tell someone meets with disbelief they stop seeking help. I've been a witness to such scenes more than once. This isn't about suspecting everyone who behaves oddly of being raped but about helping those people who asks us for help. How? By letting them know that such help is possible.

Two friends of many years' standing, who knew literally everything about one another, came to me for therapy from the other end of Poland. I had met one of them once already when she'd needed my help. She tried in every way possible to get onto the subject of ghosts which for the other woman was ridiculous, superstitious, reminding her of children's games when the kids try to frighten one another. When the first woman wanted to say anything, the other one would effectively make it difficult for her. I realized what was happening and guided the conversation accordingly. I saw relief on one face and an ironic grimace on the other. Taking no notice of that I continued to direct the conversation. I wondered why the first woman had brought the other with her. If she had been on her own we would have gone straight to the heart of the matter without going round in circles and wasting time. At a certain moment I heard once again an ironic comment: "I'm surprised that you've joined in with all those con artists we keep hearing about nowadays. I always regarded you as an authority and that's why I came here from the other end of Poland, but I can see that it's time wasted." I didn't have time to reply before the first woman tore her blouse off herself. Her body looked like it had been massacred. There wasn't a spot on it without a scar, a bruise or a scratch. She lifted her long skirt and showed us her bruised, cut legs. "Is this a waste of time!?" she shouted. "I've tried to tell you so many times but it's like you're deaf and blind. This is why I came here."

It came out that for many years she was raped by a sadist-ghost and her closest friend didn't even suspect or in any case didn't want to suspect anything. When people think about ghosts, they subconsciously feel that they do exist. The awareness that there exists a reality which they can't touch fills them with terror. They feel helpless because they think they have no influence on the other world. We started the purification. The ghost would leave and then return. When we succeeded in escorting it away for keeps, the woman's body started to heal quickly so that only faint scars remained to remind her of the tragedy.

I have come across many similar cases in my therapeutic work. You can recognize the signs of rape from scars in some people, in others there is no trace. Fortunately for the patient: they don't have to explain where the bruises came from. This can often cause another tragedy because there's no rational way of explaining where they came from, yet there is this unequivocal indication of their origin.

It can happen that someone very close to us is raped and

we suspect nothing. One of our workers, or a colleague can be experiencing this problem. These people often drink too much or are constantly tired, not getting enough sleep. There can be moments (e.g. suddenly, in the middle of a conversation) when they behave totally irrationally, only to calm down, return to normal a split-second later. I have seen many times a rape being committed by ghosts in broad daylight, in the midst of a fair number of people. People attach great importance to when and in what place they make love or have sex. For ghosts it's completely unimportant if we're alone, at home, at work, in a public place, with other people. The ghost wants sex at a given moment and starts to rape us. It is invisible to the people around and feels itself to be inviolable. It completely ignores the fact that the person being raped can be seen by the people nearby. The person concerned obviously feels terrified and embarrassed. They cannot hide it, they don't know how to react. Sometimes they do manage to go out just in time, to hide. People ask what's happened and they don't know what to do or say. People being raped can't concentrate on their work so they commit blunders easily. Then they try to put them right quickly. But sometimes the damage can be irreversible. When this happens regularly they get fired even if they used to be good workers.

How is it that such tragedies happen? As I've written already, for some reason a ghost decides to remain on this side of death's curtain. Nothing much changes in its life. If during its life its needs and thoughts circled round sexual matters then that will be the case now. A ghost wants to satisfy its needs quickly. So it searches out a living person who has similar needs or thoughts. It is easier for it to hook up to such a person. It will not hook up to a frigid person with no sexual needs. A human being always has a choice, of course. So if a person doesn't want to, then the ghost has no access to them unless of course they are not aware of themselves, e.g. after drinking alcohol, taking drugs or succumbing to uncontrolled outbursts of negative emotions. It can be a one-off hook-up, but more often the ghost remains for ever. The ghost can be a man or a woman. The raped person can also be anyone - young, old, woman, man, even a child.

It's also worth mentioning the matter of compulsive masturbation. Many men believe that since they feel this compulsion they must be mentally ill. Masturbation can be caused by ghosts. When a ghost of a woman desires to have sex with a man he feels it but doesn't see her. Sometimes he may be merely very stimulated, but most often he is raped. When this happens often and he doesn't notice the object who desires him (rapes him) he accuses himself of sensual depravity. For many men this can occur in the least expected of places, completely out of the blue. Often, in a panic, they will go into the bushes, or a stairwell, or somewhere aside to hide themselves from public view since it's hard to conceal a swollen member. Sometimes they might come across children playing in the area whereby they might be suspected of pedophilia whereas in fact the children were drawn there only by curiosity. Many men experience great stress and humiliation when they're suspected of deviance. The same applies to self-exposure: the raped man sometimes doesn't want to soil his underwear with sperm, will expose himself somewhere in hiding (as he waits for the ghost's attack to pass) and when he's seen may be regarded as a deviant. Men are in the same situation as women being raped but rape on them is more visible than rape on women. After cleansing the above problems leave along with the ghosts. This happens, of course, only in cases of possession. By no means am I saying that every deviant act is caused by ghosts.

As you can see, rape can be carried out by one ghost,

several, or several dozen. We can be raped sporadically, only in our own homes and only at night, or several times during the day and night, in every place and every situation. No therapies in psychiatric hospitals or medicines are of any help here. They can blunt our experiences but they will not remove the cause of our misfortune. This doesn't mean that we're helpless victims with which the ghosts can do just as they please. The simplest method of defense is to forbid the ghost entrance into our bodies and not allowing the rape to happen. We need to note when the ghosts attack us and simply to say: "Ghost, I forbid you to approach my person. Leave instantly!" If we say the words with faith and conviction, then the ghost will have to leave since our will is sacrosanct. Sometimes it's necessary to repeat the statement several times. We are the only owners of our bodies and nobody else has any rights over it. This is well illustrated by the wise saying: "The torturer exists only as long as there is a victim. If there is no victim there'll be no torturer". When we say "No!" to a ghost and we're unbending in our resolve then it will be forced, however reluctantly, to take our will into account. It will want to stoke up fear in us, will try to manipulate us in different ways but it is up to us whether or not we give way to it. It can threaten that it will destroy us, kill us, humiliate us or anything else that comes into its mind but these are just idle threats. It can try to manipulate us in another way, by being tender, kind, ready to satisfy our sexual needs. It's up to us whether we let ourselves be led astray or not. When we state categorically that we don't want it and we're not afraid of it, then the ghost will be forced to leave us forever. Even when we are frightened at the very beginning we must have the courage to say a quiet: "no". Later our courage will grow and grow until we become free of fear and independent.

The situation is worse when a ghost satisfies our sexual

needs but we do not like the way how it is doing it. On the one hand we would like to get rid of it, on the other we're afraid that we'll be left alone with a great sexual appetite which we won't be able to deal with since it will remain unsatisfied. We must not, however, be afraid. There are great numbers of people in the world who will fit in with us both temperamentally and in sexual preferences. Besides which, we must remember that the world of ghosts is for ghosts and the world of people is for people and it's always bad when they have interact mutually.

I've been asked how we can tell when we're being raped or sexually stimulated by a ghost. Rape by a ghost is not very different from normal rape except that we don't see the perpetrators. But the victim can feel their presence as if they were alive. Even though we don't want it, we can't switch ourselves off from it.

It is of course not rape when we express our willingness to cohabit with a ghost and are merely embarrassed when it wants to make love at a moment which is inconvenient for us.

In the chapter on homosexuality, I'll write about children who are raped by parents, grandparents, uncles etc. When an adult who committed such acts dies, he continues to rape. This state of affairs can go on till the end of the victim's life since "the child" may never rebel. It simply doesn't know that things can be different. Even when it does find out a lot of time must pass before it comes to terms with this knowledge and makes the decision to change the situation. Sometimes such a grown-up "child" may not have the courage to defy the ghost of a father, a mother or some other adult even when they are long dead. Even though life with ghosts is very hard, "the child" stubbornly identifies associating with ghosts as providing safety, love and even fulfillment, not realizing that the reverse is true. It's like a person who spends their lives in a cage. When they get the chance to escape from it, they don't do it. The new situation seems to them to be terrifying because it seems to be the unknown. For these reasons therapy for such a wounded child is usually very difficult and doesn't bring the desired effects.

I personally know of several instances where a grown man was so afraid of his father that he trembled at the very thought of him. Sometimes this might be a sickly, bowed man who apologized for everything, but there were among them men who you wouldn't want to meet on a dark night. I'm usually asked for help by a wife or one of the man's friends because the man himself doesn't have enough courage. Strangely enough, in all these cases the fathers of these men died a long time ago. After death they ensnared their children who were beaten by them from earliest childhood and often (though not always) brutally raped. Unfortunately, none of them remembered any of that consciously. They were afraid but in truth they didn't know what of. Even when the father's ghost is escorted away the fear of him doesn't go. Then it's worth very carefully, step by step, to return to those events and heal them all. The most difficult is taking the first step because the patient doesn't know what might happen to him. If he has enough courage further steps of healing come much more easily. The same applies to women who were raped in childhood.

There is at present a lot of interest in regression and hypnosis. People are keen to find out about their earlier incarnations, who they were, what they owned etc. Sometimes their subconscious, instead of taking them to a previous incarnation, will lead them to that moment in their childhood when the wounding took place. What can happen then is that a person who is unprepared for it may become panic-stricken. In the chapter on homosexuality I'll describe an event in which a "chance" session reminded a now adult woman of the sexual transgressions committed on her by her father. A wound which wasn't healed in time became the cause of several years of torture. Therapists have a great responsibility. A "problem" patient must never be left to their own resources; the memory must be healed as soon as possible even if it was not the subject of the session at the beginning.

HOMOSEXUALITY

I receive many phone calls, letters and sometimes visits from parents or guardians asking me to help their children. They are horrified to have discovered that their daughter is a lesbian or their son is gay. They are shocked, shaken by this fact and they are unable or they don't want to accept the otherness of their child. Some have rows with them, forbid them to see their partner, others throw them out of their homes, cutting off all contacts with their child. Sometimes the child will rebel and run away from home. Then a hunt for the child follows carried out by the parents or the police and forcing the child to come back home. When the child is an adult parents react in different ways: some seek help, others wring their hands. There are those who are able, through love, to accept the otherness of their child. All those who have been touched by this suffer, though they don't always show it on the outside. The parents don't understand their child's otherness even though many of them have contributed to it. They also don't realize that their children often suffer even more than they do. They are rejected not just by their family, but sometimes also by their friends, acquaintances, and society. Often they themselves don't understand why they're not like everyone else. They feel themselves to be inferior, sullied, evil. That's why they cling to their homosexual partners, because from them they get the support which they so lack from those around.

I think this chapter will explain a lot and will help people to accept this otherness. It may well be that reading it you will yourself experience various kinds of feelings. They may come from your mind or your body. You may experience tremors or hot and cold flushes. You may feel so sick that you think you're about to vomit. You may revolt and refuse to allow the information given here into your consciousness, regarding it as garbage. If you do show one of these symptoms then it is all the more important that you read this chapter. Read it in small fragments, but read it. If you believe it has nothing to do with you or if you express yourself negatively about homosexuals or transvestites, if your insides rebel and can't accept its contents, then reading this is that much more essential to you. You don't have to do anything with this knowledge, but at least you will possess it. You can not read it only when you understand, accept and are not overly affected by its contents.

I'll try to explain the reasons why some of us prefer partners of the same sex, why some people can't identify with their own bodies and decide to undergo a sex change. One of the causes of homosexuality (in a considerable number of cases) is the entrance into a child of a ghost and its partial or total overpowering of it. The most frequent reason for ghosts staying is that they haven't totally reconciled themselves with their own deaths. Even when they were alive they often thought that if they were younger and they were given the chance to relive their lives then they would live them completely differently. In their earthly existence, the personal affairs of these ghosts revolved almost exclusively around satisfying their sexual desires. After death their sexual urges pull them down and prevent them going further towards the Light. They are tied to the questions which filled their whole lives, that is the pursuit of a suitable partner. Now this becomes their motive force, an obsession in the seeking out of anyone who happens to be at hand and who would satisfy their needs and unrealized dreams best of all. From the ghosts' point of view, children are a perfect objective.

The kind of ghost I'm talking about doesn't want to be born again. It wants to get one more chance. It needs a person who will allow themselves to be possessed by the ghost (preferably someone who has the whole of their lives before them). Mourning in the home, sorrow, longing, the child's despair at the death of, let's say, its grandfather, opens the door to the child's interior for the grandfather's ghost. The child thinks about him because it was attached to him. When the grandfather appears next to the child, the child doesn't fear him, doesn't shut itself off from him – on the contrary it opens its inside to him, ready to receive him. Thus possession is easy for the ghost and the moment of possession is imperceptible to the family. The ghost is most often a close family member, someone the child knows well and is not afraid of. It can be an uncle, granddad, grandma, aunt or even a father or mother. Shortly after it is possessed, not just the child's character changes, but even its appearance. Despite that, these changes (often considerable) remain almost unnoticed because they constantly oscillate round traits common to the whole family. Someone might say: "He's so like his granddad Joe" or: "Look, our boy's just like Uncle Chuck, he even moves the same way as him". Everyone considers this to be quite normal, that they're traits carried over in the genes, but often that isn't the case at all.

When the body of a small child is penetrated by, for instance, the ghost of an aunt who, during her life, was a flighty woman, liking to dress herself up in the newest rags, spending most of her time in front of a mirror, then in time the child will also start to reveal these tendencies. This will remain almost unnoticed when the child is a little girl. What we'll say then is that she's growing up to be a little doll and no-one will think badly of it. When these same tendencies are noticed in a boy, the parents become uneasy and they start to try and drive them out of his head. This might, however, be ineffective. It can happen that this trait becomes more apparent the more rigorously the parents are against it. The child is punished for something which isn't in the least his fault and which strengthens the aunt's need as she dwells inside his body to show herself off, to dress herself up. If the boy has sisters then the impression might arise that he's following their example and wants to be a girl like them. If he's an only child then he'll secretly go through his mother's things, trying them on, wearing them. In extreme cases the aunt's ghost possesses the boy so completely he won't want to wear his boy's clothes at all. Every free moment will be spent trying on women's clothes, outfits, underwear, walking in high-heeled shoes, using cosmetics for make-up, wearing jewelry. It will take on the form of an obsession.

If a ghost having different character traits than those of a child enters the child it's obvious that the child will behave differently. It will come to similar mental harm, naturally. Signs of possession may be only slightly noticeable to those around, or maybe not at all. It depends what attitude to femininity and sex the woman-ghost had as to how the possessed boy regards his own body when he reaches the age of early manhood. If, during her life, the woman accepted her body, liked herself, then such a boy can want very much to be a girl and won't identify with his boyish body at all. If her appearance was of no importance to her, then the possessed boy, though he will feel himself to be a girl, won't be bothered about his body. If he is strong internally and undertakes to fight against the intruding ghost then he may be himself for one moment and a woman the next, or both the one and the other simultaneously.

Things will be very different if a boy's body is entered by the ghost of a man. He will, for a bit, be himself still but increasingly he will be a small adult man. He will not behave like a boy of his age. This is noticed by people around him and that's when we hear: "Our little guy is behaving exactly like his late departed granddad." Unfortunately, more often than not, we disregard such observations. We put them down to genetic similarities, but they have nothing at all to do with genetics. It's hard to come to terms with the fact that, inside our little child, there is someone else, someone who, when he was alive, we may have loved and respected. When the boy grows up he may not suffer any physical consequences of possession, but it will more than certainly be reflected mentally. If he surrenders to the ghost he'll live his life like a puppet, and if he fights then he will be internally torn apart, he'll sense that there's something not right with him. This can result in various consequences, most of them certainly negative.

However, if the ghost of a man enters the body of a little girl then her behavior will change considerably and she'll change into a tomboy. She'll want to wear pants, she'll start fights, play football, run around with boys. When she grows up she'll practice martial arts or competitive sports. As time passes she'll accept her female body less and less. She won't be able to stand the sight of her breasts and she'll want to have a penis more and more. Unless of course she remains strong and struggles against the intruder.

The self-identity of these children is severely affected. Physically, they are one person but internally they are someone else. They have had their childhood taken away from them because from the time they were very young they contended with the problems of their adult tenants. It might well be that, to begin with, the ghosts even wanted to help the small things but with the passing of time they completely forgot about that and were just themselves.

A child grows up and starts to look for sexual partners. When a woman-ghost has dominated the mind of a boy, he will seek out contacts with men. Most likely he'll join up with another homosexual who might well be in the same situation as he is. At last, the ghost of the woman has what it has been waiting for so long, namely young men. At last she feels fulfilled. She is young, healthy, in the body of a man, she has friends who are men, and even a lover or lovers. She realizes, however, that she cannot achieve total fulfillment as a woman. After all, she is residing in the body of a man. She may therefore go further in her demands and strive to change the gender of the possessed boy. Consequently, he will start writing to various clinics, asking, seeking, finding out, undergoing psychological tests, torments of self-identity.

If the ghost of the woman doesn't completely dominate the mind of the boy then he'll merely feel a desire for other men. At the same time he will, as a boy, be repulsed by them. Depending on which part of his personality is in the ascendant at a given moment, he will feel and act accordingly. This constant change of orientation will cause him to be revolted by himself. This is the reason why there is a general lack of acceptance of homosexuals. They are not accepted because they do not accept themselves. They are simply not fully themselves. The external reality shows them only what they have within.

The same thing happens by analogy to a girl who has been possessed by a man. When she grows up she looks for a partner among other women. Many parents and close relatives turn to me with just such problems. They regard it as bringing shame to the whole family when their child has a same-sex partner. What's interesting is that in the majority of cases the parents accuse their child's partner of manipulation, seduction, black magic etc. To some extent they're right. Their child is a victim, just not of their partner but of the possession which happened many years earlier.

How do I know all this? From hundreds out of the several thousand patients of mine world-wide. They recount their experiences to me, or write lengthy letters. They're finally able to express what they've been afraid to tell others. Quite often they didn't understand themselves, were afraid of the reaction of their surroundings. Their near ones also turn to me and they describe the same situation from their point of view. I find out most, however, from the ghosts themselves.

And here is an example, one of many. Parents looking for their daughter came to me: she had run away to some "depraved" lesbian friend of hers. Having examined both girls I start to doubt that the daughter's friend is having such a great influence on her. When I announce that their daughter's problems are caused because she is possessed, I'm frequently attacked by the parents. When I tell them who has possessed their daughter and what difficulties she has been struggling with for many years, they most often get up and leave, thinking they've come to the wrong person. They nearly always come back because, in the mean time, I have led the ghost away and the child has either returned home or sent a letter of apology. Sometimes, the parents receive a letter in which their child describes her tragedy step by step. Sometimes they all come back together to thank me. It's then that I hear stories that freeze the blood in my veins.

For example I discover that they wrote to various clinics looking for a sex-change. Fortunately, doctors know that this is a serious life-changing decision and they introduce all sorts of difficulties. An operation is preceded by numerous tests. Many young people go through these tests successfully, but many of them simply can't afford them. I know dozens of cases where a lack of money saved them from the operation. It's frightening to think what would have happened if it had gone ahead. Often, together with the parents, I witness extraordinary transformations during the cleansing process. One time the patient is a straight girl, saying with a shudder: "God, how could I, yuk, touch her let alone do something more" – and another time, having been possessed anew, she runs away from home and wants to throw herself at every passing girl since the ghost is very active sexually. She's furious because she doesn't have a member, she cuts her own breasts. She is so very unhappy. Girls like that were already willing to remove their breasts but that would be only half the solution because what they most wanted is a penis. The reverse is true of boys. They are desperate to rid themselves of their penis, sometimes they have breast implants. Many seriously consider performing the operation of cutting off their genitals themselves.

When a person like that is cleansed they are mystified by their own thoughts and reactions. They ask everyone to make sure they don't do anything stupid when the ghost catches up with them. Sometimes, these oscillations of emotions can last months when, for instance, her grand-father is sitting inside the girl's body and doesn't intend leaving. He possessed her body a long time ago and has completely identified with it.

The lives of these people will develop differently according to whether the ghosts have subjugated the child's mind completely or only partially. A crucial factor is also the degree to which the ghost is fixated on sex. If the ghost's sex-drive is low or moderate then it won't come to the drastic situations I've just described. A boy or girl like that will look for same-sex partners but won't have such a burning need to change and won't be so outrageous in the choice of clothes, behavior etc.

I wrote about gays and lesbians who are forced to be so. Their minds are in a state of constant conflict and they don't know how to change it. Whatever such a person thinks, the ghost will instantly confuse their line of reasoning. They won't know what's right and what's not. We have to remember that the ghost dwells within a child like that for many years, sometimes from infancy. The ghost knows the mentality of the possessed person very well. The line between the ghost and the person has been blurred. Usually, for the ghost the person doesn't exist as a being merely as a conduit for fulfilling the ghost's desires. These people find it hard to make deep relationships because that's something the ghosts aren't interested in. The ghost wants to have a great time, wants to sample as wide a variety of sexual experiences as possible which is impossible with just one partner. Hence the desire for frequent changes of partner, each one younger than the one before. Serial betrayal and abandonment among gays and lesbians is one cause of disillusionment and low self-esteem. These problems then have to be drowned quickly in alcohol or muted by drugs so as not to have time to think about them. Many of them say: "Since I'm constantly being abandoned by the partners I want to love with all my heart, what's the point of continuing to live?" That's how killer diseases like AIDS became widespread.

Another cause leading to homosexuality is sexual exploitation in childhood. From my many years' experience of psychotherapy I know that with nearly every such person sexual exploitation in childhood has played a smaller or larger part. Many children are everyday sexual objects for members of their own families, be it a father, brother, grandfather, uncle, mother or whoever. It's far less frequent for someone to be raped by a stranger outside the home. This state of affairs sometimes goes on for years and the members of the household suspect nothing, or they close their eyes to it. Not many family members stand up to defend a child raped in its own home. The children, apart from strangers, have no-one they can tell. The home should be a safe place for them. Unfortunately the adult carers often create the greatest threat. Members of the household, even when they suspect, will often pretend they don't see what's going on. There are many reasons for this. One of them is that the mother or the father quite often doesn't consider that there is anything inappropriate in it. Subconsciously they remember that they themselves were raped. What they experienced is now something they transfer to their own child. Sometimes a wife is so afraid that her husband will leave her that she shuts her eyes and convinces herself that she doesn't see what is only too evident. Sometimes she's too scared to confront him because she fears violence or a scandal.

There are daddies, uncles, mummies, aunties who are patient and prepare a child slowly for the role of a lover. To others it might happen completely unexpectedly, e.g. when they are taking their customary bath together with the child. A child may touch itself everywhere, sometimes unconsciously, most often out of curiosity. You sense its great sexual energy but the child senses yours, too. Children are very impulsive. They may have seen, or sensed, their parents making love or scenes of nudity on the television. Children imitate adults, and want to make love just like daddy or mummy. There is nothing evil in that. Every child wants to do that when they are small. Every child says that when they grow up they will marry their daddy or mummy. As the adult, you have to retain control of the situation. If you lose control then it will be just one tiny step to huge complications and suffering.

As I'm writing these words a patient phones me from the other end of the country and asks me for help for her granddaughter. I ask what kind of help and this is what I hear: "I'd like you to give the little girl some energy because she's being raped day in, day out by the wretch." "How do you mean – raped?" I ask. "You know about it and you do nothing?" "But what can I do? We're all frightened of him, he's the mayor of our town," she replies in a resigned tone of voice. I explain that this makes it better because it's enough to demand that he stops immediately. He'll most certainly do so because he'll be afraid of losing his position, not to mention his freedom. Suddenly I hear her shout: "You must be crazy! You expect me to deprive him of his fame, his success, his good position? But he's my son!" Clearly, this woman wasn't bothered about improving the girl's situation; she just wanted to work out what to do to make things right. Right, but for whom?

Another example. A single mother of a little son met a boy and they married. Shortly afterwards she became pregnant and gave birth to a daughter. She was very happy. The husband and the mother-in-law looked after the children when she went to school in another town. Whenever she returned, her son threw himself into her arms and nothing could drag him away from her. He was very unhappy to stay behind whenever she went away. She turned to me for advice. She wanted to know if she should abandon her studies or if she should send her son for some therapy. She guessed there was something not quite right with him, that he wasn't able to adapt to the new circumstances. My intuition immediately told me what was going on. I carefully started to lead her to what I had seen, and she stood rooted to the spot with terror. Everything started to make sense when she started to link individual happenings. She panicked. "Oh, God, I love my husband so much," she cried. "We have a complete family at last. What am I going to do now? I think I'll start by talking to my mother-in-law. She's a wise woman, I'm sure she'll advise me. Maybe nothing has actually happened yet."

She traveled home with a heavy heart, wondering how she could conduct the conversation without upsetting her mother-in-law. When she started, the other woman immediately replied: "I don't understand what your problem is. What are you so frightened of, and why are you so mad? Your husband's father raped him for most of his life and look what a fine man he's turned into. It won't do your son any harm either." She was horrified by her mother's-in-law approach. She hadn't expected that. She was torn, she struggled with herself. She was in love for the first time in her life and was she now supposed to give him up? She gave up her studies and stayed with her son day and night, wanting in this way to preserve both her son and her marriage. Soon she noticed that her little daughter was also increasingly afraid of her daddy. She took the children and ran away to the other end of the country. Her husband and mother-in-law are searching for her tirelessly. They have threatened to take away her parental rights. They claim that by taking them she has deprived her children of the conditions necessary for their lives and development. How much longer will she hide from them? How much longer will she have enough strength? After their departure the little boy's memory often goes back to his experiences with his step-father and he talks about what happened then. That makes her realize that she did the right thing but what will happen if she had to give the children back? How will she prove to the court that she acted in their defense?

Children are often made to feel guilty for having provoked a father or an uncle. Every child possesses an enormous energy of love which may be erroneously construed by adults as sexual energy. A small child will cuddle, kiss, touch and even wants its daddy to treat it like he does its mummy. Adults in such situations have to keep control of themselves so as not to give way to their drive. Many of them push their children away because they're afraid of that great power. If they didn't do that they would have to pit themselves against their energy and for many people doing that seems to be too difficult. Some people allow themselves to give way to their drive and then regret it, and try to recompense the child in all sorts of ways.

There are those, and many of them, who tried it and don't want to stop. In time the child gets bigger and may not want to make love to their daddy, mummy, auntie or uncle. Then people may notice that the child strangely keeps away from that person, like it was afraid of them or didn't like them. Sometimes there are more children in the family. The father will set about the next child or all of them at once. Sometimes this becomes a routine matter. Nobody rebels, daddy is the way he is and there's nothing that can be done about it. When the child is an only child who withdraws then the father feels betrayed. He won't accept his child's refusal. He may insist on his demands and take the child by force. That's when bruises on the child's body may be noticed by the nursery teachers or by members of the family.

I have written a lot about men, but women too can harm their own small children, boys and girls alike. A tiny baby is so sweet you can kiss it and cuddle it anywhere. This closeness which is full of love is good for both the parent and the child, but it's essential to know its limits, particularly when there is a lack of love in the relationship between the parents. The parent may want to make up for this lack through closer contact with its child. By fondling their tiny child they satisfy their own sexual needs while, at the same time, awakening the child's sexual energy. It might seem that there is no harm being done to the child in this way. That is not true. When the child grows up it will continue to demand to be fondled as it was before. Satisfying awakened sexual energies seems a natural thing for the child. Often it's only then that the parents come to their senses, seek help in psychiatric or psychological clinics, try to cure their child.

I can cite the case of a woman lawyer who asked me to help with her eight-year-old daughter. She began with by approaching me like this: "My little girl forces me to fondle her at the least suitable of moments. Recently she embarrassed me so badly that I don't know how I can face my friends again. Such an insult. Some male friends from work came round and my little girl came back from school in a confused and excited state of mind and she took off her knickers in front of them. You know, when my husband left me a few years ago I felt very lonely. I gladly fondled and cuddled my little daughter. You know, I had so much love inside me. I think I must have poured it all out onto her. When I was kissing her like that, it gave me so much pleasure, and she liked it, too. Sometimes we would spend whole evenings like that together. I could see nothing wrong in it. I myself wanted someone to love me so strongly and fondle me like that. I don't know when she stopped being a girl and became a young woman. Now she has the same needs as a fully grown woman, sometimes so powerful that they can't be left till later. What can I do? I didn't think I was doing anything wrong. Please advise me..." "I don't understand what help you want me to give you," I said. "I want you to perform some kind of spell so that everything goes back to normal and my daughter is like other girls of her age."

Just as you cannot stop a river in flood so you can't stop the powerfully aroused sexual drive of a child. There is a very strong likelihood that in the future the girl will equate sex with contact with a woman and her mother will wonder why her daughter is a lesbian.

I have many similar cases among girls and boys alike. Their strong sexual urges is a considerable problem for these young people. Sometimes, because they can't get what they have grown accustomed to at home they start to run away from home. Away from home their fate can be unpredictable. Often their choice falls on the first person who satisfies their awakened desires or one who does so in a better way.

It is very important to show such a young person that you accept them. That will increase the chances that they won't run away from us and that they will feel safe. They will be able to decide and choose what is best for them. Condemnation often leads these children onto the wrong path.

I wrote about a small girl, but the same process applies to a boy. Even if the father or other adult did not go as far as to rape him. A boy like that will inevitably desire men or women and men simultaneously. Even if in later life he does not remember his relations with the man that took place when he was a child, deep inside he will always associate powerful sexual energies with men. He'll wonder what's not quite right about him. Why is he attracted to men? He may deny his desire for men and lead a life with a woman but often he won't find full satisfaction in such a union. Subconsciously he feels himself to be gay which provokes fear and disgust with himself, with gays and this often leads to hatred.

Among the most virulent antagonists of homosexuality are the very people who were subjected to sexual exploitation but who can't remember it. Even when the small child is raped and feels itself to have been hurt it will still feel an attraction to the same sex. This choice stems not from the fact that the child has got to know someone and has fallen in love them; it stems from the need to satisfy a sexual drive which was frequently stimulated in childhood.

It's very often the case that damage inflicted gives rise to similar damage later. So, for instance, a man who was raped when he was a child will feel a powerful need to rape his own small child. Only the acceptance of people with homosexual problems can provide an opportunity to improve the situation and to heal. We must remember that children who have been damaged during their childhood feel themselves to be victims and so when in addition they are rejected it becomes too great a burden for them to cope with.

There are those among gays, lesbians and transvestites who really do love and are loved by their partners. It doesn't matter to them who the object of their love is, whether their partner is young or old, it doesn't matter if the person they love is a woman or a man. Love like that is real love. Love with a capital "L" is the most important thing in the world. Every human being strives for it. It is worth overcoming every obstacle, giving everything for love like that. What does real love give people, why is it so important to people? Love is everything that exists. There is nothing more important, nothing more valuable than love. Anyone who loves is healthy, happy, possessing inner riches. They are incapable of harming anyone or doing anything against Nature. They love everyone around them, the whole world. Then the whole Universe will respond with love for them. Just the existence of the other person is enough, even if they are at the other end of the world. Just knowing that they are there is enough. It's not just our well-being that counts, but theirs does just as much. We are unable to betray them or hurt them in any other way. What is important to us is THAT person, their love, their spiritual closeness, their commitment. Sex becomes an expression of love, of giving, it is not a duty. Neither is it the reason for being in the relationship. A love like that has every chance of lasting till the end of life and beyond. Have you ever seen an old couple who have passed through life in love? Outwardly they have aged but the same fire burns within them as it did when they were young, when they only just met each other and fell in love. They are still kept beautiful by that love. People who chose out of love continue to love and be loved. They are free and happy, they don't need to fear because in their hearts they have an unshakable certainty.

HEALING WOUNDS

Summing up I'd just like to touch on the question of healing injuries arising out of childhood sexual experiences. Many of us feel ourselves to be victims of those events our whole lives long. There is a strong probability that you too, dear reader, are constantly scratching at old wounds. But you can look into your past and heal it. When we face the thing we're frightened of healing follows and we become ready to move forward healthy, happy and joyful. Many people, even though they were quite big "children", sometimes almost adults, have completely scrubbed that period out of their memories. But God doesn't want us to push these events into our subconscious and finds various ways to remind us of them. He sends us many opportunities to confront the truth, to forgive and to heal. This may take the form of a serious illness, repeatedly dissolving relationships, health-destroying habits, dissatisfaction with life, constant lack of money, lack of love. It will be something which will have a sufficiently key significance for us to motivate us to start looking. We can be guided to the memories that lead to healing by a movie, a book, a similar occurrence, a story from our childhood, an old photo, a therapy session etc.

The following is a good example of this. An acquaintance of mine, Maggy, was taking part in workshops on spiritual development and volunteered to subject herself to hypnosis. Even though she is a very experienced medium she found it hard to allow the hypnotist to regress her. For most of the séance nothing much happened. The leader wanted, therefore, to bring the unsuccessful session to an end. At that moment Maggy sighed and, like a throw away remark, she said in a childish voice: "Oh, it's good he came in the evening. I'll be able to get some sleep". After a moment's pause, she cried out: "No, please, you promised you wouldn't come today". The hypnotist did not pursue the matter and finished the session. His task was to show how hypnosis worked, he didn't want to get involved in therapy. Straight after the session Maggy called me and said, her voice revealing great concern: "Imagine, when I was little my father raped me and I forgot everything about it. I have conducted sessions with other people and it never occurred to me that it's something that concerns me too. I'm mad at my father for doing that to me, but I'm mad at myself, too. I scratched open this wound and I feel that there may be something even worse underneath it." "Come over to my place," I suggested but she declined. "I must deal with this by myself," she replied. That same night Maggy's husband called me and asked me to help. "Wanda, I just don't understand what's happening to Maggy. She came back from her trip and was behaving quite normally. But when her parents visited us in the evening, she completely freaked out. She saw her father at the door and she was so terrified she crawled under the table. We couldn't get her to come out whatever we did. Has she lost her senses, Wanda?" I advised him to send the parents home. Maggy couldn't go back to her old self or understand what had happened to her for several days. In her everyday life she is the mother of two children, a wife, the owner of a business, a strong and decisive woman, but in her father's presence she became a small, terrified, powerless little girl. Her parents pretended that the situation she talked about never took place and they tried to convince her it was a figment of her imagination.

Some time later I met her mother. She must have had a strong sense of guilt because she brought the conversation round to the subject of Maggy and Maggy's father of her own volition. "I did know that there was something going on between them but I never reacted to it. My view was that it was better for my husband to keep these things at home, even though it was with his own daughter than that he should run round town chasing skirts," she said. I saw then how much she hated her own daughter, in the depths of her soul, for taking her husband away from her. Maggy persisted in wanting to clarify that situation and her parents broke off all contact with her.

Many years have passed since that session. My friend went through various therapies which brought few results because they didn't bring her the peace she desired and didn't quiet the fears. We lived far from each other and our contacts were limited to telephone conversations. I often mentioned that I could give her effective help, that patients of mine with similar experiences have long since been made well. She wasn't ready for it just then. One day, without any warning, she was standing at my door. We started a session which I tape recorded just in case her subconscious continued to refuse to remember.

This, in a greatly abbreviated form, is what I heard. "Maggy, go back to the moment when you made love with your daddy." Every time I asked her how old she was. It all began when she was three years old. She started to talk in a childish voice. "There, he's come..." "And who is it who's come to you?" I ask. "Why, daddy." "And why has daddy come to you?" "To love with me." "And do you like to love with daddy?" "Oh, yes, very much," she replies with delight but instantly adds that only in the evening because in the morning she always wants to sleep. "And how do you love with daddy?" "The usual way, daddy lies on my tummy and moves about." "And does it hurt you?" Surprised, she wonders: "No, but why should anything hurt me?" I ask: "How long how you been loving with daddy?" She thinks, furrows her brow: "Since always." "Do you like it when daddy does that?" I ask. "Oh, yes, very much," she confirms again. We go back, step by step, healing every situation as it comes up. Throughout the session her replies are almost the same. Now she is a little older, she's five, six, seven years old. She recounts everything willingly, in detail. Every so often I ask her how old she is. When she went to school she realized that her friends weren't doing this with their daddies. She was terrified. She asked her daddy if what they were doing was okay. "Well, maybe it's not completely okay," her father replied, "because what will happen when everyone finds out?"

Now it was his turn to be terrified. When she was eight years old her father from one day to the next stopped coming to her. In the first instance she was relieved because it meant that she could get enough sleep at last. However, after a few days her powerful drive demanded to be satisfied but daddy didn't come to her. She wondered what she'd done wrong, why her daddy had stopped loving her. She asked him, but he only shouted at her. She was terrified, she didn't know what to do. She went down with a severe fever and was ill for a long time. She wanted to die. During the session we healed these experiences, we came to understand them till there was a sense of complete relief. I ended the session. When she opened her eyes she was calm and smiling. I could see she was very pleased. When we discussed the session she was very surprised that she hadn't remembered anything of those times. After all, she was quite a big girl by then. We both reached the same conclusion, that the fact that she had been rejected by her father had been a profound shock. She started to be very afraid and pushed those experiences into her subconscious. She decided that since daddy no longer wanted her there must be something wrong with her. Now when she saw it all and heard the tape she suddenly understood everything.

"I was afraid of my father not because he once made love to me, or raped me, but because I was afraid of being rejected," she said. She also saw that she was jointly responsible for what had happened and rid herself of the sense of being a victim of sexual exploitation. She desired to have sex with her father just as much as he did, so she couldn't blame him for it. This understanding and healing allowed her to rid herself of the fear of her father, of rejection, and to forgive him, her mother and herself. She no longer has any problems with the relationship with her parents and her mother has opened her heart to her.

I have conducted many such sessions quite similar to each other. The differences come from the fact that some fathers were tender while others were less so. When a child said "no", some would respect its will, while others did not. Some parents wanted to have sex despite resistance, and then might resort to rape. For a parent, however, rape is not the same as consensual sex and with time many of them stopped it. Sometimes my patients are surprised that they aren't victims forced to have sex but that they provoked and even demanded that their adult lovers have sex with them. Sometimes at some moment the children didn't want any more sex and everything finished, sometimes the adult would turn them away and then they experienced great distress.

Very occasionally situations occur where children are assailed by demands for constant sexual readiness or when the adult is drunk and demands compliance regardless of the child's resistance. These children are in a very difficult situation. They have nowhere to run to and no-one to complain to. They often suffer great distress. They see themselves as victims of compulsion, they feel a paralyzing fear. The only real cure is to look with an experienced therapist into that area of one's life despite the huge fear. The greatest problem is the patient's assumption that they are the victims of someone's transgression. Looking outside for the guilty party will not help.

When a patient has the courage to look deep inside themselves they will see that they chose that experience before they came into the world. It was that lesson they wanted to do. Every person is the creator of their own destiny, including a small child. If a rape was committed on you then it was meant as a lesson. Maybe in a previous incarnation you raped your tormentor. Nothing happens by chance. Even when it seems to us to be terrible and cruel. Nobody will do the lessons for us. Only you can take the decision that you want to make changes, and then the Universe will help you with them. You don't have to know how to do it, it's enough that you make the decision.

Sometimes we relive the same experience afresh. That happens only until we fully comprehend its meaning.

WHEN A MOTHER DIES

We have to be conscious of the fact that the chain of births is a form of repaying debts. Our parents were given life by their parents, they gave life to us and we give it to our children. If we look at it in this way then we will understand that parents have an obligation to nurse their children up to the moment when they are capable of looking after themselves. Many wise parents do just that. They appreciate that when their children grow up they will become independent and will set out into the world along their own paths. This path may run close to their own, or it may run thousands of miles away. They bring their children up as best they can without demanding anything in return. To do that you need great wisdom and courage. Courage because when we grow old we may be left on our own. At this time it will help us trust that life will look after us. In that way we will succeed in protecting our children from the paralyzing fear of old age and death.

That's how love proceeds. It gives everything without expecting anything in return. Our children will then feel free, strong and will reciprocate our love with love. If they are unable to do so personally, then life itself will reciprocate in the shape of good people, their support, friendship and care.

Unfortunately many people don't appreciate that their children are not their property or their insurance for old age. From the moment of conception they subconsciously plan, in front of them, their old age, tying them to themselves every which way. They have (usually subconsciously) expectations of them in accordance with the principle that "I'll give you something now, but you must pay me back later". I'm not saying we're driven by cold calculation, though that happens, too. Usually, however, this kind of thinking is unconscious, governed by our fear for ourselves and for our children. Where fear motivates our actions there is no love, though it may appear that everything is being done in its name. Parents like that won't let their children spread their wings. For then they might fly too high and that would be dangerous for the parents.

How can one keep one's children by one's side for the longest time, best of all till the end of one's life? Simple – by not letting them grow up. When a child wants to do something by itself, it constantly hears remarks like: "Leave that or you'll break it", "Don't touch it if you don't know how", "You're so clumsy", "Stupid child, what have you done now?", "Oh, you dummy, is that the best you can do?", "Well, you couldn't have done a worse job". When a child wants to express an opinion it will instantly hear: "Stop talking nonsense". When it does so in company we say: "What garbage is that you're saying?" At the very moment it has a chance to take an independent decision, it hears: "Do this and that" or, worse still: "You must do it this way!" Does that sound familiar?

The period of maturing is the time when a child has the right to make mistakes in the sight of adults. Unfortunately, they are not allowed to. When, in that case, is the child to learn independence, self-sufficiency? When it grows up it will find it hard to undertake any step at all since it has heard so often that it is useless, that it can't do anything, that it makes all the wrong decisions. This isn't down to the parents' malevolence. That's how their parents behaved with them, now they behave this way with you, and in the future you will behave this way with your own children. We call it love but it is a blind love and has nothing in common with true love. There are so many adults running their own companies, having children and grandchildren, who ask for their parents' permission about literally everything. Although they have revolted many times in an attempt to free themselves from this bondage that is, nevertheless, the way they were brought. They are incapable of taking even the smallest independent step. You'll ask: How can that be? They have their own family, children, grandchildren, business, therefore they must be independent. Indeed, in these areas of their lives they are independent because those areas are to do with their family, but as children of their parents they are not independent.

There is an excellent movie dealing with this subject – "Very Annie Mary". When Annie's mother dies, her non-independent "child" suddenly has to confront the mass of obligations of everyday life. Earlier she hadn't dared to start her own family because according to her dad she wasn't good enough to do so. She is alone, abandoned and embittered. I suggest that everyone who has come across this problem or sees it in their near ones should see this movie: it will touch your subconscious deeply.

Families in which there has been a divorce are in an even more difficult situation. Both parents try their hardest to recompense their child (children) for the situation that has arisen. They can go to town helping, rewarding, doing things for their children without noticing that their child has grown up long ago. They forgot that you can only bring children up, you cannot live their lives for them. Sometimes, one of the parents will recognize the dynamics of such a situation and will take steps leading to making the "child" independent. Unfortunately, the ex-spouse, often blinded by love or driven by a desire for retaliation will offer more help without realizing the harm done to the "child". It can also happen that the adult "child" might see through the parents' games (the fight between them) but finds that they're quite useful to him or her. Such a "child" goes for the easy option and steers things in such a way that it keeps getting instead of taking care for what it really needs. When it does not get what it wants it starts to manipulate the parents, awakening in them a sense of guilt, ensuring that neither of them will uncover the true nature of the situation. They know that the parents are competing for their love and will do anything for that love.

Why do they behave this way? Don't they sense that such behavior is inappropriate, that what they're doing isn't advantageous to them? I think they do know. Most likely they once felt wounded and subconsciously they continue to blame their parents for the divorce not taking into account the fact that it all happened long ago. They behave on the basis that they will cut off their noses to spite their mom and dad, thus punishing them. Subconsciously they rebelled against their parents and said to themselves: "I won't do anything, I won't be successful, I'll be an alcoholic or a junkie, let them worry". Despite the passing of the years, they have not grown up. They don't take into account the fact that if their parents had stayed with each other despite everything (e.g. for the sake of the child), they may well have come to live in a real hell, that their separation was the lesser evil. The years pass, their peers have long since started their own families but the poor "little child" subconsciously continues to rebel, hurting their parents as the price of their own tragedy.

Sometimes, when a father dies or abandons the family, exceptionally strong ties develop between the mother and the son. The mother often doesn't arrange her life afresh, tying it up with her son (including the sexual aspect). When the son grows up and wants to start his own family, she is often very antagonistic towards his plans. When, despite everything, he does marry she demands to be allowed to move in with the newly married couple. There she will dominate and the young wife has no chance of victory in this contest. The mother will iron the shirts better, she will prepare a tastier meal, bake a better apple pie.

Many women of various ages call me to tell me about just such problems. They often ask me: "What chance do I have to win back my husband?" Or I hear: "During our engagement we were a perfect couple but ever since we married and moved into his mother's house my opinion simply doesn't count. Even moving out of there didn't help much. His mom instantly moved in with us." Or: "My husband is a very loving, warm, sensitive and generous person but only when his mom isn't close by. When she appears he changes 180 degrees". Some women hold on in the hope that someday something will change, others, even though they love their husband, are forced to give up the relationship. It has a lot to do with what kind of woman the mother is. Sometimes she fills the couple's entire living space, not leaving even a tiny space for the wife. If, despite everything, the mom doesn't manage to break up the marriage, the life of the couple is still like hell itself. Separation, even though it is a

painful move, may well be the happiest solution for all concerned. It cuts through once and for all something which doesn't
bode well for success. Often a different woman comes to take
the place of the previous wife, but neither that one nor any subsequent one is good enough for the son of a mom like that.

There are many daughters-in-law who just wait for their
mothers-in-law to die. They don't realize, however, that their
hopes are futile. In a relationship as strong as this the mother
simply does not leave. She possesses her son and continues to
rule him except that now she has him totally to herself. The
same formula often repeats itself. The mother dies, the wife,
though full of hope to start with, admits sadly that things are
worse then ever before. She explains her husband's behavior by
his grief after the loss of his mother. Months, then years pass by
but her husband's heart grows into an ever greater stone. In such
cases I ask: "Then why do you stay in this relationship?" The
women explain it by referring to the good of the children or saying they couldn't manage without him. Sometimes, the husband
deals quite normally with the children but treats the wife like she
was air. The therapy for the ghost of the mother-in-law and the
husband is a real challenge, but miracles do happen.

Sometimes similar bonds can be seen in father-daughter,
or father-son and mother-daughter relationships, but these occur
much less frequently.

Let us return to parents and immature "children". What
do you suppose parents like that will do after their deaths? Will
they go on, beyond death's curtain? Will they let their "small",
twenty or thirty or forty year-old "children" function independently? They will not. The parents will remain next to the children. Even if they wanted to leave, the "poor little things" will
not let them. They don't know how to be independent, they
haven't been taught how to be, and now they have been left

alone and abandoned. I'll just mention here the torment that the spouses of such "children" experience in their everyday lives when their views don't count for much because mom and dad have to be asked about everything. I'm not talking here about advice on an important matter, nor about using the wisdom and experience of an older person. What I'm talking about here is asking about even the smallest step, about the most trivial of decisions. In families like this nearly everyone is possessed by ghosts. Within the mother is her father, within the grandmother are her parents, within the children one of their grandparents and so on. A similar thing happens when one of these non-independent "children" dies. They will not have the courage to go through to the Light and will cling onto their parents, possessing one of them.

When things start going wrong in families like these (one of the family members falls ill, others start to drink, separate) then they ask me for help. Life has given them such a bad deal that they are ready for anything. I lead the ghosts off but after a few days or hours they come back. Then I often hear them say: "When you cleansed me I felt so good. I never felt so wonderful but once again something has gone wrong". When I remind them that they must permit e.g. their mother to leave because she is the cause of the troubles, I hear them say right away: "Mom? Oh, no, how can I demand that my mom leave me, I mean she's done so much for me, I want her to stay". I then explain that when she was alive the mother suffered from cancer and the person she is haunting now will also suffer from cancer. To begin with I pick up surprise, terror and most often denial. "But my mom would never do me any harm, this is some mistake, it's impossible," they reply, insisting they're right. In cases when the terror is sufficiently strong they are faced with a dilemma, and the question arises: "What to do next?". Often, even when they are confronted by death these people are not capable of giving up their mutual bonds. What follows then is exhausting therapeutic work with the ghost. I want to make it understand that it is harming its own child. Understanding takes a long time because the structures of dependence are often built up over many generations. It's easier when several years have passed since the moment of death because then the bonds are much looser. Sometimes the ghost wants to depart but is pulled back because the person with whom it is involved on earth calls it back so strongly. This kind of leading a ghost off can take months, years or in very rare cases can turn out to be completely unsuccessful. Does the exorcist in such cases prove to be ineffectual, too weak? This bonding has tied these two people together with chains. It is probable that in such a case they will be separated only by death.

A woman once asked me to help her brother who had spent many years in a psychiatric hospital. She looked after him conscientiously, visiting him twice a week, traveling fifty miles one way each time. She confessed: "I won't be able to perform my duties any longer, I love my brother but I have fallen in love with a magnificent man who asked me to marry him. When our mother was alive my brother had a marvelous future, he finished his studies, got a doctorate, he speaks four languages fluently, but after her death it all went to pieces". Straight away it was clear to me who was the cause of these troubles but just in case I checked if there was anyone else involved. When I told the sick man's sister about it, it didn't even surprise her. "You're right, they had an unusual relationship, those two. My mother couldn't see the world outside my brother, everything was done for him, neither I nor my father counted at all. When she was alive my brother didn't reciprocate her affection so strongly, he was just a normal, healthy boy. It was only when she died something strange started to happen, maybe because he did love her just as strongly". I escorted the mother off, and after three days the hospital doctors said: "You're a lucky man, you're well, go back home, you don't even need to miss us".

They released him from hospital and he went to his sister's. They called me right away and I could hear them shouting with excitement: "My brother's come back, and can you believe it, he's talking normally, he even remembers everything. This is the first time in twelve years that we're drinking coffee together". They cried with joy, laughed, then cried again into the telephone. They must have talked for about an hour. Their joy, however, did not last long because their mother had no intention of staying away for ever and when she returned so did the illness. In fact it was even worse than that because the brother, in a terrible rage, very nearly burned down the sister's property. She called me, I escorted the ghost away, and he immediately calmed down. Luckily he realized what the cause of his misery was and he resolved that he would no longer allow it to happen. Before that he had surrendered – now, even though he loved his mother, he wanted to live his own life. He understood that his mother wanted to help him as she had done previously but was now harming him. He very much wanted to be well and he wouldn't permit her to stay. It was exceptionally difficult, but he didn't give up. His mother returned from time to time until in the end she left for good. He said goodbye to her for ever. Today he is a renowned academic and he is making up for the time lost. His mother was domineering and the son had to stand up to her. If he hadn't wanted to do that then even escorting her off would have been impossible because he would always have summoned her back.

The situation is a little different when one of the parents dies and leaves small children on Earth. A parent like that often doesn't think about their own good but about those they've left behind without care. This is not, however, real love but action driven by fear, a lack of faith in God, in the Higher Order, in the fact that God will look after those that remain. The children will be orphans because that is the lesson they have to carry out. If the dead parents had this awareness they would pass through towards the Light and to God from where they could care for their child. They have, however, been blinded by fear for their near ones. Acting under the influence of this fear is not altruism, it is going against Nature. The decision to remain has painful consequences for everyone. To begin with the mother is only slightly hooked up to her child. After a while she has to use the child's energy which weakens it greatly. Then she penetrates the child's body and it makes no difference here how old the child may be. From that moment on, the child starts being a little bit itself and a little bit its mother. The mother thinks that by standing guard over her child she will protect it from the dangers of the world. That's what happens in the first phase, immediately after her death. After a while, the boundary between the mother and the child starts to fade. Often the mother quickly starts to control the whole of the child's body and mind. She didn't notice when the boundary between herself and her child got erased. And again – if the child is strong then it will be a little bit itself and a little bit its mother, or alternate between being itself and its mother. What is also important is what phase of the process we find ourselves in – at the start the mother will want to play the part of an adviser and will more often allow the child to have its opinion.

A person's body is a house for the soul. When a mother takes control of a person it's like she stole that house. Unfortunately, this happens quite often. When a person dies they retain the memory of who they are, what is happening to them, what's happening with their near ones, and in this case with their child. With the passing of time this memory begins to weaken. Soon the mother completely forgets who and what she remained on this side of death's curtain for. This is not down to her, it happens automatically. Then the child becomes a stranger to her. A battle for its body begins, just as it takes place in every case of possession, to establish who is to remain in the body – the mother or the child, and if both of them, then in what proportions. There is nothing particularly cruel about this because with the passing of time every ghost loses its memory increasingly, although the stronger the bond between two people the longer the memory. The same principle applies to living people. Immediately after a funeral we suffer greatly from the loss of the dead person. The more time elapses the weaker become our suffering and our grief until the time comes when we remember the dead person, with pangs of conscience, only on the anniversary of their death. Everything is arranged so that ghosts forget about the world of the living in the shortest possible time. The world of the living belongs to the living, and the world of the dead to the dead.

I wrote here about the mother, but her place could well be taken by a father, a grandmother, grandfather or other members of the family. Little children often cannot understand why their mom or dad have abandoned them. A child like that will start to look for the fault in itself and will find some scarcely rational reason to burden itself with responsibility for the event. For instance: "I was naughty and that's why dad died". A sense of guilt like that will often stay in the subconscious till the end of the child's life unless it is discovered and healed. The child, wanting to fix what it had apparently done wrong, will call the dead parent for days on end. That may well lead to possession, caused in this instant by the child's intense thoughts and feelings. Children who are possessed often experience an inner chill. They feel cold in all conditions. They have to have extra gloves, socks, sweaters, hats and scarves. Even in the summer the sun isn't always capable of warming them up enough to let them undress. When the ghosts haunting the child are escorted away, all these additional "warmers" becomes superfluous.

In cases where a child is possessed by someone who was sick, the child, too, will be sick. What's said in such cases is that the sickness is hereditary. I know of numerous cases where the escorting away of a ghost was accompanied by the immediate disappearance of chronic and even incurable illnesses. I'll give you a rather unusual example. I was called by a woman who asked me to help a neighbor's child, a semi-orphan. The child had cancer and had undergone several operations. The doctors had diagnosed a tumor in various parts of the body but during the operations it transpired that there were no tumors. They had operated on the liver, spine, kidneys and several other organs. When I heard about the case it was a few days before the doctors were about to open the child's skull. They were delaying the operation because the tumor was situated in a place which meant it was life threatening. When I checked I found that it was the father who'd entered the child. During every operation he disappeared only to appear again after a short time. After subjecting the ghost to psychotherapy and persuading him to depart, the child miraculously recovered. That dad had no idea that he was the cause of his child's suffering. He wanted to protect it from danger and all he was doing was driving it into danger himself.

I'm by no means claiming that every tumor or serious illness is caused by possession. Such a claim might give false hope in situations where there is some other cause of an illness. It is, however, worth checking in every case to see if the patient's ill-health is the result of a disease or of possession.

Sometimes doctors come to me for help when they or members of their families are afflicted by an illness. They are professors, consultants which many people find strange – after all, they have access to the best medical achievements. They reckon that where all hope has gone it's worth trying unconventional methods just in case.

What you have to do is liberate yourself from the fear that exorcism or checking out possession may in some way be harmful to the sick person. I can assure you that freeing someone from ghosts is like taking a heavy weight off a person without intruding into his or her body. A ghost is just such a weight taking not only a person's energy but also their will to live. It can also provoke an illness which doctors are unable to treat.

DISEASES

It might be thought that a disease is something bad, something that happens to us and over which we have no control. When it is serious we might think of it as a punishment for evil deeds, when's it's less serious we blame external conditions e.g. bad weather when we catch cold, an epidemic when we get the flu or unfresh food when we get a stomach upset. Thinking this way we feel ourselves to be victims of external circumstances over which we have no influence. Most often we then reach for some pill or turn to the doctor for help. Doing this we don't want to take advantage of the opportunity that the disease is giving us.

We do not realize that every illness, every ache is our ally and plays a very important part in our lives, namely its purpose is to draw our attention to something we are doing inappropriately. It is a messenger informing our consciousness, just like a mailman ringing at our door warning us by letter of the consequences of our activities. When we feel pain, or when we fall sick, is a good time to consider what isn't quite the way it should be in our lives. When we reach for a pill we ignore this very valuable warning sign. What is our great ally we treat as an enemy. We feel sorry for ourselves for being so wretched because we're in pain when somebody else isn't. We feel unhappy because we have been struck down by an illness instead of celebrating that we have been given a chance to develop.

When someone in my company complains about e.g. a headache and reaches for a pill I ask straight away who is it they're so mad at that it's given them a headache. Almost always what follows is a moment of outrage and reproaches like: "What are you talking about?" or "How can you be so insensitive, I've got such a fearful headache and you're making jokes about it." But that brief moment gives time for reflection. Usually it's enough for that person to see who or what they're angry at and to understand their problem. Usually, too, at that same moment they reply, astounded and incredulous: "How is it possible for that terrible pain to pass so quickly?" Sometimes it's being mad at someone else, but most often it's being mad at themselves.

When we come to understand why and with whom we're furious, the pain goes like it's been touched by a magic wand. Pain only gives a signal – "Attention! There is a situation which is getting on your nerves. Heal it." It doesn't matter who or what is getting on our nerves. We suffer while that "someone", the perpetrator of our suffering more often than not, doesn't even realize he or she is its cause because it's not he, or she, but we who have something to see through and we have to deal with it ourselves. Sometimes that person has to be forgiven, often we have to forgive ourselves. When we know what the cause of our pain is then it's up to us alone what we do with the situation next. If we reach for pills the headache will pass, true, but what will also pass is a marvelous chance to understand ourselves and to feel masters of the situation instead of victims. Instead of taking our lives into our own hands we give it up into the hands of the doctors and the pharmacists. Does it not make you wonder that God gives us such simple solutions and we don't want to be aware of them? All it needs is to be vigilant the moment we feel a pain somewhere and to ask the pain: "Why are we suffering in that part of our body?" We will most certainly receive a reply and then we will know what is not functioning well in our lives. The body always informs us, all that's needed is to pay attention to it. Every part of our body reflects a different problem and tells us what needs mending in our lives. It's enough to identify the symptoms and to fix them.

There are numerous books that teach how to listen to ourselves insofar as we don't know how to. It's a bit like we were learning to read ourselves, just like we once learned to read elementary books. When we become adept at it we become real experts. Our lives are in our hands. When we don't do it, we want to give our fate, our life into the hands of other people. Why? Because we believe that they are wiser, more important than we are. Of course, that simply isn't true. Every one of us, regardless of what kind of education we've had, is his or her own best doctor, needing only to want to be and to believe they are. That doesn't mean to say that medicine isn't necessary. It simply won't heal us by itself if we do not help in the process. It will not work if we don't help. The doctor prescribes the pills, but we have to swallow them ourselves.

In the chapter "Death and Then What?" I gave two examples of cases where the subconscious punished itself with a disease when it accepted something we had done as an evil act, as a misdeed. Sometimes it can happen that we are sick because our subconscious has misunderstood our longings.

One time a young woman came to me for help. She was a psychologist. She suffered from cancer and, as a result, had many and various pains. She was treated in a hospital but she also tried to get at the cause of the disease herself. She couldn't manage it herself so she found her way to me. Even though she was a very intelligent woman I had the impression that we were speaking different languages. Whatever I said she replied straight away: "Yes, I know all about that, I mean I am a psychologist". I kept repeating: "Knowing is one thing, but applying it to life is something completely different. Our subconscious may totally not want us to do it". She was a single mother, an orphan who had no family, she was dying and had no-one to leave her little daughter with. I tried in every way possible to release in her the will to live but it was like throwing things against a brick wall. "You have a little daughter, she has nobody in the whole world except you, don't give up. Do you want her to be left completely alone? Remind yourself how hard you found it in all those children's homes. Do you want her to suffer the same fate? You have someone to live for, and if you can't live for her then live for yourself," I kept repeating.

How did I know that she could live on and it was only up to her whether she chose life or death? Because the cause of her illness was the ghost of her aunt who had also died of cancer at a very young age. Whenever I escorted the ghost off the tumor vanished completely, but when the ghost returned the disease became more severe. Just before she died she called me and right at the outset she said: "It's probably too late for me now, I sense that I'm dying, but I asked God for understanding and it came to me but only today. If I had listened to you then I would most likely have recovered and my little daughter would still have a mother and not become an orphan through my stubborn stupidity. Please promise me that one day you'll describe all this in your book as a warning to others who find themselves in a similar situation. Let my death not be in vain if only in this way." I promised, and that's what I'm doing now. That's what she came to understand a few days before her death. When she was living in one of the children's homes a photograph of her distant aunt fell into her hands by chance. The photograph was a picture of a beautiful, but very emaciated woman sitting in a pink dressing gown on a bed. From that time that photograph became something of a talisman for her, because whenever she felt unhappy she used to sit in a corner and dream about growing up to be just like her aunt. That photograph was all she had in terms of a family. Her aunt died shortly afterwards, though no-one informed her of the fact. When she grew up she bought herself exactly the same dressing gown and her life followed the same path she'd dreamed of in her childhood. She lived just like her aunt, and she died like her, too.

When someone dies as a result of some illness then death does not automatically free them from the disease. After death they are ill in the same way as they were when alive. Though when they die they leaves their physical body in the grave, they takes with them all the other bodies including the one where the illness is written down. Only when they pass through to the other side of death's curtain are they subjected to a cure. This, let us call it, quarantine lasts just as long as the person's state demands. If their mental state demands a longer time then that is what they get, till they are completely cured. It is treated individually, depending on the person's needs. It happens only if we pass through to the other side of death's curtain. If the person, for whatever reasons, resolves not to pass through to the Light, then they remain in the world of ghosts with all their mental and physical afflictions. The disease which was the cause of death exists within them just as it did when they were alive. It will afflict them for just as long as they continue to exist on this side of death's curtain. If they passed through to the Light they would be cured, by remaining they continue to be ill.

When someone we love and are close is dying after a long and serious illness, we are incredibly sad. We want them to stay with us for as long as possible. We are afraid that we may never see them again. Though this isn't true, at such moments we don't really want to know it or remember it. Finally, the moment of death approaches. We feel very bad, our heart bleeds from despair and we're often in no state to let them go from us. It's quite frequently the case that we want to die together with the person we love. At such a moment we are in pain and indifferent to everything, we don't have a healthy outlook on things and we lose our instinct for self-preservation.

This is a very crucial moment which will decide the fate of the departing soul and our own. Why? There are many reasons. One of them is the fact that we cling on to that soul, we don't want to let it go, and the soul, unable to free itself and to leave, will be forced to stay behind. I'll try to illustrate this – we tangle this soul up in our sorrow which is like chains, from which it is unable to escape. It might seem we are doing it out of love, but this has nothing to do with love, what we are really doing it is imprisoning it. Real love is freedom. Freedom at every moment and in every situation, even at the moment of death. It appears to us that we are gaining something when we limit this freedom in the name of love. We can submit to such delusions in the very first moment, but we will always be harming not only the soul that is trying to depart but also, and even more, ourselves.

The question may be asked: what to do if the soul of the dying person wants to stay for our sakes. In such cases we must explain its erroneous reasoning and ask it to quit.

Let's return to where it's we who don't want to release the beloved soul since it seems to us that we're doing it out of love. We don't realize how very mistaken we are at such a moment. We don't even recognize that we're thinking only about ourselves and not about the person we love. We think that our despair is caused by love, but the truth is we are terrified of the thought that from now on we are going to be on our own. We are terrified and we can't imagine what will happen with our lives from now on. It isn't always to do with financial matters, either, though they sometimes do come into the equation. We are more afraid of the possibility that in the future there will be no-one to love us, that we will have a lonely old age, but most of all we are afraid of death. A very pertinent characteristic of this spiritual state is that we are very open to the other side and thereby helpless and susceptible to possession by ghosts. Many people have no objection to having someone close to them who has died possessing them. In the first moment they feel happy, they talk with them, they want to keep them by their sides for as long as possible. The family nods sympathetically, look how hard it is, for instance, for our gran to be apart from our granddad. No-one will say anything, no-one will remind her not to do this, that this is harming granddad as well as her. Often what happens is that shortly the whole family suffers because the ghost will possess one of the other relatives. There is nothing malevolent about it, as some people claim. If we do not release a ghost in the period that has been ordained for it then it's like its time for leaving this world is through. Then there is no longer the possibility for it to pass over to the other side under its own strength. And therefore if we restrain it with our despair it's like we were detaining it by force, a force that will disarm it and deprive it of the opportunity to pass through to the Light. Such a ghost has no alternative but to enter our or someone else's body.

Let us assume that, after some time, you, too, die and without any problems you pass through to the other side of death's curtain. But you can't take with you a ghost you forced to stay behind. You do not have sufficient energy for that. At the moment of death you have only enough energy for yourself, not for both of you. Consider then: is that the fate you want for a person about whom you say that you love them? The fate of a perpetually wandering soul?

It does happen that a ghost will stay behind of its own volition. As I wrote in another chapter, it may do so for various reasons. I went through them all. Now let us consider the consequences. It makes no difference at all if the ghost decides to stay or if we in some way restrain it. Sooner or later it will hook up to some living person or, worse still, will enter the person's body. If, when it was alive, it was ill then it will continue to be ill as a ghost. The ghost's first reaction, for various reasons, is to be drawn to members of its own family. Firstly because it will feel safe among them. Besides, by constantly thinking about it we involuntarily draw it to ourselves. Thirdly, when we are grieving we are open and willing to welcome the ghost not just to our homes but into our bodies.

When a ghost penetrates us or one of the members of the household it is, to begin with, almost imperceptible. Our character may change a little but, because we are still thinking about the dead person, we do not notice it. It may be that people around us will notice before we do that something isn't quite right. We notice it only at the end, if, that is, it comes into our heads at all. Even if everyone around us mentions it we will deny it and the ghost will help us to do that. The truth is that it will be the ghost who will be doing the denying, questioning and doubting what others say. This takes place only in our minds. In time we will doubt what others say more and more. Indeed, what can our near ones tell us? That within us there is, for instance, our dead grandfather? He knows that he continues to live though it is through our lives, so he must deny everything. This isn't a question of the ghost's malevolence, although that can happen, too, but looking at the matter from two different points of view. For us the ghost is not alive which for the ghost is an evident untruth. That's why it will forcibly deny it.

Aspects of the ghost's character may be but if it was suffering from some disease before its death then similar symptoms will start to appear in us. Doctors will often explain such an occurrence by calling it a family or genetic predisposition. Such diseases are considered to be family illnesses because, for the sake of argument, a grandmother will have had heart troubles but having died she didn't go through to the other side and entered her daughter. She, in turn, accepted her mother most willingly as a result of which she herself developed a heart disease and shortly thereafter died. Now her son became ill with heart disease. If we look at this chain of events from the standpoint of conventional medicine we may well be satisfied with the explanation that this is a hereditary disease. If, however, we look at the case more closely we will notice that it's not hereditary at all. The kind of illness is of no significance. In every case events occur in exactly the same way.

One of a pair of identical twins fell ill with cancer. He was a young, unusually good-looking man: it was heart-breaking to watch him dying so quickly. The illness lasted less than six months. In the spring he had been promoted to a crack army regiment and before Christmas he was dead. When he joined the army he underwent a medical examination which showed that he was perfectly fit. By the time I was asked to help he had been through several operations and was in the last stages of the disease. I discovered that the cause of the illness was the ghost of his uncle who had not so long ago died of cancer. The young man ridiculed my diagnosis, called it rubbish. He was of the view that his uncle had loved him so much when he was alive that he couldn't possibly harm him. He was unswayed by any persuasion. For me, his attitude was quite comprehensible, I'd often come across similarly strong resistance from my patients. The family, however, continued to look to me for support and renewed their pleas for help particularly since every time I escorted the uncle off the patient's state of health improved radically. The doctors in the hospital noticed it, too, and were very perplexed by the changes in him - from healthy to sick. It would probably have been possible to save the young man if he had wanted it, too. That's not to say he wanted to die. He wanted to live but in a situation which was so difficult for him he looked for safety in the wrong place. Instead of trusting himself into God's hands, he gave himself up to his uncle's ghost. Whenever I escorted the uncle off, the young man drew him back to himself. He was incapable of believing in life, in recovery and whenever the pain became intense he always cried out loud: "Uncle, help me!" His family, which sat with him day and night, tried to restrain him. They tried all sorts of ways to persuade him not to do it. His twin brother was the first in the family to understand what was happening in all this and was the most strongly engaged in helping his brother. Unfortunately, the boy could not be saved. He died.

Very shortly after his death a tumor was noticed in the other twin. This twin, however, had acquired knowledge through his experience during his brother's sickness and he turned to me for help. After a thorough examination it transpired that his recently dead brother had entered him as had his uncle. Even though he suffered greatly and missed his dead brother, he was in no hurry to die. He very much wanted to live and obediently did everything I asked him to. Not only did he not hamper my work, he himself tried to convince the ghosts to leave him in peace. But they stubbornly wanted to take him to their world. It was clearly evident when the ghosts departed and when they returned because the tumor, just like in his twin brother, appeared and then, when the ghosts departed, quickly vanished. This went on for several weeks, the ghosts returned less and less frequently until one day they did not return at all. Even though this was the same disease suffered by his brother, he did not follow the dead man's footsteps. Even though the doctors tried to persuade him, he did not submit to any operations or radiotherapy regardless of the fact that his disease progressed just as quickly as his brother's had. He stood up against the ghosts and he won because he knew that his problem was that he was visited by sick ghosts. That's not to say that he didn't love his brother. He loved him very much indeed, but he did not want to die at such a young age. Added to which he was aware of the fact that it was very likely indeed that he would be the cause of illness in the next living person. He won not only for himself, although he was the most important person there, but also for his family and for the ghosts who were imposing themselves on him.

If the second brother had not been saved, then this instance of the illness would have been explained as being hereditary and everyone would have anxiously asked who the next victim would be. In my practice I have seen many cases that subvert the theory of hereditary diseases. The fact that a disease affects several members of the same family does not mean to say that it is hereditary. When the ghosts have been escorted away it may leave for ever. I do not, however, want to give false hope where it is not appropriate and that's why I state clearly that not every illness is caused by ghosts. It can happen that even when all the ghosts affecting a family have been escorted away the illness continues. The patient and their family may feel aggrieved. What has to be taken into account, though, is that even then the patient is still in a much better situation than previously. They are free of ghosts and so have a lot more energy to combat the disease. Before then what was happening was that the patient was struggling against the disease while at the same time being burdened by one or several ghosts who were constantly drawing the energy out of them. Now, though the patient is still fighting the disease, they are free from that added burden.

The fact that members of the same family succumb to the same disease for many generations may have another source. Every family has a specific outlook on life, similar habits or tendencies and it's this that may be the cause that the same kinds of disease afflict them. Let's assume that members of a family have suffered from heart disease for generations. At first glance it might seem that this is hereditary, that the family has it written in its genes, but when we look at the family more closely we may see that there is no love in their home, no joy, everything is taken literally, the atmosphere is usually gloomy, there are constant complaints about everything. In such a situation their hearts cannot be healthy, they don't have the right conditions for it. A child brought up in such a house must grow into a future heart-attack victim, just as a flower growing in the shade must remain weak and frail.

Let's take an example from another family. Everyone sticks close together, no-one takes even the smallest step without having someone else alongside them. At first glance it may look like they're doing it out of love, that they can't live without one another, but they are living in fear, of which they are not even conscious. When we look more closely at them we will see that they're sticking together not because they feel good in each other's company but because when they're with the family they feel safer. They believe in a terrible and cruel world which is outside their home just lying in wait to harm them. They're afraid of everything, they feel threatened at every step. Members of this kind of family will suffer from ulcers and stomach cancers. Because they transmit this way of thinking from generation to generation, their disease may well be regarded as hereditary.

In another family anger, rancor, and even hatred hold sway. There no-one will give anyone any slack, no-one will forgive anything. The livers of these people are subjected to great stress and diseases of the liver are frequent. This conforms to the old saying: "I'm so angry it make my bile spill over". Where there is so much anger and rancor the liver cannot cope and the bile duct is filled with stones. Every stone is another unresolved matter, something we weren't able to forgive.

It's possible to describe in this way every part of our body which corresponds with a different area of our lives, or - and this follows from it - a different emotion.

Once I was phoned by a woman who had an unusual request. She wanted to stay with me up until the day of her operation, which was to take place in two weeks' time. She announced that she will look after the house through the whole period of her stay. I had a home help anyway, so I didn't need anyone, but there was such determination in her voice that I agreed. There was a little more room in the house because members of my family had left to various places. Besides, I'd always planned to open a center where I could have patients stay. This woman's proposition was like a foretaste of some-

thing I'd intended to do in the future. Her family brought her
and left her with me.

     Christine was suffering from cancer of the colon. To me
this meant that she wasn't able to forgive herself or others for
her past. I checked whether the cause of her illness was a ghost,
but it wasn't. We started on therapy which, because of the short
time before the operation, lasted all day long. When, after ten
days, her daughter came for the weekend I had to acknowledge
sadly that, despite the huge amount of work we'd done, her stay
with me had brought very little benefit. I accepted that this was
a case I couldn't crack and I let it go. During a random conversation her daughter said: "How enormously lucky your children
are to have a mother like you". I looked at her with surprise not
knowing what she meant. She went on: "I have never in my
whole life heard my mother tell me that she loves me, but your
children hear it every minute". Christine's daughter left and
there were just two days left before the operation when I asked
her straight out: "Please tell me: was your daughter born as a result of a planned pregnancy?" She replied that yes, of course,
but her whole body was saying something different. I realized
that I'd finally found the right track. We started everything from
scratch. I gave her a pile of loose sheets of paper and advised
her to forgive everything and everyone for that old situation.
Her husband for not being careful and impregnating her, her
daughter for crashing into her life when she wasn't ready for it.
Her parents, her family, her neighbors for judging her, and of
course God for letting it all happen. She was to do that until she
felt a noticeable effect of her forgiveness. I left her till the next
day in peace.

     When I saw her in the morning, at breakfast, she ran up
to me, seized my waist, and twirled me round and round. I
asked her to let me go because she might do herself some harm.

But she had no intention of letting me go, she was so happy. When I'd finally freed myself I wanted to find out about everything. We went for a walk and she started to tell me: "When you told me to write down my forgiveness on sheets of paper I thought that I'd often done that and it had given me nothing. But I didn't want to upset you so I started to write, without much conviction, though. The longer I wrote the more it started to draw me in, until I began to do it more and more from my heart. At one moment I badly wanted to go to the bathroom and it was lucky that it was close by otherwise I'd have soiled my knickers. Do you realize what performing that function has meant for me till now? How much trouble it causes me? How many tears I've wept wanting to relieve myself? But now, if only you knew how it all poured out of me. I cried with joy. After a while I went back to the writing and the whole situation repeated itself afresh. That happened nine times".

When we returned from the walk, which lasted a couple of hours, her husband was waiting for her anxiously. He started to speak straight away: "I don't know what's happening here, but since yesterday I've not been able to cope. I keep seeing you before my eyes and you're forgiving me, I thought something terrible must have happened. That's why I came and I'm taking you home". The day of the operation was approaching so this was the most appropriate moment for her to leave. The doctors in the hospital carried out tests, then kept repeating them because they showed that the cancer had vanished. Her bowels were clean. The damage done by the tumor had also healed. I knew that complete forgiveness would help Christine but I had not supposed that it would give such amazing results in such a short time. Christine got her health back, and her daughter finally got her mother back. To begin with, Christine had thought that the cause of her illness was a ghost. It turned out that it was a feeling of guilt and being a victim of a situation many years ago.

Christine's husband was very happy because he thought that my care would give her the only spiritual support possible before an operation that was so difficult for both of them.

Another example: I got a call from a man who was asking me to help his wife Barbara. His wife was suffering from breast cancer and in two weeks' time she was going to have a double mastectomy. She was taking it very badly and that's why I was asked to help. The wife knew nothing about this plea for help and the husband wanted it to stay that way because she completely didn't believe in that kind of therapy. The next day I ascertained that the wife didn't have cancer but had inside her a ghost who most likely died of that or a similar disease. Unfortunately, the husband didn't know of anyone in the family who had died of cancer. Meanwhile, I received a letter containing a photograph of the wife. Many people send me their photographs or those of their near ones. She was a very beautiful woman with unusually large breasts. There was very little time left before the operation and so I asked him to tell his wife about his plan. Then she phoned and told me about an aunt whom she had liked very much when she was young, and by whom she was liked, and who had died of cancer a few years before. I checked and it was she indeed. But there was not enough time before the operation for me to be able to intervene effectively. I asked for at least two weeks' delay. They were to go to the professor together and make up some reason for postponing the operation. For some unknown reason the professor was against it and set a second time but a week in advance. Barbara went onto the ward and phoned me constantly. She decided she would pretend to have a cough which she hoped would postpone the operation and give me the necessary time. Unfortunately, the aunt kept coming back. On the day of the operation I was very careful to make sure that she wouldn't be close to the patient. At about midday the telephone rang and I heard her crying helplessly. I couldn't understand what had happened. "Since she's calling it's obvious the operation didn't take place, but then why is she crying so terribly?" I wondered. Finally she stammered out that there will be no operation at all since there was no evidence of a tumor. "Since it's not going to happen, why are you crying like this; are you missing the cancer?" I asked. She replied, weeping, that no, but what is she, poor woman, going to say to the professor, after all he'll be asking her but she doesn't know if she's to lie or tell him the truth. She burst into tears again. At this moment I lost my rag and what I said to her is not suitable for publication. I reproached her, saying she was a stupid cow who instead of rejoicing and thanking God that she was well at last, was worrying what she was going to say to the doctor. Then she suddenly understood, stopped crying and said, astonished: "You are absolutely right. That's how I should look at the whole question. Why didn't I do that? I must have lost my head completely. Thank you". From that time on she never called me again. When, six months later, I was visiting her home town she found out about it and, with her husband, brought me a bouquet of flowers by way of thanks. She decorated the place I was staying with hundreds of the most beautiful roses, and this was in the middle of winter.

I don't claim the right to pontificate on medical matters. What I have written are my observations collected over many years' practice with very many patients. I also rarely set out simply to cure patients though I can do that with good results. I believe that when we are ill it's either caused by ghosts that possess us, or the disease is put upon us to persuade us to understand that we have to work through some problem. In such situations no treatments of a bio-energo-therapeutic or any other kind will have any effect. Even if they do help to begin with, then their effectiveness is very short-lived. Nor will treatment or cures of conventional medicine help. It's a bit like a doctor and a patient subconsciously coming to an agreement: "I'll pretend I'm curing you, and you'll pretend you're being cured". I don't wish to hurt doctors' feelings, I'm simply drawing attention to the specifics of the phenomenon which is disease. When we get to the bottom of what the problem is that causes it and transform ourselves, then the disease will depart by itself just as it came even if it had been regarded as incurable.

It is my view that if we come across a problem then we are sufficiently mature to be able to deal with it. Often it's a constantly repeated situation which drives us to distraction, we can't bear it, but it does help us reach a final decision about changing mistaken convictions. There comes a moment when we have so heartily had enough of a certain something that we say to ourselves: "That's it, I can't put up with this a moment longer". That is a very good moment. It's at precisely such a moment that we have the highest motivation to understand our problem and to change. It doesn't matter how much we don't want to do so, it is nevertheless worth seeking out the solution in ourselves. As soon as we want to we will find it and, at the same time, heal the problem. We can do this by ourselves or we can turn to someone to help us. This can be a specialist, but it can equally well be a friend who will hear us out. I'm not talking here about whinging, complaining and returning to the previous situation. If we open ourselves up we ourselves may find the trail which will lead us to the source of our problem. If it requires inner understanding and healing then the whole of the Universe will in some way be showing it to us. It will be like a mirror for us, saying: "Look, now you have to understand (work through) such and such".

Let's assume that something or someone maddens you. You may sulk, argue, take offense, even go away from the person but the thing that maddens us is the very problem we have to work through. Parting will solve nothing because you will soon find yourself in a similar situation. If, for example, we have to work through the problem of victimhood, then we'll keep finding ourselves in situations where the circumstances incline us to feel that we are victims, be it in our own homes, on the street, or at work. We can put the responsibility, as before, on "others", convincing ourselves that "they" are at fault - your boss at work, the sales clerk in a store, the husband or kids at home etc. We can turn our faces away from it all and pretend that we don't have a problem at all. But we should consider where, within us, is that same part that maddens us in others and this will be enough to heal us. If we don't do this then situations and people will press down on that part for as long as it takes us to recognize the problem and heal it. If we overlook it or do nothing about it, then a disease will begin and that will force us to stop and consider that part of ourselves which we least accept. It is to that part of us that ghosts will come. For example, a person who will not accept his anger will draw to himself a whole host of angry ghosts. On the outside a person may appear to be very calm but inside everything is bubbling like a volcano waiting to explode. More often than not they are unaware of it. That's why, when they lose control of themselves, e.g. after drinking alcohol, they change in a moment from the proverbial still waters to a monster. A person who has a problem with addiction will attract addicts to himself. If a person has a problem with jealousy they will attract jealous ghosts, if with lying - liars etc. It's often the case that they aren't deceiving anyone from their milieu, but they are deceiving themselves or not keeping a promise made to themselves.

A person constantly thinking about illnesses will attract a ghost who suffers from the disease they most fear. For instance, fearing cancer we will draw to us a ghost with cancer, fearing a heart attack we will most probably be possessed by a ghost with coronary disease etc. That's why ghosts with some disease find it so easy to infiltrate us, because we draw them to ourselves through our fear. The ghost merely fulfills our expectations. We can later explain this "coincidence" by saying: "Well, yes, I always had a premonition that I would be struck low with cancer". The same can also be true, of course, with every other disease, not just cancer.

When we are completely well ghosts have no way into us; if, however, we let just one infiltrate us then others have an open road in. There can be a multitude of them. I mentioned earlier that when, during its life, a ghost suffered from some disease then the person possessed by it will suffer from the same disease. In this way many diseases can find a home in the same person. Some ghosts can be stronger than others just as some people are stronger than others in life. When a ghost takes control over a person's body the disease will appear along with the domination. It can be that, inside a person, there is a constant battle being waged to decide who will be controlling the body. In such a situation first one ghost rules, then another. The person may not be aware of what's happening, but his acquaintances will notice that the same person is quiet one moment, then exuberant, then again another time prey to attacks of rage. We say that such a person has mood swings. When they occur frequently or when we can't control them then that can be a reason to consider if we haven't been possessed by ghosts.

THE HYPOCHONDRIAC

———————————

A hypochondriac is what we call someone who barely has to hear about a disease before they falls ill with it. One day, or over a longer period, they complain about one illness, and the next moment about some completely different one. People around them and their doctors suspect the patient of having imaginary illnesses or of faking. And that's because when the patient is examined none of the diseases appear. It often happens that they are in severe discomfort, doubled up with pain, but when they go to the doctor there is neither an illness nor any pain to be seen. They suffer a lot, they complain, but the doctor can find absolutely nothing. Even though at the time of the examination the patients can't feel any symptoms, they know that they're ill. After all, they remember the symptoms or the dreadful pain. They are really suffering but the doctors cannot help them. Not because the doctors don't want to help or don't know enough about the illness, but because at the given moment they cannot find evidence of it. When a situation like that repeats itself on a regular basis the doctor will start to regard the patient as a faker or a hypochondriac. The patient, finding no help from one doctor, starts to look for a different one. The situation repeats itself. Why does it happen? Are such patients deceiving themselves or are they really ill?

Well, this situation arises when a given person is possessed by many ghosts which are carrying within themselves some disease. Depending on which of the ghosts is "ruling" at a given moment, the person will feel the symptoms of its disease. I hear you ask: "Why then, when the person is examined by a doctor, is there nothing there?" It's precisely because the sickness belongs to the ghost and not to the person. Its symptoms are clearly experienced by the person when there is a ghost inside them, but impossible for the doctor to recognize if that same ghost is no longer "ruling". It can also be the case that the cunning ghost will simply hide itself during the examination, just as in the case of a child undergoing numerous operations when it was possessed by its own father, which I mentioned in the chapter "When a Mother Dies".

I'll now give an example which is somewhat extreme but even such examples unfortunately do take place. Let us assume that a person has been infiltrated by one ghost with diabetes, another with asthma, a third with poor eyesight and a fourth with coronary disease. A person like that might become ill with all these diseases simultaneously, in other words be a diabetic, have a heart attack, have poor eyesight and suffer from asthma. What I want to talk about, however, is when at given moment the person is ruled undividedly by just one ghost. That will influence which of the diseases the person will suffer from at that moment. When it is the ghost with diabetes, then at that precise time the possessed person will suffer from diabetes. As a diabetic they will have to take insulin since without it they wouldn't be able to manage, but on other days they will simply not need it at all. At another time the patient's body will be controlled by the ghost with poor eyesight. The patient will start to lose their sight, the optometrist will prescribe spectacles for them, but after a couple of days the glasses, which were essential earlier, now become a positive hindrance. It may turn out that the patient sees very well without the help of glasses. Another day the patient may start to complain about their heart, need trinitrateglycerol, because the ghost with coronary disease has taken charge, but another time the heart will be perfectly fine. When the ghost who suffered from asthma during its life takes charge, the patient needs an nebulizer. All of these are chronic diseases, people usually suffer from them till the end of their lives. And therefore, from a medical point of view, we are dealing here with an impossibility since the principle of chronic diseases precludes the option that the same person can use thick lenses one day and have perfect sight the next. One day they can't take even a couple of steps at speed because they become short of breath, and the next they run up the stairs to a high story. Diseases like that don't just go away on their own only to return after a while. They need medical support, drugs, otherwise the person could die. It is therefore all the more surprising that there are instances where a person suffers from a given condition, a couple of days is completely free of it, only to fall ill with another disease and then, after a while, to fall ill again with the previous condition. Many people say: "Well, even these things happen", but I know of cases where, after the ghosts were escorted off, all the diseases stopped.

If, despite that, the disease remains then either the ghost for some reason doesn't want to leave, or it does leave but then comes back, or it is the person's disease and the person himself has to deal with it. In every case, however, we must take the matter into our own hands and decide if we want to be healthy or sick. Once we've resolved that, the disease will be much easier to treat and the ghosts much easier to escort off.

LONG-LASTING DISEASES

I'm sure many of you have been puzzled by the fact that some people cure themselves of their illnesses quickly and con-

clusively, whereas others have the illness drag on for years, resistant to all forms of treatment. This can also often be caused
by ghosts. If we are dealing with a disease suffered by a ghost
then treating the person will have no effect. That would be like
giving medicine to Johnny to cure Andrew's illness. The medicines are taken by a person who is most probably healthy
whereas the ghost is, for obvious reasons, not in a state to receive them. That's why sometimes an illness drags on for years,
sometimes till the end of someone's life. But when the ghost is
led away, the disease stops.

EPILEPSY

I know little about this condition, but in the cases where
it was caused by ghosts (I have had more than a dozen of them)
I have cured it once and for all. I was once phoned by a woman
with an authoritative voice who demanded that I help her.
Lately her epileptic fits had intensified to several each week and
this made it difficult for her to function at the very responsible
level which she occupied. She was peeved that I hadn't recognized her name, which apparently was well-known. A few days
later I received a letter containing several photographs and it
was only then that I realized who it was. I worked on her for
some time and I succeeded in leading off the ghosts that were
troubling her. She was, as she told me, very grateful because
she was able at last to work calmly, receiving delegations, repre-
senting the country abroad. I even received a letter with thanks
and congratulations for performing my "service". After about
three months she called me greatly excited and said: "To begin

with I regretted very much that I turned to you. I missed those fits so much it was driving me crazy. It was only yesterday that I understood the nature of the problem after the violent argument in our department. You probably know about it because the newspapers are full of it". Unfortunately, I didn't know. I'm not much interested in politicians' arguments. She started to tell me that someone had insulted someone else, people started fighting etc. She was describing it to me with exaggerated excitement. "Now I know," she said, "that I need these emotions which epilepsy ensured I got. But I don't have to be ill to provide myself with them, all I need is to provoke an argument in some way, isn't it?" I calmly explained to this woman that she doesn't need to argue to experience emotions. All she needs is to open herself up to them and to accept them all.

Emotions are very important for people. We need the energy that flows through us in the form of emotions. Unfortunately, the majority of people is closed to experiencing them. That happens for very many reasons. Gary Zukav and Linda Francis have written the best book I have ever read on the subject of emotions: "The Heart of the Soul: Emotional Awareness". It describes the subject of emotions in a magnificent and simple way, and gives exercises to help us recapture our ability to experience them. To be totally open to emotions is a magnificent state of being and that's why I whole-heartedly recommend the book.

ALLERGIES

We get allergies when something or someone literally "gets under our skins". It can be any situation which we don't accept and which we do nothing to change. An allergy can also be caused by ghosts. When we are dealing with such cases, then leading the ghosts off will completely remove the allergy. When it is caused by something other than ghosts then all we need to do is realize what is hindering us and what it is we don't want to accept. Then the allergy vanishes as if by magic, never to return. Sometimes one needs to work on it a little, maybe one has to forgive someone. An allergy is an alarm bell telling you that there is in your life something you don't like, something you won't accept. Sometimes even after a cure we return to our old habits. At such times the allergy can return for a short while, but by then we know how to deal with it. Instead of being victims, we are masters of the situation.

ASTHMA

Asthma can be caused by ghosts, but in the majority of cases it is the result of an excessive, demanding love which doesn't allow the person suffering from asthma to breathe properly. This can easily be noticed in a child suffering from asthma who is surrounded by the overly protective concern of adults. When the child leaves home for a time, or even goes to school, the asthma will go, but when the child returns home the disease returns, too. When a child like that grows up and has a chance to change its environment, where it lives, the illness passes. It can happen that when the person starts their own family, the childhood situation may repeat itself this time with the wife (husband). Then, unfortunately, the person will fall ill again.

Often the sufferers, even when they know the cause of

their condition, do not want any changes since they're afraid of a life without excessive "love". Life with a suffocating love is bad, but without it it's bad, too. They choose what to them seems to be a lesser evil and with that the illness, too. It often happens that when the person who loves excessively dies, the disease vanishes instantly. Then everything will depend on whether the ghost leaves or whether we will want to let it go. If we don't, then the problems with the condition will start anew.

ALZHEIMER'S DISEASE, MEMORY LOSS

Both conditions can be caused by ghosts. I know of cases where the leading off of ghosts has led to a complete return of memory. I have mentioned in other chapters that our brain works on principles close to those of a computer. When we have a ghost inside, it can sometimes happen that the data is written on the ghost's hard drive and not the person's. It's hard then to expect us to find the data on ours. We won't remember what the ghost did when it was controlling our mind. What follows from that is that we can remember what we did in our youth but not what we did an hour ago or yesterday. After the ghosts have been led away we will start to write the data on our own disc completely from scratch. If we were under the influence of ghosts for a long time, then the gaps in our memory can be quite big. It is always better, however, to free ourselves from their control than to agree to functioning like a plant, to accept that the ghost will live the rest of our life for us.

PAINS

Any kind of pain may be caused by the action of ghosts. The most frequent are headaches and stomach aches. They can have various degrees of intensity. Unfortunately it's sometimes very hard to withstand the pain. I'm talking here about pains for which the doctors can find no cause. No remedies are able to soothe them because we are giving Agatha the pills or injections for a pain suffered by a ghost with the name Walter. In the chapter "Haunted Houses" I wrote about a girl possessed by the ghost of a woman of the Warsaw uprising. For a number of years she experienced terrible pains through the night. The moment I led the ghost away the pain left along with the ghost.

Ghosts most frequently take up residence in the stomach (at the level of the navel) and in the solar plexus. During a conference for healers I was approached by a woman with a twelve year-old daughter. The girl had been suffering from severe stomach pains for many years and she was very lethargic. The doctors couldn't reach a diagnosis, they could find no evidence of any illness. After I'd examined her I found that she was possessed by many ghosts. I asked the girl if she had ever summoned ghosts. The mother, as normally happens in such situations, protested. The girl replied that she had indeed, and often. I explained that that was the reason for her ailments. I instructed her in how she should collaborate with me. The mother was shocked, she didn't want to believe it, but she understood that she didn't really have any choice in the matter. After a few days they both phoned to tell me that the pain had gone and the girl had started to enjoy life again. On the same day I was visited by a father whose daughter had literally identical symptoms. The cause of her pains was also ghosts. The parents, however, had no intention of letting the daughter know that they'd turned to me for help. They decided that she was too young to understand anything. They were afraid she'd be terrified and the pain would intensify. All my explanations that I had just had an identical case and that that girl had been able to take in my words perfectly calmly came to nothing. I tried cleansing the child for months with poor results. The ghosts went away, but only for a short time. No amount of persuasion could get them to let the child participate in the therapy. The parents' actions were the consequence of ill-conceived concern. If they'd had the courage we would most probably have managed things right away. Unfortunately, the girl's suffering continued for many months.

ANOREXIA, EXCESSIVE WEIGHT LOSS

Anorexia and being excessively thin are not the same things, but both may have the same cause, namely ghosts. Many people wonder how it is that some people eat as much as others but look like coat hangers without an ounce of flesh as if their bodies consisted only of skin and bones. There may be a combination of several reasons. I'll describe only those I've come across during my practice, in other words those cases that concerned possession by ghosts.

As I wrote earlier, those who are possessed may show various disturbances of a physical or psychological nature. They may suffer from various diseases or fall into addiction. It all depends on what kind of ghost has possessed them. Ghosts very often take up residence in the region of the stomach. Such a person may either have no desire to eat anything, or if they do eat then they instantly want to vomit it up again, which they frequently do. This form of eating often leads to excessive thinness. When a person eats normally and yet despite that is thin it could mean that the ghosts are taking away more energy than the person is able to get from the food.

In the chapter about suicides I write about ghosts which are unable to get out of the person they've infiltrated. It can happen that they will do everything to make life unbearable for the person possessed in order to persuade them to take their life the end result of which would be to liberate the ghosts possessing them. To people such a course of action may seem very cruel, but a ghost is no longer living, it has gone through the process of dying and so to the ghost it may seem to be a perfectly normal action. The ghost will sometimes act on the principle: "Since I'm not living let them die, too". Ghosts like that may make food disgusting to the person possessed relying on his or her death by starvation.

One day a woman who was extremely thin was brought to me. Being one hundred and eighty centimeters tall (five feet eleven inches) she weighed thirty-seven kilograms (eighty-one pounds). She was supported, and when she tried to walk by herself she had to hold on to the walls. She came with her husband and two tiny children. She had undergone a series of tests and the doctors could find no cause for her problem. When I examined her it transpired that inside her was her grandmother and it was most probably she who was the cause of the thinness. When I told her this, she recoiled. "No, granny would never. No, I'll never believe it, I am sure you're quite wrong. We looked after her, my husband and I, to the very end, she died happy and reconciled. No, it must be someone else". Afterwards her husband phoned many times in her name, asking me to check the facts again. They insisted that this ghost was not their beloved granny. I told them it was, they insisted it wasn't. When I spoke with the grandmother's ghost, she told me a different story. She was full of resentment against her granddaughter. I began to conduct long conversations with her and discovered that she would never leave this "trollop" (that's how she expressed herself about her grand-daughter) in peace. She would be happiest if the woman "died like a dog" and all because she once kicked the grandmother's little dog. During our next telephone conversation I asked if such an incident really had happened. She said nothing, she was so surprised. That evening she called me back and remorsefully told me that when she was a little girl she really had accidentally kicked her grandmother's dog. She hadn't imagined that her grandmother could still hold that against her, particularly as she had apologized for it many times. The grandmother wouldn't relent or leave for another few weeks, wishing her grand-daughter's death. When she finally did leave, the grand-daughter started to put on weight at such a fast rate that her family joked she would beat the Guinness Book of Records in growing fat.

BULIMIA, EXCESSIVE WEIGHT GAIN

For many people, eating is the only pleasure in life. They get up from the table and already they're thinking what they're going to eat at the next meal. They're not necessarily fat. I know slim people who do just that. When such a person dies their attachment to eating won't let them pass through to the other side of death's curtain because of an imagined fear that they won't have anything to eat there. The ghost is afraid it might die of hunger not realizing that it is no longer living. These ghosts hook up to a person for whom eating is a pleasure. This happens most often while the person is eating. The ghost wants to "eat" together with the person, taking pleasure from doing so, as it had done during its life. The person will eat for as long as the ghost hooked up to them wants to eat. Unfortunately, our body is in no state to digest the calories we provide for it with this excessive eating. No slimming diets, no counting of calories will help if we are unable to leave the table the moment we've consumed sufficient calories to sustain us. A person like that may be aware that if they eat too much they will grow fat. So the solution that may come into their mind is this: they'll overeat and then they'll vomit up what they've eaten.

When I was visiting in the capital, a dear colleague of mine invited me to dinner at a popular restaurant known for the fact that the food there was good and plentiful. It was busy, there were people waiting for a table. Our dishes were brought to us on huge platters and, surprised, I asked who was going to eat it all because my portion would last me several days. I thought: I'll eat as much as I can and leave the rest. The food was delicious and there was quite a lot still left on my plate and hers when she asked: "Well, is it good?" I replied truthfully: "Oh, yes, you were quite right, the food here really is very good but there's just too much of it". To which she replied: "Let's go to the bathroom, we'll have a good puke and then we'll be able to eat some more". I looked at her with amazement, and she riposted that that's what she always did. "That's the only reason I'm so slim. If I let myself eat all of this, and I do like to eat, I'd look like a tank". It was only then that I noticed that she had a problem with her skin, which she kept carefully hidden under layers of powder. There were ghosts hooked up to her, and when I cleansed her she no longer felt the need to absorb such large quantities of food and, as she called it, "to have a good puke".

Sometimes people come to me for therapy for a specific problem and I help them overcome some completely different restraint which revealed itself seemingly by chance. That happens when it's very difficult to get to the problem the patient has come to solve in therapy. In such cases I decide to apply hypnosis or regression. Sometimes during the session something happens which is completely unrelated to the problem about which the patient complains. A watchful therapist will take the chance to seize on the phenomenon. But it can easily be overlooked and that's what usually happens; after all the client has come with a different problem. The therapist does not want to add another one. In the chapter about homosexuality I write about the sexual molestation and abuse of children by their adult guardians. Many adults may blame the children for it. This sense of guilt and the need to be punished that goes with it (for every other reason, too) may cause us to start putting on too much weight.

When I visited the United States, a woman therapist working on obesity, said to me: "You know, Wanda, maybe it's just my luck but it seems to be the rule that all my patients were either raped or sexually exploited in their childhood". I replied that one can't generalize such a question but the fact is that many people have had that experience. It wasn't even necessary for anything to have taken place: just the attempted molestation or rape could induce just such a result. When, during therapy, the moment when the injury took place is reached and then healed, the obese person loses pounds at an astonishing rate even eating the same as they were before. In my view, obesity is nothing other that surrounding yourself with fat like with a great wall so

that nobody and nothing can hurt us. The location of this excessively collected fat indicates what kind of problem we are dealing with.

MENTAL ILLNESSES

It can happen that a normally functioning person may suddenly, from one hour to the next, stop knowing who they are, what they're saying, what they're doing; they see visions, they hear voices. They can sense that they're being touched, forced to do things, they feel compulsions. They may notice scratches or wounds on their bodies and not know where they've come from. They may be aware of the moment the injury occurred, see the blood flowing, and feel pain even though they are far from any sharp objects. A person who till then had been active, sociable, cheerful may suddenly become closed in on themselves, it may be hard to make contact with them, they themselves may start to have suicidal thoughts. Or vice versa: a calm person may become aggressive, ready to destroy everything in one moment, sometimes even to kill someone. Their eyes emanate hatred even towards those they'd loved till now. A refined person may suddenly become vulgar, swearing at people for no reason - in a streetcar, a shop, a church or the street. They may smell some scent everywhere, anything from a pleasant one to a terrible odor. Or vice versa, people around them may smell an unpleasant stench coming from the person, even though that person may wash constantly.

These symptoms don't, of course, appear simultaneously in one person, though even that can happen. These phenomena can be barely perceptible to the afflicted person, but very obvious to those around him, or vice versa. They may be annoying, interfering considerably in a person's normal behavior, and can even stop them functioning normally, but may be completely imperceptible to those around them. A person like that, when he's with other people, may see or hear something very clearly which no-one else can, even though subjectively these signals are of a very powerful intensity. Doctors have classified this kind of behavior or state as a manifestation of schizophrenia or some other mental illness. This kind of person is universally regarded as insane. When these symptoms grow more intensive or cause a threat to society's safety, these people are locked up in psychiatric hospitals. These symptoms, and many others I've not mentioned, are a clear sign of the presence of ghosts within a person.

Every psychiatric illness presents symptoms similar to the ones I've mentioned above. It occurred to me that since there is a similarity then maybe its cause is also the same. The cases of psychiatric illness I've come into contact with have confirmed my conviction that that really is so. I have collected several thousands of them and they are all very similar to each other. My many years' experience have taught me that every mental illness arises when the afflicted person allows themselves to be not only possessed, but surrender their body and their mind in their totality to the ghost, yielding themselves to its will. Every case is, of course, different. In some cases, a person is himself for a moment, then somebody completely different, and then himself again. The moments when he is "somebody else" are not noticed by the patient, nor indeed remembered. The human mind can be compared to the activity of a computer. The information when the ghost is present within the sick person is written onto the hard disc of the ghost, not the sick person. It's a bit like the sick person giving himself a vacation from being himself. During that time it's the ghost that directs his body and mind. That's where the memory gaps in the sick person come from.

Other times the sick person is someone completely different constantly, and only very rarely themselves. This happens when the body and the mind are surrendered to the will of many different ghosts. In extreme cases a person's spirit may be ejected from its own body by ghosts and be forced to exist outside it. Such cases are not at all rare. They depend on the level of a person's possession. There may be hundreds of ghosts possessing just one person. In the Bible they were called "legion" (Luke 8,30).

A sick person may be aware of themselves but may be too weak mentally to stand up to a ghost or ghosts. They steal a person's body, and the sick person doesn't know how she can defend herself. A lot depends on the environment she lives in. When it is a friendly one and supportive then her chances of staying healthy are greater. But if she is alone with her problem or meets with disbelief when talking about it then she may give up and fall ill. A lot depends, too, on the reaction to the ailments of doctors, psychiatrists, and ministers. If they're unable to explain to the patient the reasons for her state then they drive her ever more deeply into a state of illness.

To make the splitting of personality and many other

mental illnesses more comprehensible, I will draw a comparison of the body with that of a ship at sea. A mentally well person is like a captain on his ship. He steers it competently, avoiding the dangers it comes across. He steers confidently because even in the greatest storm nothing can threaten him since he is in the care of God. A captain like that won't allow unauthorized passengers come aboard his ship. He will always know where the ship is and what its course is.

But there are other kinds of captain. They rarely stand on the bridge and steer, allowing the ship to drift aimlessly in the ocean, usually because they're afraid. They also allow unasked passengers to come aboard and do whatever they like. A person suffering from schizophrenia is just that kind of ship filled with passenger-ghosts, without a captain on the bridge. The captain, as the owner of the ship, can be present on it throughout the trip but the passengers, or the ghosts, won't let him near the wheel. When some passenger grabs hold of the wheel he will ignore the presence of the captain and steer the ship in his own way. Sometimes, the captain won't grab the wheel even when there is no-one steering. In extreme cases the captain may be thrown overboard (in other words out of his own body). The passenger-ghosts, seeing the bridge free, will steer the ship in their own way but even they, after a while, will abandon this pastime for various reasons. Sometimes, the passengers know nothing about the presence of the captain, or the other passengers, on the ship. The captain may also not apprehend the presence of passengers on the deck. Every one of them considers the ship to be their own property and behaves in accordance with that belief. Sometimes all the passengers want to steer the ship at the same time and they fight amongst themselves for power. That's when attacks of mental illness are exacerbated in the owner's body-ship. When there is no volunteer among the passengers to steer the ship and the captain resolves to stand on the bridge at last then we may notice a momentary improvement in the sick person's condition. His self-awareness returns and he may be released from hospital. He is not well, though. The ghosts are still there inside him, and have only taken a vacation from steering his body.

If such a person knew the reason for their problems they would most probably fight. But they do nothing about it because they think that they're in a situation over which they haven't the slightest influence. Sometimes it seems to them that they really have gone mad. They are in great error. This is the best possible moment for the person, ill till now, to resolve to stand at the wheel as the captain of their ship. But somebody would have to appraise them of it, repeat it to them more than once until they acknowledged it. Then the sick person could regain control of their own life.

Every disease can be cured and not be endured. Anyone can at any moment take advantage of the opportunity offered by God, but few do so. There are many reasons for this. So much time may have elapsed from the moment when they gave up the wheel that they have forgotten about their role as captain. Maybe they have grown accustomed to the fact that someone else is standing on the bridge. The patient often doesn't want to make the effort thinking that someone will take it away from them at any moment. This happens particularly often to people who since childhood haven't been allowed to make decisions about anything. When they become adults they continue to submit to someone else and are not fully independent. In their childhood everything was decided for them by dictatorial parents, now other people do this, or ghosts, often the ghosts of the dead parents. In the chapter "When a Mother Dies..." I described the fate of a man who spent twelve years in a psychiatric hospital, suffering from severe schizophrenia. Its cause was his own mother. Instead of going to the Light after her death, motivated by a blind love for her son she remained and looked after him just as she had done when alive. She drove him to severe illness. When he discovered the cause he demanded the right to his own life. Even though he had to wage war against himself and his mother, he didn't allow her possessive affection to continue deciding about his life. He fought for his life and he won.

Many patients decide to take that step when they discover the cause of their misery. They do not allow the ghosts to continue to interfere with their own lives. Even though the ghosts occasionally return they courageously keep steering their own ship.

You see, in truth nothing has changed in that person, they have the same number of ghosts as before, but their awareness has changed. This gives them strength and leads to a full recovery. They don't give up the wheel even when they doubt that they can cope with the challenge. Now they know that if they allowed themselves to weaken it would be the same as being ill. They want to get better and the very awareness of their state gives them strength in the battle against the invading ghosts. When an exorcist leads the ghosts away, the person will certainly not allow them to come back in.

Sometimes the family and friends, even when they know that the cause of the illness is possession, continue to conceal the fact from the sick person. They judge that he is not in a state to cope with the knowledge about himself, about ghosts and about possession. They don't realize how great the error is in their reasoning. When a patient finds out for the first time about the cause of her illness, she says joyfully: "Mrs Pratnicka, now at last I know what's wrong with me. What you tell me is an explanation for my ailments, and it's proof that I haven't gone mad.

Now at last I see that I can be free of it!". From then it's just a tiny step to a full return to health. This awareness gives the patient the strength to take the wheel of her life into her own hands. For there are many people who are possessed just like her, not mentally ill. All the time that they are afflicted they don't allow the ghosts to steer their ship even when those ghosts fight to do so.

The cause of mental illness is not so much being possessed by too many ghosts or ghosts that are too powerful, but the fact that the sick person, not knowing what's happening to them, becomes very frightened and gives up without a fight. I know of a case where a person was possessed by hundreds of ghosts and he continued to function normally, whereas with another person just one ghost can enter and he won't be able to deal with it or with himself.

I dare to suggest that the chief cause of mental illnesses is the patient's, and their family's, ignorance of the fact that their bodies and minds have been taken over by ghosts. If the knowledge of that were widespread, then people would respond to it quite differently and more appropriately. Even if they didn't know how to lead the ghost away they would avoid it like they avoid an annoying fly. When a ghost visits someone who is unaware of these matters then that person becomes frightened not just of the ghost but of everything around him or her. Being frightened that person surrenders their body to the ghost without any resistance. From that moment they start to feel differently than before and, unable to understand the cause of it, they start to get even more frightened. Thus they attract to themselves more ghosts on the principle that "we attract the things that we fear most". Soon, they are afraid of everything, even of fear itself. What frightens them more than anything, however, is that what they're experiencing may be a figment of their imagination.

The result is that they reach the conclusion that they have gone mad. And they do go mad, on the principle that "reality is what I believe it is". A person whom ghosts are trying to possess can be helped just by believing what he says. Do you hear voices? You're right, you didn't imagine it. You have the right to hear the voices of ghosts. You see something? You didn't go mad, I personally don't see it but you have the right to see, you must be more of a medium etc.

Whereas the patient is not believed even by those who are supposed to help - the doctors, the priests. This does not stem, of course, from any ill will on their behalf, but from ignorance. This can easily be seen when a member of the clergy or the medical profession succumbs to possession. After they have been cleansed they can see how their lives have been changed, recognize what it was all about and from then on they help their patients in a completely different way. Some will become zealous propagators of this knowledge, others again remain silent about it not wanting to betray that they themselves were possessed. However, they send their patients to me or help them themselves if they are capable of it. I want to tell those who are ashamed of it that theirs is a false shame. Possession can happen to anyone and those who help others are even more exposed to it.

Even though I have had many successes, I am conscious of the fact that it's not possible to help every sick person permanently. I can help only those people who wish to help themselves. But even those who haven't yet decided to do that can be helped for just a short while. They are given a chance by God and they can consider whether they want to continue being ill or whether they want to get well.

A considerable number of people don't wish to be healthy. As a sick person they can put the responsibility for their lives onto the shoulders of the doctors, the family, or the community. Many exploit their illnesses to achieve aims of which they are not conscious. People have various needs and sometimes, if they are unable to demand them directly, they retreat into illness. For instance, a person who feels unloved will fall ill because they erroneously believe that only in this way will they get what they need so much, namely some affection from their family and friends in the form of their sympathy, care, and interest. A mentally ill person thinks that he'll get this affection from the ghost. Someone else may use the illness to manipulate his surroundings on the basis that: "you won't give me what I want, so I'll be ill which will make you feel guilty and in the end you'll concede". They don't realize that they're manipulating. Nor do they expect that their manipulating tricks may find a ghost-manipulator hooking into them. Alive or dead - every manipulator will come across another manipulator. Please don't imagine that this all happens on the conscious plane, these are deeply hidden tendencies though easy for an experienced eye to read. When a sick man desires to be healthy and wants to confront his or her subconscious problems, then he or she returns to good health permanently. This is the moment in which he may well become one of my patients. He wants his health but doesn't know how to get it back, and I help him get out of the labyrinth into which he has stumbled.

Till that moment even the best medical help wasn't able to help him permanently, only for a short while at best. The description of a young sportsman's case will illustrate how this works. It's not a case of mental illness but I chose it because it is very transparent. The responsibility for the patient's decisions cannot in this case be put down to mental confusion.

Peter had had many successes in his sporting career. Jumping into water in an unauthorized place he damaged his spine and became totally paralyzed. About a year and a half after the accident the family asked for my help. I very much wanted to help him and I set to work eagerly. He was driven over to me regularly and after a few sessions he started to feel pins and needles in his legs. This was our first success, then there were more and more visible steps towards a return to health. In time the moment came when he could make minimal movements of his toes. Our joy knew no bounds. The doctors were amazed. Immediately after his accident, Peter was in all the mass media. He made many new friends, he even fell in love, which was requited. Now there were more and more friends appearing. He was the center of attention, just as he had been during his sporting successes. One day Peter started asking questions filled with doubt: "When I'm well again, I won't go back to sport. I have no chance to get good results... and then I'll have to go to work. God, I mean I can't do anything. I always found learning very difficult. Maybe because I was always training. At least now I have a disability allowance, but how else could I get money? I'll probably end up sweeping the streets. At least now I have some friends. Before I was always alone, nobody liked me". He was increasingly scared. None of my arguments or those of his family could persuade him. He wanted to return home immediately. That same day, in the evening, I received a call from his parents. They informed me that he'd lost all feeling in his legs again. His mind had chosen sickness rather than health. For a while he was satisfied with his choice but after a couple of years when I saw him again he was a lonely, bitter, crushed human being. By way of welcome he said: "Mrs Pratnicka, if I could have one more chance I'm sure I'd make a wiser choice. As you can see, I have a lot of time to think about my life and the decisions I've made. Right after the accident I was mad at God because I was an invalid. That anger concealed what lay below it. I rebelled, I convinced myself that now, just to spite Him, I would not get well. That's how I explained it to myself to feel better. When the anger passed I started to question my own life, just like you taught me. I reached the conclusion that I had created that accident myself in the exact same way as I hadn't wanted to return to health. It happened when I was starting to get poorer results in my sport. Subconsciously, I was very afraid of leaving the sport as a loser and unconsciously I made the accident happen".

Naturally, there wasn't one moment when Peter had thought: "I'll make an accident happen now" and it took place immediately afterwards. It was the consequence of many subconscious thoughts stretching over a long period. I helped him unravel the next knots in his psyche. I knew that he had completed that lesson. Though he didn't recover control over his body he did regain control over his life. He started to use the healthy parts of his being and his life acquired sense and momentum. He helped himself and now he is able to help others. Despite his handicap he is a happy, fulfilled human being.

Peter was so afraid of losing that he missed losing his life by a hair's breadth. And what is Agnes afraid of? She had been suffering from schizophrenia for many years. Several times each year she would be sent to a psychiatric hospital. When she came home she would take powerful psychotropic drugs. One day her mother asked me to help. I cleansed her several times which, in cases of psychiatric illness, is quite normal. I noticed that each time she had different ghosts, but there was one that was always the same. I thought that she must be emotionally involved with it. I asked her mother for a list of people who had died in the family. Unfortunately, it was not someone from that list. I asked her to look through close and even distant acquaintances, but that came to nothing. One day I sensed a teacher in the ghost. I followed that track. I asked her mother to consider whether any of her daughter's teachers had died, and she suddenly had a revelation. When her daughter had started high school she often talked about one of the teachers in a manner which suggested that she had a crush on him. "Mrs Pratnicka, he has been dead for so long," the mother said dubiously. "Besides which, he was an old sick guy with a wife and kids. What connection can he have with my daughter's illness?". It transpired that he could and he did, in a big way. I demanded from her mother that she let me talk to the daughter who had hitherto refused claiming that it would drive her even deeper into illness. My aim was to make the girl aware that her state was caused by the presence of a ghost. The mother beseeched me not to say anything about ghosts to her daughter because she thought it would terrify her. When I started my conversation with Agnes I noticed that though she was interested in what I had to say she gave evasive answers to my questions. I was getting discouraged by this constant equivocation when she told me straight out: "Now that my mother isn't here I can tell you: I feel good the way things are and I don't want to change anything. It's only my mother who wants to force me to change". She explained that she was living with her teacher and she was summoning him quite consciously. "I feel good now. Earlier it was hard for me because I was molested by some thick-skinned, vulgar drunk who made me curse in shops and in church. I was ashamed of it but I couldn't withstand it. It was like something talking to me. Thank you very much for taking him away from me, but I won't give up my lover. My mother worries about me so I tell her all sorts of rubbish, e.g. that I've got a fiancé who's going to marry me. I do it so she'll stop guarding me and leave me in peace instead of sending me to hospital. The hospital stays do nothing for me, I don't take the medicines since you started to cleanse me. Please explain to her that it's she who's going mad, not me. I know that what I'm doing isn't entirely normal, but I'm used to it. Although I'm not that bothered about him any more but you know something? I'm quite old now. Who'll want me now? I've no other way but to stay like this. At least I've got someone to make love to when I need it. Does my mother want me to stay alone for the rest of my life?".

The girl knew perfectly well that in order to "get better" in the eyes of those around her she would have to let the ghost leave. She knew that the price of that love was hospital, ridicule and contempt from her surroundings, but that's what she chose. She had the right to do so. The mother, on the other hand, refuses her that freedom by asking me to help. She wants me to support her plan and, working behind her daughter's back, to do something against her will. That can't work. Her daughter isn't a madwoman but a girl who has made inappropriate decisions.

There are often cases where two people are so strongly tied to one another that they won't let anything separate them, not even death. It can be two friends, lovers, a married couple, but it can also be a parent and a child. That's what they chose and, in their view, it's okay. However what had seemed at the beginning to be a good solution may result in becoming the greatest shackles. When one of the parties changes their minds and wants something else for themselves, it may prove to be very difficult or even impossible to put into effect. Sometimes the living person won't want to release the ghost and keeps summoning it, sometimes it's the ghost which won't leave the living one.

Agnes's example is one of thousands. It reveals an interesting dependency. When a person is open to one ghost then other ghosts, too, have access to them. That's when various complications can arise - health, financial, mental. When the person comes to an exorcist, the exorcist will lead away all the ghosts. After cleansing, the person misses the "wanted" ghost, and when they summon it others come in, too. A vicious circle is formed. This behavior harms both the ghosts and the people. It is essential to understand that the ghosts' place is in their world, and our place is in ours. A clear grasp of this matter would improve the lives of many people and many ghosts.

During my years of practice I've noticed that a large number of patients could get better but at the same time, like Agnes, they want something else. There is a conflict: receiving one thing they have to do without the other. They choose what, in their view, is more precious. However, it's not unusual for something which was once valuable to lose its price. When the patient's system of values changes then they may want to return to health. If we discover what is of value to the sick person then, jointly, we can look for a similar value which is not in conflict with their health. That is what happened with Agnes. Some time elapsed but in the end she comprehended that the world is full of living people who are just as lonely as she is and who are waiting to become friends with her and to love her. Today she is a happy wife and the mother of two children, and her mother won't stop thanking me for helping her fulfill her dream of becoming a granny. Agnes spent such a long time waiting for her happiness because she didn't have the courage to try.

Now I'd like to write about other causes of mental illnesses which have quite severe consequences.

Looking back on the history of the world we see that at the start of every century there was an increasing rush by mankind towards changing itself and the world around it. The same is happening now. At the start of this century a great number of people all over the world are starting to take an interest in spiritual development, esoterics, looking for power. Much of what earlier was regarded as secret knowledge is now generally accessible. Earlier the effective schooling of an apprentice of the secret art took place slowly, over a period of years, and it didn't always guarantee success. Secret because very few had access to it. Now the same effect is demanded from a course, schooling or initiation without any deeper preparation. In every bookshop, not just specialist shops, one can buy books from any field of esoterics from how to meditate and open the third eye, increase the kundalini energy, all the way to precise instructions for using black magic or writing death letters. These things are taught not only by books but by other mass media. From this comes the mistaken belief that this knowledge is suitable even for a pre-school child, that everyone not only has to know about it but has to use it on an everyday basis. This approach awakens curiosity and persuades people to reach for it without any preparation. The other side of the coin is that it blunts any sense of caution. Approaching this question in such a light way can easily obscure the truth that sometimes employing this knowledge can lead the participants to very sorry results.

There was a woman, a shop owner, who often heard from her clients about a healer across the ocean who helps by sending energy at a distance. Her husband had for some time been unwell, it was later discovered that he had cancer, so she decided to ask the healer for "energy" for her husband. At the moment that the healer was sending the energy, at the agreed time, she sat down with her husband "in the line of fire" as she described it, so she, too, could take advantage of it. She thought she was being a very clever and sharp woman because she was paying once but taking double. The cancer developed at an astonishingly rapid rate and the husband was dying, while she was, at the same time, going mad. One day she noticed that one of her clients was radiant. She started to laugh hysterically. A moment later she noticed that another client was radiant too. When she discovered this she started to walk along the streets laughing at the passers-by. Now she was seeing not only the person's aura, but also their insides along with their diseases. She also saw the astral world, the world of ghosts. She wasn't aware that what she was seeing is the reality in which we are all living but about which the majority of people have not the faintest idea. She didn't appreciate that she had received from God a miraculous gift which many people all over the world dream about. She could at least have used it to save her dying husband. It's possible that it was given to her for just that, but she was frightened by it. Her gift became a curse. So as not to feel the enormous fear caused by what she was seeing, she drowned it with noisy laughter. Many people when they are very afraid of something, get attacks of laughter. She also laughed at her husband, showing him the places in his body which were devoured by cancer. He was dying and she was taken to a psychiatric hospital. When I was asked to help it was too late for both her husband and for her.

If that woman had known what a dose of energy like the one she'd succumbed to can do, then she would have prepared herself, at the very least theoretically. She would have known what a person's aura was and, having seen it, she may not have been frightened at all. Furthermore she would have started to examine with interest the various facets of its presence like its size, color, shape etc. Surely the same would have happened with every other phenomenon she saw. Acquainting her with this after the event did not bring the required response. I noticed that she was most terrified by the fact that other people didn't see what she saw, thinking she was a madwoman. She didn't want to hear words of confirmation from a clairvoyant. She assessed that she was dealing with the same sort of madwoman as she judged herself to be. What she wanted most of all was confirmation from priests and doctors. She is in a psychiatric hospital to this day, terrified by her otherness.

I write about these cases because many people who are being treated for mental illnesses come to me for help. After close examination of the causes of their illness it turns out that their beginnings have something to do with Reiki initiation, tarot reading, performing magic, participating in a spiritualist séance or, as in the example quoted, opening oneself up to the activity of energy. There is nothing wrong with these fields of esoteric knowledge, the problem arises from a lack of a theoretical basis in that person about the particular field they've come into contact with or started to practice. The apprentice will often consider that there is no need to fathom the knowledge in depth, that it's enough to explore that fragment that particularly interests them. These explorations are usually undertaken out of pure curiosity and don't aim at a professional involvement in the subject like fortune-telling, clairvoyance, telling the future. The person involved in this doesn't aim to become a healer, a master of Reiki, or bioenergy therapist. Such an attitude ignores a very crucial aspect of the knowledge which can decide whether we succeed or fail or even suffer a disaster.

We also ignore a very important fact namely that esoteric knowledge is given to us to help us better understand the reality around us and ourselves. It is to help us develop the most crucial accomplishments for which we have come to this earthly school, namely our capability to love ourselves, other people and God. Our investigations, meanwhile, are often concentrated on acquiring aspects of knowledge aimed at leading us to manipulate ourselves, other people and to gain external power over the world.

It can happen that a poorly prepared person will want to earn a living by exploiting their esoteric knowledge. They want to help people by, for instance, healing with the aid of bioenergy therapy. They have completed a short course on which they're taught how to transmit energy. They give it out here and there to everyone who just comes and asks for it. Having no knowledge, however, of the specific illness and its cure they don't know if the illness arose as a result of a lack or an excess of energy. They don't know, therefore, when to add energy, when to subtract it, or when to balance it. That's what happened in the case I described of the man suffering from cancer. The energy, instead of helping him, simply accelerated his death. The powerful stream of energy opened the woman's third eye as a consequence of which she went insane. Despite the negative results all three people involved (including the healer) acted in good faith. Esoterics is a science which deals with invisible things. "Invisible" is not the same, however, as "unreal". I fear that not one of that threesome was conscious of the processes which took place. Unfortunately, the consequences of these processes don't always appear at the moment of operation.

To understand this better let me return once more to the example given above. The healer sends the energy intended for the husband part of which is taken up by the wife. It happens at her own request so in some sense it is her own fault and she has to suffer the consequences. The healer, however, could easily have avoided this turn of events if he had been aware of the processes that take place during the sending of energy. He could easily have tracked what was happening to the energy on its way to his patient. He should have directed the energy in such a way that it reached only the recipient. Not out of cunning but out of foresight so that it would not harm anyone. He did not do so. I suspect that he simply wasn't aware that it could be harmful. To harmful. To some extent he was right. Energy on its own can't harm anyone. It is the energy of God, and there is plenty of it everywhere. However, receiving increased doses of it can cause harm just as anything can that's taken in excess. And so it's not the energy that does harm but an excess of it.

There is also a large number of mentally ill people who became involved in playing games with ghosts without regard for the consequences. Once the wife of a famous professor came to me looking for help for her husband. The doctors had diagnosed a mental illness in him. They claimed it was one of the most severe mental illness for which there is as yet no therapy. The woman demanded that I as good as cleanse her husband instantly. All attempts at persuading her that it was hard for me to do it in a hotel and that I'd do it when I returned home were of no avail. In the end I promised I would start cleansing the next morning. She insisted on knowing at what time it would start and what course it would take. I thought all this was because of concern for her husband but shortly it turned out that there was something else behind it. This lady was a clairvoyant who had invited several other clairvoyants to her house so they could all watch from close up while I healed her husband. If I'd known about it I would have categorically forbidden it. They didn't know what they were exposing themselves to. If it was as safe as they considered it then I would carry out cleansing in the patient's presence, and not at a distance. They apparently were going to experience it on their own skins. I started the cleansing. I was horrified by the ghost's strength and viciousness. After about an hour he left calmly for the other side and never returned. I was very surprised by the joy and gratitude it showed as it was leaving. I, too, felt joyful and grateful. I was quite tired but the satisfaction I felt with the successful completion rewarded me for it. The telephone rang and I heard the familiar voice of the professor's wife. I was just about to inform her that I had cleansed her husband when she, very perturbed, started to tell me what she had seen and what had happened in her home: "Before leaving the professor, the ghost started to demolish the whole apartment in a great fury. He hurled the professor against the wall and threw anything he could lay his hands on at the people gathered in the room. He wouldn't let anyone run away, nor open a door or a window". "Just as well," I thought, "otherwise they'd all have leapt out of the windows and they lived high up in a multi-story apartment block." "An hour later the apartment looked like a battlefield, the people were all beaten up and terrified," she continued. I have never come across such an aggressive reaction from a ghost. I suspect that the people present there had done something which the ghost didn't like or maybe its nature was that of a raving madman. "Mrs Pratnicka," she said gratefully, "the furniture can be replaced or restored, and the apartment can be refurbished. What's most important is that my husband is free at last of that terrible ghost. Right after the cleansing he got into the car and drove over to the university. He even asked me not to wait with dinner for him." I said that this wasn't a particularly sensible move because the ghost may well come back. "Mrs Pratnicka, please don't worry, my husband is a very wise and a very strong person. I am certain that he won't allow the ghost to enter again. He allowed it to enter because he wanted to see what it was like. He thought that since he had the power to let the ghost in he would have the power to get rid of it. It turned out, however, to be too difficult. Now he knows that it's a one-way trip." Since then the couple have often phoned to tell me that the doctors can't believe how well he's recovered. They claim it's only a temporary remission, that he might relapse at any moment. Many years have passed but the illness has not returned just as the ghost which was its cause has not returned.

Now you can see what people's curiosity can lead to when they haven't much of a clue about a given subject. It's like putting your hand in boiling water just to see what it's like in the mistaken belief that everything will be okay. The professor isn't so exceptional. Many people delve into the knowledge of ghosts out of pure curiosity. Many play with magic and energies. And how many raise the kundalini energy, aim for opening the third eye, seek to attain the power in any way possible? You think it's a harmless hobby, but you are wrong. If you don't believe me then visit the psychiatric clinics or hospitals where you live.

There are those who desire esoteric knowledge as a way to peering into their own or others' futures, or to become healers, magicians etc. Some do it on their own, others sign up for seminars and courses. They often see it as getting a new profession which will, in the future, bring them money or even, perhaps, fame. There is nothing wrong with that, but since it's going to be their profession they should prepare themselves for it more thoroughly just as they would for any other profession. A short course on a given subject won't solve the matter, it will give only a very hazy idea of it. Many people armed with just this minimal knowledge start to practice in the hope that no-one will check out the level of their qualifications. They deceive themselves into thinking that by practicing a non-material subject they cannot be checked. I, too, have been approached for lessons and this is quite normal. What isn't normal, however, is to demand that I show the apprentice in short time what the knowledge is more or less about instead of giving them a thorough grounding in the subject. If a chemist learns about chemistry only superficially then he might well pour water into an acid and get burns for life. The same is true of the knowledge of the laws governing ghosts. One must know one's own specialty very precisely indeed, and the subsidiary specialties very well, in order not to harm anyone, and above all oneself.

A healer from abroad would often come to Poland to visit till finally she settled here along with her family. It was a pleasure for me to watch her work. There was something beautiful in her movements which I've not seen the like of since. We became close friends and so I was very surprised when she suddenly vanished without even saying goodbye. In the places where she used to go nobody had heard of her. I guessed that some important matter had forced her to leave the country. In some inexplicable way she stubbornly kept returning to my thoughts, as if she was trying to tell me something. Usually I find it easy to read the messages sent to me, but not this time. I was uneasy especially as she made no contact with anyone. After nearly a year, when I was at a conference of healers, I suddenly saw her. I stood rooted to the ground because this beautiful woman had turned into a wreck of a human being. She was unnaturally twisted, she couldn't stand up on her own. There were two people holding her up. With the greatest difficulty she babbled out: "I've got a pass from the psychiatric hospital, I've only got ten minutes, I've got to get straight back there, I beg you, I can't cope with it, help me, you're the only one left". She turned right round and left. She was returning to the hospital in great fear that she wouldn't get back before the allocated time as if there would be terrible sanctions for the transgression. I wondered what had happened to this magnificent, strong, independent woman. Since she had turned to me it meant that she was being attacked by ghosts. Now I understood why the messages had been so unclear. In my thoughts I had seen her as healthy and it hadn't occurred to me that she could have been possessed. When I returned home I started to cleanse her as soon as I opened the front door. Even though it was a very powerful ghost, it left comparatively quickly. I waited for some news from her impatiently. I knew that now she would be released from hospital. The doctors usually notice my intervention immediately because the patients quite simply become normal. It happened that way in hundreds of cases. A few days later I saw her in the street walking towards me: she was healthy and straight-backed. She ran up to me, seized my hands like I was a little girl and twirled me round and round in circles. She hugged me, kissed me and hugged me again. A crowd gathered round us but still she wouldn't let me go. When her emotions had calmed down, she put me down on the ground again. We made our way to a nearby café and this is what I heard: "A very sick man came to me and I, instead of sending him to you, started to heal him myself. I don't know what tempted me to do it, I must have just wanted to try to see what it was like. You've told me so many times not to undertake cleansing in the presence of the patient, but I didn't listen. It all happened in the twinkling of an eye. I knew right away that that ghost had possessed me, but I couldn't do anything about it. I told my husband about it and asked him to call you straight away. He wouldn't agree as if he didn't believe me. Throughout our union he's been against my activities as a healer and now he'd found the opportunity to discourage me. I thought it was transitory, that I would be able to manage it, but it didn't go away. I felt worse and worse, till in the end I lost my awareness and my consciousness. My husband called the ambulance. That's how I ended up in a psychiatric hospital. I was there for more than a year. You saw the way I looked after the injections. They constrict the muscles, it's impossible even to talk after them. During the electric shock treatment I thought I was going to die. It was lucky that shortly after going into hospital I recovered my self-awareness and I preserved that more or less till the end. I asked the doctors for a pass to see you, but they wouldn't agree. I couldn't get my husband to agree to phone you, he claimed he didn't believe in all that nonsense. He kept saying: 'She's just as stupid as you were till now. You can see for yourself where it's got you'. Now that he's seen what you've done for me in such a short time he can't forgive himself. He knows that if he'd agreed to your help I'd have been well long ago and wouldn't have had to suffer all that in hospital. But I suppose it was there so we could learn something from it. What's happened cannot be undone. It's taught me humility in doing what I do and it's taught him - we'll see, time will tell".

My friend had been a healer for years. She had many successes on her account, yet despite that she suffered a catastrophe when she wanted to do something she didn't know about. As she herself said, she did it out of a lack of humility in the face of knowledge.

A large group of mentally ill people is comprised of those who got involved in various kinds of esoteric practices. They did so out of curiosity because it's now quite fashionable to indulge in such activities. Some read books, others attended courses or workshops. There are those who were initiated by the teachers of various schools of spiritual development. They submitted, for instance, to Reiki initiation whereby they start to see with the third eye. They are terrified, not understanding what's happening to them. This hasn't, however, occurred by their volition as in the case of the woman who had hooked up to the healer's energy. Some of them had to work very hard at it. When they achieve the aim of their attempts they suddenly start to hope that it's just a temporary disturbance which will pass shortly. They see people's auras, the astral world, and this provokes in them a state of panic. This uncontrolled fear is hooked into by ghosts and the next step is schizophrenia. Maybe they

had ghosts before and now seeing them has terrified them so
much. If we start to observe them without any preparation it's
easy to fall into a panic. People who forced the opening of the
third eye often can't switch off its function and that can be very
burdensome. The fear grows and every day they ask God to
take away from them what they had wanted so much before.
But what can happen is that, with time, the vision becomes ever
more clear instead of fading. Many people tell me how much
they regret having gone down that road. They feel like they've
been cheated by fate. They had expected something attractive
but what they got has disappointed them greatly. They nearly
all ask me: "Mrs Pratnicka, why did nobody on the course tell
me what would happen to me?" or "Why wasn't I told what I
could expect after my initiation? I mean, the course was led by
the finest specialists". I suspect that the teacher had assumed
that this was fundamental knowledge which every apprentice
should be aware of. No teacher in a high school asks the students if they know the alphabet.

Here I would like to remind all those who lead any kind
of schooling and workshops of their responsibilities. Maybe
you don't realize that shortly after such courses some of the participants start to go mad. Of course, it's not the schooling that is
the cause but the fact that a given person hasn't matured sufficiently for it. A teacher's fundamental duty is a thorough assessment of the apprentice, to ascertain whether or not the student has matured enough for the knowledge being presented at
the course. My patients frequently don't associate the causes of
their illnesses with a course or initiation they took earlier.
Sometimes these problematic students turn to their teachers with
their problems. They often hear then: "You're a schizophrenic
so stop bothering me. I don't wish to see you here any more!".
It's not out of the question that these people were ill before the

course but before starting to teach one must select the volunteers even though it can be difficult. They should also know about the complications that can follow. There's no certainty that they'll listen to you but you'll have a clear conscience if you inform them. Sometimes the desire to earn an income can obscure common sense. I'm not writing this to pass judgment on you but to draw your attention to it. It is becoming a problem for an increasingly large number of people.

Many workshop participants believe that energy channels can be opened with immunity. Whereas the participant's whole being is not prepared for it. It's just like a beginning body-builder going up to huge weights and, without any training of his muscles, wanting to lift them. Starting on any discipline one has, first of all, to get to know the subject theoretically, then practically and only after years of exercises does one become a master. Esoteric knowledge has to be acquired thoroughly and from all aspects.

I also wish to add that anyone wanting to delve into the mysteries of spiritual laws must be not only mentally well-balanced but must also be a very good person. When such a person takes that road every dishonest act will turn against him or her. What till now he or she had got away with will now not be allowed. I sometimes get to see masters of various schools, chiromancers, tarot readers, bioenergy therapists and exorcists who have, unfortunately, forgotten about that.

MOOD SWINGS

I mentioned earlier that there can be many ghosts residing within one person. Each one of them will have a completely different character, a different approach to various matters, a different assessment of reality. One of them may, in a given situation, switch on fear, another one may withdraw or become aggressive and create an argument. Another one still may not react at all, treating the matter with stoic calm or indifference. The person's character will depend on which ghost is at the wheel of the possessed person's mind. From the outside this will be perceived as constantly changing moods. When there are many ghosts present, the people around the possessed person never know what to expect. One time a dish will taste good to them, another time they will throw the plate against a wall with disgust, or one time they may like to go to the opera or a piano recital and another time they'll cover their ears at the very sound of music. One time they may like to play some game and be very good at it, playing it like a champion, another time they don't even know the game's rules. One time they may paint, write or sing brilliantly, another time they'll make a mess and sing off-key. One time they'll have perfect vision, another time they'll need to wear glasses. I could give many more examples but by now you've probably realized what I'm talking about. When ghosts enter a person then their problems become that person's problems. When they are led away, suddenly everything returns to normal, including moods and competencies.

AUTISM

There are those who call autism childhood schizophrenia. The condition is one in which the child, from its earliest years, fails to make contact with its surroundings. The child won't allow even those closest to it into its world. The child develops and looks quite normally but often it won't even want to learn to speak or carry out the simplest of tasks like those involved with its personal hygiene or with eating. When it grows up, nothing much changes. Since the outside world doesn't interest it at all, the child is totally reliant on the help of those closest to him. When there are none they have to rely on welfare. If they were left to their own devices they would be unable to look after themselves and would most likely die of cold or hunger. Just as in all diseases this one, too, can be more or less severe. An autistic person is usually so strongly aroused that they have to take psychotropic drugs throughout their lives. Conventional medicine can do little to help, regarding autism as an incurable disease. I have a different view and I have many proofs for it. Here is one of them.

A few years ago a young mother with a son of four and a half years, Bill, came to me. The little boy couldn't talk, hooted like an owl, wriggled about constantly, strongly aroused he took no notice of anything around him. Absolutely nothing interested him. He didn't look round the inside of my surgery where he was for the very first time, nor did he look at the people there. The toys which were put into his hands didn't interest him, nor did the kitten and puppy playing on the floor. He was in the care of doctors and the daily help of therapists but even they weren't able to make any contact with him. The doctors examined him many times and they were unanimous in diagnosing complete autism. His mother knew what she had to do to force some sort of contact. She was very severe which shocked me somewhat but she claimed it was the only way to reach him even in a minimal way. I asked if Bill always behaved like this, if she could leave him to himself even for a couple of minutes. It seemed that unfortunately he was always like this twenty-four hours a day. "What do you mean twenty-four hours, when does he sleep?" I asked. "He almost doesn't sleep at all, if he dozes off it's for a couple of minutes and then he's awake again," she replied. I asked how they put up with it. The reply I heard was that during the night, and when her husband was at work, she looked after him, and when her husband came home from work she slept. "That's the way our life looks," she said. I thought that this constant waking was the work of a ghost. I checked and it turned out that that was indeed so. He had a very strong ghost. It seemed that he was born normal and only when he was about a year and a half old did his autism start to manifest itself. I asked if anyone in the family had died while she was pregnant or during Bill's life. The parents couldn't remember anyone like that.

My intention wasn't to find a way of curing autism. I wanted to help the child by ridding it of the ghosts possessing him. I hadn't come across autism before. I felt very moved by what I saw. As they were leaving I promised I would try to help but I didn't know if it would have any results. I believe that giving hope and then taking it away is worse than a complete lack of hope.

I cleansed Bill immediately after they left. As I found out later during their return journey a great change in his behavior was apparent. His mother told me over the phone that at a certain moment he started behaving like a normal child. Even though he hadn't taken his psychotropic medicines that day (at my request) he was completely calm which had never happened before. He looked at the surrounding countryside through the car window with amazement, he even pointed to things with his finger. I wiped away tears of emotion and asked God for that state to remain for ever. At that moment I felt a sense of relief like I hadn't felt for a long time. I was afraid I might be disappointed, that this was only a momentary improvement caused by tiredness or by the journey. Bill's parents got home and went to sleep. Their son slept peacefully through the night for the very first time and the next day behaved quite differently to the way he had done till now. It looked like he was seeing everything for the very first time. He was calm, interested, curious. His mother phoned me every so often and let me know what was happening with him. He wanted to absorb everything like a sponge, like he was making up for lost time. He found learning words very difficult, but he was doing it eagerly. His parents and grandparents were very happy. At the same time they worried that this might end, like a dream. The therapist who looked after Bill on a daily basis was amazed and uncomprehending. The parents were afraid to tell her that they had turned to me for help.

A couple of days later Bill returned to his earlier behavior, and it was even worse than before. As things turned out, the cause of the illness was his great grandfather who had fallen so unfortunately that he had lost his memory and never regained it. When I was leading the great grandfather away, Bill recovered for a while but when he returned Bill became autistic again. This continued for a good couple of months.

After some time Bill himself started to reveal that his great grandfather wanted to possess him. He started to show it in a characteristic way which his mother could read immediately. Bill's mother asked me if there was anything she could do which would help to lead away her grandfather. I told her she could "talk" to him. I taught her how to do it and she willingly made contact with him. Every evening as Bill was falling asleep she asked her grandfather why he didn't want to leave for the other world and why he was hurting her son. For a couple of days she received no reply, then, as usual in such cases, came a string of curses. She wouldn't give up, though, until one evening she got a reply: "I'm not hurting Bill, you stupid cow, we're just playing together". "Don't play with each other because when you do that he shuts himself up in himself and is ill." "You stupid cow, that's not an illness. We don't want anyone to interfere and that's why he doesn't say anything." These conversations went on for several weeks. I led the grandfather away regularly, and the periods between returns were longer and longer. It wasn't just I who wouldn't let him stay, but the whole family was doing it, too. The school year was just starting. Bill was ready to go to the first grade. For the first few days his mother accompanied him. Then he stayed there for longer and longer until he could finally be left there on his own. Meanwhile, the great grandfather decided to pass through to the Light. Today Bill is a grade three student and is just like all his classmates in every way.

Since then I have cleansed many people from all over the world touched by this condition. The parents of a child in Canada whom I helped have told me that a professor there recognized this case as worthy of an academic study and he's describing it as regressive autism. The parents don't have the courage to tell him that it was a case of possession and that it was exorcisms that helped, not medicines and doctors. I have many more similar cases. Doctors cannot explain how it is that one child gets well and another doesn't.

This condition, like every other condition, has another facet. There are many children who could be helped but the parents have grown so accustomed to it that they won't even think about giving it up. They find themselves in the circle of interest and sympathy of many people. They ask for help everywhere but only for as long as they have a subconscious awareness that they won't get it. When they start to suspect that help may be effective they back away, wanting to remain in the same old state.

A single mother asked me to help her eleven year-old autistic son. I managed to cleanse him and suddenly a dilemma arose: what's this boy supposed to do now? He's well but he doesn't know this world at all, like he was thrown into the deep end without warning. He can't talk and he's way behind his peers. The mother's greatest problem, however, was that when the son recovers he'll have his disability allowance withdrawn. She was afraid that the family wouldn't be able to cope with that financially. She started to demand that under no circumstances was the boy to be helped any more. I agreed, but the ghost didn't want to return. It was lucky that the boy started to learn very quickly and was soon catching up. When the allowance was stopped he was awarded a scholarship and he graduated with distinction. Then his mother died suddenly. I think that God didn't want him to have the life which his mother had prepared for him and that was why He placed me in his path. Right to the end, however, she was of a different view. She held a grudge against me and against God for it. I sometimes wonder what would have happened to the boy if he'd remained an autistic child.

This is not an exceptional case, it happens very often. I usually do everything I can to persuade the parents to help their children get well. When the parents are no longer there, what is their children's fate? You must try when the children are still small otherwise with every year they'll have more and more ground to make up.

And this is a story I want to tell as a warning to many parents. At my grandmother's house, in the attic, I found an old, yellowing photograph of two beautiful women sitting with two tiny children. This was my mother with me in her arms and a boy, more or less the same age, sitting on his mother's lap. The photograph was taken before we could walk. Both of us were diagnosed with the same genetic condition (congenital hip displacement as a result of which one leg grew normally and the other didn't grow at all). My mother wouldn't give up. She looked for help for me everywhere, a way of curing me. This was just after the war and at that time nobody was performing operations on such conditions. She went from clinic to clinic until she came across a professor who agreed to do it. This was the first operation of its kind in Poland. The first operation did not bring with it the hoped for results and more operations had to be performed. In the village where both the women lived there was a lot of talk about this. My mother was accused of being an unnatural mother who was condemning her child to unnecessary suffering. The parents of that boy refused the operation and they were regarded as the good ones. My mother, on the other hand, was hounded out of the village. The operations and rehabilitation lasted for close on seven years. Then I went to school. From that time my legs are agile and healthy and, in addition, quite elegant. When I became an adult I came across the boy from the yellowing photograph. He was in a wheelchair and one of his legs was normal and the other half its size. There was not one muscle in his legs.

Seeing him I understood what it means to make the correct decision at the correct time. I saw what I'd gained thanks to my mother. The boy holds it against his mother to this day for the decision she made. The roles have been reversed and what was once a curse is now a blessing and vice versa. My healthy legs remind me again and again that it's not worth giving up but on the contrary, one must try and try again until when gets the right result.

I sometimes wonder what would have happened if my

beloved mother hadn't trusted God and not made me undergo the operations. I admire her great courage and determination. Even though, as a young woman, she was ostracized by the community of her village, she did not give up. Today I would have been like that crippled man, driving a wheelchair. Thank you, mother.

Why have I given my example as a warning to parents? Because many of them look for help for their sick children for as long as subconsciously they know that the illness is incurable, whatever it may be - autism, brain damage etc. When something can be done about it they suddenly back away as if they were saying: "I won't give up what I've got thanks to this illness, the sympathy that everyone extends to me" or "I am so extraordinary. Any other mother in my place would not have managed". Such an egotistical attitude will bear bitter fruits in the future. Have you thought what will happen to your child when it grows up and you're no longer on this earth?

This is such an important subject that I'll describe another case history. The mother of three very gorgeous children noticed, when visiting a cemetery, three tiny graves. She was seized by a feeling of guilt for having these three little ones, that they were healthy, growing up well, whereas another mother had just one and it had died. This feeling would not leave her. The next day she took the children to the cemetery and showed them the tiny graves. From then on they went there every day. The mother decided that the cemetery was an excellent place for walks, and for educating the children. One day during one of their walks she started to tell the children how lucky they were to be alive, to be healthy. She told them to think about that constantly. She thought she was doing the right thing, but the very next day, at the cemetery, one of her children felt very ill indeed, started to faint, and was taken away by ambulance. When they returned home something strange started to happen to the second child. Only the eldest was all right. From that time on two of the children succumbed to two hitherto unknown diseases, each one different. They needed help day and night, and the mother was collapsing from exhaustion. Then she remembered me. She told me everything. For me the strangest and most incomprehensible thing was her admission that when the children fell ill she finally gave a sigh of relief. She felt that now she was at last like other mothers, suffering and unhappy. After I checked the cause of the children's illnesses, I realized that they'd been possessed by very many ghosts. When I had cleansed them, they started to recover their calm, and the state of their health improved. A couple of hours later the ghosts came back and everything returned to what it was before. I knew that the children had been possessed by ghosts from the cemetery. They were not tied to them emotionally and that being so they should leave immediately. But that didn't happen. Why not? It turned out that the mother had inculcated in them such a powerful feeling of guilt that when they grew healthy they started to feel guilty and subconsciously drew the ghosts back to themselves. This phenomenon was explained to me by the eldest child: "When mum told us to be sorry that we're healthy I thought I won't do it otherwise I'll die. I didn't want to die. My brother and sister obeyed my mum and now they're very ill". I told this woman that since she'd planted these truths into the children's subconscious then she must now start to implant others. Then the ghosts will stop returning because the children won't be summoning them. She willingly agreed, but two days later she called demanding that she no longer wished to have the ghosts led away. I asked why. She replied that there are so many illnesses in the world, so much poverty, misfortune. She reckoned it wasn't right that only other people should carry this "cross".

Since this has affected her children she will carry her "cross" with head held high. Several years have passed, the children live like weeds, they don't get out of their beds, they don't even speak, they just sigh. The mother looks after them on her own since her husband took the healthy son with him, wanting to save him, and moved to another part of the country. Does a mother or do parents have the right to exploit their children for their egotistical ends?

I have just described a very extreme case. Not every visit to a cemetery ends this way. Let us remember, however, that cemeteries are not the best places for walks. When children are possessed it often turns out that their parents used to take them to a place where there is a particularly large number of ghosts, and in circumstances like that it's not hard for disaster to strike.

I am approached by parents who want me to help them, advise them because they are afraid of their own children. Sometimes the child merely hits the parents, but there are cases when, full of hatred, the child hurls itself at the parents wanting to kill them. These tragedies play themselves out in many homes though they are carefully concealed by parents because of inappropriate embarrassment. When a child like that is a teenager or an adult we usually put the blame for their behavior on the influence of unsuitable friends at school or in the street, on alcohol or drugs. Often children displayed aggressive tendencies from birth but at that time we took no notice. We hoped they would grow out of them. Unfortunately, these aggressive tendencies intensified. I have come across extreme cases in which a three or four year old child seizes a knife with which it can kill. It lies in wait through the day, and often at night, too, to pick a convenient moment to attack its parents. Sometimes it manages it, too, and tragedy is only averted because it is not strong enough to push the knife in deeper or to do something equally cruel. The parents are terrified, they are in fear of what the child will grow into, they also fear for their own lives.

In these cases we're not dealing with a one-off whim, with a child angry with its mother because she didn't give it something it wanted; we're dealing with a constant searching for an opportunity to kill. The child may turn on any member of the family, but more often than not it targets one specific person. Its eyes speak for themselves - they are cruel, full of hatred and ready to attack at every moment. A child like that has not had the chance to be spoiled by school or its environment: it is often brought up exclusively by parents who are warm, well-balanced people. In such a house knives, scissors and other dangerous tools are kept hidden. Most often the matter is never talked about. If someone does mention it, they do so quietly, with shame in their voices, judging that there must be something wrong with them since they have such a bad child. If the parents do not look for a definitive solution to this problem then their old age will be a miserable one. All the cases that have come to me have not been caused by genetic factors but by possession by ghosts. It can happen that a child may be good and helpful when it's young and only when it starts to grow up does it start to be aggressive towards its parents. These are by no means isolated examples. Here is one of them.

A woman came to me because her adult son was mistreating her. She was prepared to continue suffering it, but she was afraid that the matter would come out and her reputation would suffer. She was a Supreme Court judge, a very strong woman and she could easily have dealt with her son by giving him up to the law, but she noticed that one day he was a generous boy and the next he could be a mean-spirited ruffian (who couldn't remember anything the following day). She looked for help everywhere before she came to me. She brought him up on her own, they got on very well together until suddenly her well-balanced, loving son started to transform himself into a real tormentor. After examination it turned out that he was possessed by a very powerful ghost. When I cleansed him there would be an improvement, but the attacks kept returning. We couldn't work out who the ghost inside him might be. It was only a year later that it turned out to be an uncle, someone for whom there was mutual dislike. Though things never came to blows there was a decided lack of affection between them, and when they were in each other's company there was always tension. When I told her whom I had discovered in her son, the woman fairly jumped up. He had bothered her all his life and now he had possessed her son. Unfortunately, this discovery was of no use because the ghost had no intention of leaving or, if it did, then it would do so for only a very short while. Finally, however, something did change. The ghost announced that he wants to make contact with her, but only one-to-one, there was to be no-one else taking part. She didn't really wanted to agree to that. I taught her how to do it. I promised that if anything unexpected should happen then I would be ready to help at any moment. Since she didn't know how to make contact any other way than through her son, I advised her to wait till he was asleep. She was to sit in the next room writing down questions addressed to the ghost on sheets of paper. If she was to sense any thought or feeling she was to write it down. Finally, she consented. The first time she asked why the ghost was tormenting her son, her mind was filled with very vulgar thoughts. It was a mountain of the worst insults. I had warned her in advance that it was most probable that something like that would happen. It surprised her because in her family no-one swore, not even the uncle, so how could he do so now as a ghost? But she was to write down everything, even if they were the most stupid and most vulgar thoughts. That's how it continued to the end of the session, and every question provoked only insults in reply. The next day the same happened, but after about a week the ghost's rage lessened. It stopped its insults and started to reply to the questions. When she asked why it had possessed her son, it replied: "Because I chose you. You are the only suitable one. Nobody in the family is as wise and as sensitive as you, and I have a lot of important things concerning you all to convey". To the question why her son was behaving like he was, he answered: "It was me hitting you because I was so mad at you, because you were as deaf as a post when I tried to say anything to you". A couple of days later, now in a more amicable way, it conveyed to her "secrets" relating to various members of the family, after which it left once and for all. She recovered her peace of mind and her son. They are best friends again. That woman often asks herself what would have happened if she hadn't found me to help her and hadn't wanted to listen to the answers. She says that it makes her skin crawl just thinking about it.

I'm touching on this subject so that whenever a child's behavior steps outside the norm the parents should search for the reasons for it and not accept their fate, blaming the child, or genes, God, or everyone around. There is a way out of every situation, for every ailment there is a remedy. More often than not behavior like that indicates possession by ghosts. In my experience out of a hundred such cases, ninety-five will be possession by ghosts and only about five will have some other cause. As we've discovered, it makes no difference how old the child is. Whether the child is an infant, a toddler, a school child, a student or an adult, if their behavior is abnormal then they must be helped.

This can be done by parents, guardians, friends, teachers or neighbors. Here is an example. Once I was called by the head of one of the elementary schools of a large county town with this request: "I've heard about your skills and I'd like to ask for your help in a very delicate matter but I beseech you to keep it just between ourselves. Unfortunately, I will not be able to pay you". I agreed, and the head teacher described the problem which the school was completely unable to deal with. "There is a student in our school who is very poor and comes from a broken family of alcoholics. He must be the devil's spawn, because he hits the other children, bullies them in the most cruel way, extorts money from them, what he gets up to is simply horrible. I think he's behaving like this because he wants revenge for the fact that other children have normal homes and he doesn't. I've heard about your approach to matters like this so I was wondering if you would like to work with us on it. Our educational psychologists have given up on him long ago. If you didn't manage to do anything then we already have in our hands a statement to send him to an institution of correction. But I know that prison has never yet converted anyone, and that's why I'm turning to you. Nobody in the school must find out about this, though, because I'd lose my reputation and maybe even my job if people found out that I believe in the things which you deal with."

At this point I'd like to reassure the headmistress that by writing about this case I am not betraying any confidence, either hers or the child's. I have many cases which are all very similar to each other, only the names of the school and the places change. Even though I knew little about the boy I managed to reach the ghosts which were possessing him. They thought they were helping the boy this way. They didn't want him to be hurt. When I explained to them that rather than helping him they were harming him, they left willingly. From one day to the next the boy became a different person: polite, helpful, and his knowledge was greater than that of pupils in the higher classes. Thanking me for my help, the headmistress was extremely happy with the results of his learning and she recounted all his qualities which had been uncovered along with the cleansing. There was, however, one problem. Before, the boy had beaten the other kids, and now he is being beaten by them. He behaves as if he has forgotten how to fight, he can't even defend himself. The headmistress noticed that he is attentive to children he'd formerly beaten but not because he's afraid of them. It look like he can't remember anything. I confirmed the headmistress's suppositions. That almost always happens after a cleansing. It happens when a ghost has completely taken command of a person's mind. I asked for the boy to be given protective care because it hadn't been he who had been the bully but the ghosts which had possessed him. The headmistress promised that she would look after it and I heard no more from her. In this case I managed to lead the ghosts away quite quickly. At other times, however, they do not leave quite so willingly or they return frequently after being escorted away.

The same applies in the case of street gangs, bands and hooligans. When the presence of such a group bothers us then any one of the neighbors, acquaintances or parents can seek help. The effect will be peace for everyone. Sometimes one of the members of a group might get fed up with life in the gang and will ask for help themselves. Their example may be followed by others until the gang disintegrates on its own and everyone sighs with relief. In the majority of cases it turns out that the young people are good - it's just that they have difficulties in coping with the prevalent reality.

PHOBIAS, OBSESSIONS, FEARS

Some people suffer from various kinds of phobias and obsessions. Sometimes they are able to function to a lesser or greater degree and people around them may not notice anything. But other people's phobias are so intense that their whole lives are subordinated to them. And occasionally not just theirs, but the lives of the whole family, too. There are instances when a phobia is so strong that it ruins a life. The majority of people tormented by a phobia believe that it's just something they have to live with for ever. It often never enters their heads that the phobia could have anything to do with ghosts or with possession. It makes no great difference if it's a fear of infection we're talking about or a fear of heights, open or confined spaces, an obsession with hand-washing, constant cleaning, checking or correcting. They all function in a similar manner. The patient doesn't realize that they could live differently until the moment arrives when, cleansed, they can suddenly do something which, till then, they had feared so much. Once liberated, they may be-have like little children, constantly repeating the very action they had regarded as prohibited. If they feared heights, they will now climb wherever they can. If they were afraid to go out of their rooms they now don't want to spend any time there, etc.

A few years ago I took part in an event during which I was being interviewed. Suddenly, a woman confronted me: she was very frightened and out-of-breath. She seized my hand. She held on to it tightly, refusing to let it go, as if she were look-ing for help from me. This happened in front of many people present at the time. She turned to me and she wouldn't talk to anyone else. There was a commotion. I went with her to a room which the organizers made available. It transpired that for fourteen years she had not left her home, and more specifically her tiny room. She wasn't capable of going to the bathroom on her own, which was across the hall from her room. I asked her how she'd got to be in the building where I was. It turned out that she had been watching television where the interview with me was being broadcast live. Without a moment's thought she had leapt up and run out of the house. The motive force for her was the fear that she may be too late to find me. After a few minutes her phobia had paralyzed her, but it was too far to go back home so she ran straight ahead. "And that's how I ended up here," she cried. There was so much hope and determination in that statement that it pierced my heart. There were tears in my eyes. We spent a couple of hours together, she calmed down, eventually she said that the fear that had gripped her for so many years had now left her, that with me she was afraid of nothing. Her family came for her, expecting the worst. They had been anxiously searching for her the past couple of hours. I returned home. It was very pleasant and at the same time amus-ing that she called me every few hours telling me where she was at the given moment and that she was hardly ever in her room. In fact she only goes in there for a while to sleep and then she goes out again to enjoy her new-found freedom.

Nor is this an isolated incident. I know people who were so afraid of open spaces that they stayed in a small, cramped and darkened room for years, performing all their physiological needs there. They spent more than a dozen years in such an enclosure, sometimes more than twenty. This would probably have continued till death if they had not been cleansed of ghosts. This "voluntary" shutting away can be compared with serving a sentence in the hardest prison with the longest tariff. A real prisoner will, after a time, grow accustomed to prison society and will serve their punishment in peace. A person staying for years in a tiny space, however, undergoes torments, being afraid all the time. Many can't bear the tension and commit suicide. So some people sit in cramped tiny cells, whereas others would die of fear if they had to spend as long as a minute in an enclosed space. They feel they will suffocate or will be crushed by the walls.

Another phobia, or rather obsession, is constant handwashing. I know of a case where a person washed her hands so often that the flesh was coming away from her bones. She bought bags full of soap and used them straight away. Having been cleansed of ghosts she now finds that one bar of soap lasts her longer than a whole bag used to before. Some people wash their hands, others wash something else. An inner compulsion will not allow them to stop even for a moment. I have seen people who fell into an indescribable panic at the sight of a tiny spider and when it approached they froze motionless for many hours or even days. They would recover only after heavy doses of psychotropic drugs. Once they had been cleansed of ghosts, a spider made no impression on them at all. Different people fear a variety of things which the average person cannot even imagine.

How is it that we or someone close to us is attacked by a phobia to such an extent that we are in no state to accept any arguments to show us we are in error? We are incapable of noticing that other people in similar circumstances don't have any fear at all. What doesn't get through to us is that it's something not right with us and not with the situation we're afraid of; in other words, we're reacting to a situation in an inappropriate manner. I'll try to clarify why that happens.

After an unexpected, sudden death many ghosts are simply unaware that death has occurred. It's a little like they overlooked it. They can scarcely work out that there's something strange happening to them. They remember how they died as through a mist and they go through it again and again like in a dream. This process has a very important function to fulfill, namely to remind the ghost that it is not living, to awaken it from unconsciousness. This constantly re-experienced death allied with the unawareness of its happening becomes a cause of fear. Unfortunately sometimes this, instead of awakening the ghost, inclines it to even greater caution. It desires, paradoxically, to guard against something that's already happened. Let's assume that it died crushed by some great weight. Now it constantly goes into a panic that it could die in just this way. So, wandering thus in the astral world it will, sooner or later, awake and be given the opportunity to pass through to the other side of death's curtain. There does exist, however, a large probability that it will manage to hook up to some person. When it possesses the person it will transfer its fear to them. It will avoid at any price all situation that remind it of the circumstances of its death.

To return to other examples - a ghost which fell from a

height will be afraid of falling again and will not allow the person possessed to climb anywhere, even if it's quite low. A ghost which died crushed by some weight will be afraid of cramped spaces and won't even enter an elevator. The possessed person won't even know why they're afraid. And that's how a phobia will start. If the person was afraid for some reason then they would be susceptible to a cure through some kind of therapy. But in the case of a ghost being frightened, helping the person is futile. For we are healing John while it is Andrew's ghost that is sick. That's why a person who has been tormented by a phobia for many years will be freed of the fear immediately the ghost is escorted away. This can be seen most vividly when the ghost leaves only to return after some time. What we see is the sickness returning. But by then the person knows how to live without the ghost, how good it is not to be afraid. From then on the person is far less prone to surrendering their body and mind to the ghost.

Some ghosts willingly leave for the next world, others do so with certain reservations, others again don't want to leave at all. Many factors will have an influence on that. A ghost often finds out it is no longer living quite by chance and then goes through a considerable shock. So what has to be done first of all is to give the ghost some therapy. Once they have understood their situation, many ghosts resolve to depart. Others might like to leave but may be paralyzed by a fear of the unknown. They may also feel unworthy of passing through to the other side, or they may be restrained by an attachment to earthly matters or to a particular person. Quite often a person may not want to release the ghost that has possessed them.

Not all powerful fears are caused by being possessed by ghosts. They may be caused by great stresses experienced in childhood. It may also be the case that we experienced something exceptionally cruel or traumatic in a previous incarnation and we have carried the memory of the event into our present embodiment. It might be, for example, being burned alive, dying of starvation or any other death involving great stress. These fears may be very powerful but they leave easily when the source of their cause is reached. This can be done through regression or through hypnotherapy.

I was once asked for help by an acquaintance called Christopher. He said that he'd always suffered from a terrifying, irrational fear but he couldn't specify what it was he feared. He insisted that I record a session with him. I agreed but without much enthusiasm. I know from experience that it's difficult for people who are friends to reveal themselves. It's much easier to work with a stranger. But exceptions do happen and this was one of them. Before the session we agreed that when we got to the occurrence that triggered the fear and it turned out to be too difficult, I would cut short the session. Christopher, however, was so exhausted by his situation and, through that, so determined that he staked everything on this throw of the dice. In his innermost self he believed that this would be the very thing to help him and rid him of his constant fear for ever. He even asked me not to bring the session to a close regardless of what happened. He only said: "With you nothing bad can possibly happen".

I asked him to go back in his memory to the moment when the fear started. We got to the source quickly. I recognized it from the complete change in his appearance and his behavior. His face contorted with pain, his body changed position, he panted, he groaned. "Where are you? What's happened?" I asked him. He did not reply. I gave him a little time knowing he had to grow accustomed to the situation even though he was going through it a second time. When the silence was beginning to grow too lengthy, I asked the same question again. He answered: "I don't know where I am, I can't see anything, there's a very thick mist." "Wait for it to lift, take your time. Tell me how old you are. What do you look like? What are you wearing?" I gave him a series of questions, which he couldn't answer. "I don't know where I am, I can't move, I am crushed by something." He was breathing very heavily, and groaning. "Try to describe the place from the position you're in." He couldn't do that. It was only after a long period that he started to respond, with difficulty. "I'm lying on the ground... I'm holding a banner in my hand..." he started patting himself. "I think it must be armor I've got on me... God, I'm wounded. There are scattered bodies all around me..." He started to strain his eyes, like he'd seen something. "I can see an outline," he murmured. At this moment he started screaming terrifyingly: "Oh, God, they're going to kill me!" "Who's going to kill you?" "The people who are walking round and finishing off the wounded." He was extremely frightened. "I must save the standard... I must save it. They're coming closer. I can't get up. God, if I didn't have the standard they wouldn't come here. The standard... Why do I have the standard? I promised... To the end, to the last drop of blood. Now I'm going to die because of it. If it wasn't for the standard I might have saved myself. Now they're going to finish me off. Just a few more bodies. Just two more, one, now it's my..." Suddenly, he broke off. Everything happened so quickly I didn't even have time to react. I brought him out of the seance slowly. I asked him if he remembered anything. It turned out he remembered everything, down to the last detail.

After a seance, even the most successful, I don't let the patient go home straight away because there's never any way of telling what such a regression to traumatic events might evoke. We started to talk about what he'd been through just then.

Christopher was amazed that he had felt and seen everything so clearly, just as if he'd really been taking part in the events at that moment. He said that now he understood where his fear came from. Going through it a second time had to some extent given him relief. I knew, however, that he still felt himself to be a victim and I wanted to heal that. "In your view, was the fact that the soldiers were finishing off the wounded a good or a bad thing?" I asked. "Of course it was bad!" he shouted. I, however, had a different opinion. I asked him if he judged that he'd have had any chance of leaving the battlefield under his own strength. He doubted it because of his very serious wound. In that case, what was worse? To be left by his enemy on the battlefield and, being wounded, to die in agony of hunger, thirst and exhaustion? Or to be ripped to pieces by dogs or wild animals? Or to be finished off by the enemy? Which is the most humane? Was this an act of cruelty or of mercy by the enemy? "I never thought of it that way before," he said. "Subconsciously I always thought of it as evil and I was afraid of it. Now I'm even grateful that they did what they did". I said that in this world there are no things which are only bad or only good. Everything is relative, dependent on the point of view from which we look at it. After this session, Christopher no longer felt fear even in the most extreme situations. He had been healed.

Very many people want to discover their previous incarnations out of sheer curiosity. I categorically advise against such experiments. Most often people want to get to know their previous incarnations in the hope that they'll see themselves in a very glorious role, e.g. a king, a saint, someone of importance, a rich or admired person. Most often, however, we remember moments that are associated with the most negative emotions. What will we do if we see ourselves as a murderer, a thief, a rapist etc.? How will we cope with that? The exploration of earlier incarnations was supposed to help the seeker of powerful emotions to raise their self-esteem in the present gray and mediocre life they are leading. Whereas what happened is that it crushed them even more because the past was much worse than the present. What I am saying here is no exaggeration. There are many people who are simply not capable of coping with what they will see. One can know about very many previous incarnations without it bringing anything into our lives except disenchantment. It is only worth doing in order to heal an injury sustained as a consequence of a traumatic experience. Then our subconscious together with the Higher Self will lead us to the moment where it happened and tell us what we need to understand, heal, forgive. In every other case it's like putting your hand into a vice: it hurts but brings no benefit.

Once, a colleague of mine returned to an earlier incarnation out of curiosity. She cried for several hours because she saw herself in a great palace among a crowd of servants, but she saw that nobody loved her, that she was terribly lonely. Someone else recalled how he used to live in a hovel, in one room with a huge mass of children and felt so much love, such inexpressible happiness that he would have given away everything just to return there. But there's no going back.

Many people, and this includes members of the Church, believe that there is no such thing as re-birth. I don't share this view. Here is a story I heard almost immediately after it occurred. Friends of mine from the United States, a married couple with two children, came to Europe. The parents came from Poland but the children were born in the States and had never been abroad. After flying to Paris they hired a car and visited town after town. After a couple of hours, the younger girl suddenly said: "In a minute I'll show you where I used to live". Nobody took any notice of it, regarding her words as a four year-old's imagination. "Round this bend there'll be a little white bridge and then if you turn right I'll show you where I used to live," she repeated. They drove about a mile and, sure enough, after a series of bends, there was the little bridge their daughter had talked about. It surprised them. How could she know that? They were just about to talk to her about it when she ordered them to turn into a side street. The parents looked at her with astonishment but, out of curiosity, they went that way. About a mile further up she pointed to quite a large house where she told them to stop. When they'd pulled up in front of the gate she suddenly opened the door and ran out of the car before they could say anything. She ran through the gate and the household dogs greeted her joyfully, whining loudly, like they knew her very well. She, too, knew them because she spoke to them like she was calling them by their names. Some people were standing at the front door; it later transpired they were the owner and her grown-up children. They were equally surprised by the behavior of their usually very dangerous dogs. A moment later everyone was truly stupefied when she started to address the owners by their names, greeting them tenderly. Then she started reproaching them like an adult for the mess which she saw in the yard. She spoke in French, a language she had never been taught. She went into the house. She knew its lay-out and all its nooks and crannies. She had, of course, never been there before.

It turned out that six years earlier the owner of that property had died leaving his wife, children and grandchildren. The little girl behaved just like that dead owner. They agreed that the family could stay there for a time, especially as the little girl didn't want to leave. They all waited tensely to see how things would develop. For the first two days the daughter behaved like the adult owner of the house. Then she showed less and less interest in that family. After a week she'd lost it completely and insisted that she wanted to continue her travels with her parents. When I was told about this occurrence she told me without any enthusiasm that she has her old family there but she prefers to be with mom and dad. In time, she also forgot her French.

In my life certain events occur in pairs. At almost the same time, an acquaintance of mine went on a mushroom-picking trip and after returning from it she told me about an unusual incident that had taken place there. After successful mushroom picking, the evening was drawing in. There was a problem because one of the party, a twelve year-old boy, could not be found. The mother went back to the bus in the hope she'd find her son there. With growing terror she started to say that they'd been together all day and suddenly he'd gone off. All the people on the trip started to look for the lost boy. The residents of the local village joined in. It was dusk when someone saw the boy standing waist-deep in water. He was standing motionless, like in a trance, reacting to nothing. When the mother ran over to the pond he slowly started to walk straight ahead. Everyone stood watching, bemused. The boy went on like that till he reached a nearby ravaged mansion house inhabited by villagers. He opened the door like he was going into his own house. Hanging on a wall in the entrance hall was an enormous portrait of a boy similar to the one standing before it. Those present compared the two faces with astonishment. It created a stir. The inhabitants were asked if they remembered who had been the property's owner before. It turned out that there were still people alive who remembered that before World War I there was a family living there whose child had drowned in that pond. The next day the press wrote about it extensively but the boy remembered very little of the incident. The members of the trip, on the other hand, talked about nothing else for a long time to come.

And now let me tell you about an experience of my own. I was on a trip with some friends when I had a most unusual adventure. On a pretty hot day, after a couple of hours' visiting an open-air museum, we were all very tired. At a distance we could see benches arranged in a circle and shaded by trees. This sight made a very strange impression on me. Someone suggested we all sit down for a moment and rest. As we were walking towards the benches I unexpectedly asked: "And what will you do to me if I don't go with you?" I wondered why I was saying that; after all, I also wanted to rest. Sitting down I wouldn't let anyone sit on "my bench". Despite my desperate protests, they all sat down where I was sitting. I was surprised myself by my behavior. I looked ahead and at the same moment I smelt something burning. I like the aroma of a bonfire, but this offended me. I asked what was burning, but no-one replied. Only I could smell it. Even though I was tired I wanted to get away from there as fast as possible. They all looked at me with surprise but no-one moved. Suddenly it seemed that there was meat burning and smoke from a bonfire was obscuring my vision. I leapt up from the bench like a scalded cat. I sensed that it was from my body that the smoke was coming - through my eyes, ears and nose. I felt like I was burning. I ran away further and further from that place, shouting and beating myself. My friends, very surprised by what was happening to me, ran after me. Inside I felt that they were in no position to help me, indeed I wanted to run away from them. My clairvoyant colleague suddenly shouted to the others: "She's burning!" She was terrified, not knowing how to help.

Before my eyes, in slow motion, I saw an event from hundreds of years ago. All of those acquaintances present there took an active part in it. Taking various roles they were witnesses or executioners of my being burned at the stake. I saw all this, of course, with inner vision, the others passing by saw nothing. Nor did a colleague who once led me to the stake see it. He approached the whole thing with stoic calm. He pulled out a camera and made a series of photographs of me, on which we later saw a red glow around me. It wasn't just the photos that recorded that happening. The next day I could still see the smoke emanating from my body. My eyes, nose, lips, throat and the back of my head were severely burned for the next two or three weeks. Luckily, all traces vanished completely with time.

I have had several other similar returns to previous incarnations. They took place at short intervals of time, almost one after another. They were all equally drastic. Each time I had with me people who took a part in those events. I wondered why there were so many of them at once, what they were supposed to teach me. What were they supposed to change in my life? Some of the people who were witnesses or perpetrators of those happenings withdrew from me. Some permanently, others returned (sometimes only to apologize). Evidently some of them were to free themselves in this way of a subconscious sense of guilt. At the same time they sensed that they had rid themselves of a huge burden when they forgave themselves for those actions. I saw that those events, despite their drastic nature, made it possible for me to understand many issues in my relationships which were, in some cases, negative for me. They showed me that I was going along the same, unprofitable track. I spotted it and changed my conduct. They also helped me at a deeper level to understand those perpetrators and to forgive them. I became free as a bird. I hope that this example will help you to understand that when God wants to reveal to us our previous incarnations He does so without any effort from us.

SUICIDES AND MURDERS

As I have written earlier, it is easier for a ghost to enter a person than it is for it to get out. Also, it can turn out to be an inappropriate place for it to stay. If during its life a ghost had carefully planned his future then after its death it will seek a suitable subject. The person it chooses must suit it in every respect. It's a bit like choosing friends. Some friends suit us, others less so. With some people we are like proverbial blood brothers, while in the wrong company we don't have anything to say to one another. Most often the people about whom the ghost knows just about everything, knows them in depth, are members of its family or friends. The ghost's task is then made easier.

Immediately after a funeral and during mourning we are very open to a ghost and we willingly, albeit maybe unknowingly, allow it to come inside. For we are not aware of the consequences of doing that. It can well be that somebody suits a ghost in every respect but that person still has to allow it to enter. It happens that a ghost can't possess the selected victim in any way. It lies in wait waiting for an opportunity, but it depends on the person as to whether or not it succeeds. The ghost may never find a way in. In our normal state of consciousness there are defense mechanisms, like sensors, warning us that someone is trying to break into us. But there are situations where people lose control over themselves and aren't aware of themselves. This happens after the consumption of alcohol, drugs, in any alternative state of consciousness (even after smoking a cigarette!), after the loss of consciousness, a strong blow to the head, during an operation when we are under anesthetic. That's when a ghost can take charge of our body without our knowledge or permission. Sometimes, after death, a ghost may be so sorry for the people it has abandoned that it decides to stay with them just for a short time. It stays at the optimum time for leaving, when it still has the strength to. Then it has no possibility of choice. After a while it may stop suiting it to stay, it would like to leave, but is unable to. The same situation applies to a ghost which has found its way by chance into a person who is not an appropriate subject for it. It is of no importance for our discussion to wonder the way or reason why the ghost entered a given person. It simply wants to leave, tries various methods, but without any effect. It feels like it was in prison, or even worse. In a prison cell it would have more freedom of movement whereas here it feels like it's in a cramped cage. It then has two options. To wait for the person to die and be free of them in that way, or persuade them to die. The kind of death is, of course, neither here nor there. Persuading someone to kill themselves is far more difficult for the ghost than might appear at first sight. A normal, healthy human being has encoded in him or her a very powerful need for life. If someone wanted to take it away from them, or if they were suddenly about to lose it, additional powers are released within them to save that life.

How, then, does a ghost manage to carry out its plan? First of all by cutting a person off from their surroundings by fully occupying their consciousness with its presence. Not knowing about this, a person will close in on him or herself, become inaccessible to dear ones. With a great effort he or she will do what they have to and no more. The ghost forcefully pushes away everyone from the person possessed. We feel uneasy in that person's company, we get shivers, it feels unpleasant, so we avoid them more and more, and they avoid us. The ghost will make the possessed person have an aggressive attitude to their surroundings, they may pick on minutiae, start arguments. The possessed person will often feel so bad that they will look for escape just so they can forget even for a moment about the nightmare they find themselves living. They seek to forget through alcohol, drugs or relentless work. Sometimes their dear ones, friends, acquaintances won't interfere with their life judging that what someone does is their own affair and that everyone has the right to live their lives any way they want to. Sometimes this stems from general indifference. Most often, though, it's because people are so preoccupied with themselves, their family responsibilities, their work that they don't notice that the person next to them is in need of help. After prolonged struggles with the ghost residing in the body of someone we know we come to the conclusion that the possessed person has upset us so much with their behavior that we have had enough of them, and it would be best if they vanished from our sight. This is exactly what the ghost wants most of all - to have the possessed person completely to itself. What the ghost does to us we ascribe to the possessed person's malice, and they in turn think exactly the same way about us. We don't realize that there is an enormous gulf between us and the possessed person which is completely filled by the ghost which is pulling all the strings that are, of course, invisible to us. We move away from the possessed person, and they from us. The ghost doesn't need to bother about us, the possessed person sinks further and further into hopelessness and is just one step away from deciding to commit suicide and releasing the ghost from the unsuitable subject. It starts to prove to the possessed person that their life has no point at all. How? By making everything vile to them. Whatever they may do is wrong. This isn't constructive criticism aimed at pointing out errors which can be put right. The ghost wishes to persuade the possessed person that they are worthless, garbage, not even someone but something that has no value. It's most difficult for the ghost at the start when a person still has a lot of awareness and knows that they can achieve something, are loved, accepted etc. When a ghost arranges or stumbles across some psychological low it exploits the opportunity since then it will be much easier for it to immerse a person in depression. If, despite all these procedures from the ghost, the person continues to have support from their family or friends the ghost would have huge problems in persuading them to commit suicide.

When close friends notice that someone has symptoms of closing in on themselves or a constant feeling of hopelessness, they should be aware that this is a warning sign and that they should start looking for help. It's very easy to overlook this moment, then one regrets it for the rest of one's life, when all that was needed was to find a good exorcist. One doesn't need to go to them, it's enough to inform them by phone or letter, and the exorcist will cleanse the possessed person at a distance. Many people have told me that they made light of the symptoms mentioned above. Sometimes there are families where several suicides follow each other. Some people have experienced this in most macabre ways. A ghost persuaded members of the family to commit suicide and now it's persuading you to kill yourself. Could this not have been prevented? Listen to what happened to one family in England. The husband committed suicide. Though the wife was sad, as one is after the death of anyone with whom one's spent several years of one's life, she didn't despair for too long. They had rarely been able to come to an understanding together. A few months later, the daughter committed suicide. This loss shook the mother to a far greater extent. She explained her daughter's death by the strong emotional bond she'd had with her father. Suddenly she noticed that a voice had appeared urging her, too, to commit suicide. It was only then that she realized what the cause of the previous two deaths had been. She started to look for help and she found me. She understood that if she's been more watchful she would very likely have saved those two lives. It was easy to lead the ghost away and no-one else in that family suffered.

And another example. A woman with fear in her voice phoned me. She asked me to help her husband who, she suspected, might commit suicide. I asked her why she thought that. Is her husband talking about it? "He's not, but this year there have already been four suicides in our home and my husband has changed just like the others," she replied. I asked how he was behaving, was he drinking, picking arguments, is he closed in on himself? "No, he's not drinking. My father-in-law, his brother and brother-in-law all drank and often. Only the mother-in-law didn't drink. He's acting as strangely as they did. He sits like he was far away and says nothing. We have four small children, you must help me, what will happen if he kills himself? I won't be able to cope". She started to cry. I checked and he was indeed possessed by a murderous ghost. I fought with it for about a year until it finally went away. It was exceptionally vicious. Besides, it kept bringing a disgusting smell into the house. When it left the person it was impossible to sit in that room. They ripped up the floorboards, stripped the plaster several times before I heard about it and told them that the cause of the unpleasant odor was the ghost. After it had left the danger passed. Nor is the odor there any more.

It can happen that a ghost will try to persuade someone to commit suicide and the person doesn't respond. It might then persuade the person to murder. In many countries the punishment for murder is the death sentence and the ghost knows that. It is all the same to the ghost how it is released from the unwanted person. The eventual effect will be that person's death and freedom for the ghost. When a ghost frees itself from the person it often doesn't know what to do next. It doesn't know how to pass through to the other side of death's curtain. It remains on this side and shortly it runs out of vital strength and, sooner or later, it will have to hook up to another person. It can happen that that one, too, is unsuitable for it.

After the first suicide the ghost might think that the punishment awaiting it for that death is hell fire and won't want to do it again. Another ghost won't harbor such fears and will decide that punishment awaits it whatever so it's all the same to it. Sometimes leading people to suicide or murder becomes a kind of game for the ghost, something akin to a gamble, a challenge. It will see nothing wrong in it. Since there is no death for the ghost, there is no death for its victims, either.

One time I was visited by a woman of about forty who asked me to help. "Mrs Pratnicka, please hear me out. If you're to understand me fully I have to start at the very beginning." I agreed and didn't interrupt her. "When I was young I got to know a boy whom I married in quick time. We had two children. One day he went out, I thought it was for cigarettes, and he never came back. To begin with I worried that something bad had happened to him, but I was told he was fine and living in another town. From one day to the next I had to learn to manage everything myself. The children very much wanted their daddy. They talked about only him for most of the time. One day my little son asked some man in the yard if he'd like to become his daddy because his real daddy no longer wanted him. The man was kind-hearted and agreed. He thought: 'What harm can it do me? I'll give the child some joy, when he grows up he'll get over it, but for now let him be happy'. A couple of days later, when I came back from the shops, my son introduced me to his 'daddy'. We were both astonished. I explained to the children that one doesn't find a daddy like this, but they wouldn't concede. One day Roger (that was his name) and I both decided that, for the children's sake, we would play at being a family a bit. After some time we grew closer to each other and we became a successful couple and a magnificent family. The children were quite big when, one day, their real father appeared in the doorway claiming he had a right to the home because it was in his name. He also demanded to be part of the family since I hadn't divorced him. He was very insistent, so Roger had to leave the house for a while. He moved into a rented bachelor apartment and missed us all very much. And we missed him. We all started meeting with him at his place. We would most willingly have moved there ourselves, all three of us, but it was simply too small. Besides, everything in the house was what I and Roger had put into it. We were a family even though not legally speaking. My former husband was in no hurry to leave his new abode even though nothing in it was his. We waited for the court's decision regarding the division of the property and the separation. One time I visited Roger without the children. We both wanted each other very much and I stayed a little longer than usual. We made plans for the future, we wondered how to get out of this situation, then we started to make love. Suddenly Roger leapt out of bed like a scalded cat and ran out naked, carrying his pants in his hands. I was amazed by this behavior. I had known him for more than ten years, he had never done anything like that before. I quickly threw something on and followed him out into the corridor. From the doorway I could see a shaken Roger standing over an old man who was lying on the floor looking like he was dead. Suddenly Roger recovered his senses, looked down at his hands in surprise, then down at the man lying there and just stood there like that for a while. He ran into the room and quickly dialed a number. It turned out he'd called the police and told them he had just killed a man. Before the police came he told me why he had done it. He said that while we were making love something was very insistently ordering him to kill me. It was so strongly hypnotic that he couldn't resist the command. However, his love triumphed. He ran out into the corridor to calm down, and light a cigarette. The old man was walking past at that moment. He had no idea how he did it. Between his leaving and my appearing in the corridor only the shortest moment had elapsed. Roger didn't know this man and even if he had known him he wasn't capable of harming him. The police arrived and without asking about anything they manacled him and took him away. Now he's under arrest and awaiting the verdict. Mrs Pratnicka, how is this possible? I think I'm going mad, you must help me. He's such a good man, everyone will testify to that". I checked and Roger did indeed have inside him a killer-ghost. I had a dilemma about what to do. If I cleansed him, the court would find him guilty of murder and sentence Roger for the deeds of the ghost which had lived in that apartment. I could do nothing and count on the possibility that they would find him insane and

leave him to a psychiatric doctor. On the other hand I knew
only too well that while he was in his cell he could do it again,
to himself or someone else. I knew the truth and could do nothing with it. I couldn't appear in court as an expert witness because my truth would be no kind of evidence for the court even
though I would have stated categorically that it wasn't Roger
who had killed that man but a murderous ghost. Fortunately, the
psychiatrist diagnosed schizophrenia and he was detained in a
psychiatric unit. He is now free. And he is also free of the
ghost which possessed him.

What helped me in taking my decision about Roger's fate
was a documentary I saw a few years ago about murderers in
prisons around the world, made by French television. The con-
demned people were men and women. The prisoners answered
questions given them by the reporters. They talked very openly
about their lives, about what had led to the murders, like they
wanted to warn others that their lives and those of those dear to
them can end just as quickly. Some of them spoke straight to
camera, others covered their faces, ashamed to show themselves,
others again spoke only into a microphone behind the closed
doors of the prison cell. Every one of them had killed someone
very close to them. The common feature of all the cases was
that the prisoners remembered absolutely NOTHING about the
moment the murder was committed. They claimed that they
loved the murdered person very much indeed, that at the moment of death they didn't love them one iota less, that the murders weren't preceded by any argument or disagreement. One of
the women killed her brother. She spoke about him with great
love and tenderness. She couldn't understand how she could
have done such a thing. If she had been indifferent to him, or
hated him, then the event would have been in some way expli-
cable. But they were exceptionally good to each other. The

brother used to drop in on his way home from work virtually every day to say hello and ask her how she was and to give her a kiss. That day he had done the same thing. She was in the kitchen, cutting something... It lasted a fraction of a second and he was dead. All of these accounts, even though they were filmed in different prisons and the crimes were committed by people of various nationalities, faiths, and levels of education, were almost identical. These people were concentrating on something, then came a gap in their awareness and... someone close to them was dead. One could claim that this was completely impossible, to think that the prisoners were only justifying themselves in front of the camera and that their accounts were highly embellished. This would make sense if they were all waiting for the verdicts, but each of these people had been inside for several years and they were therefore telling their stories long after the murders and they'd had a long time to consider them. What's more none of them wanted to get out of jail feeling that there is no punishment fitting the crime they committed.

As I write these words the television is showing a documentary from a German prison where a serial killer of women is doing his sentence. He is a young, intelligent man whom nobody would have suspected of doing anything untoward. In the interview he said: "I wouldn't have done it if, at the moment of the murder, I'd been able to control my self". The moment of the killing is like a film to him which he isn't taking part in, just watching. He felt a compulsion over which he had no control. I checked to see if in his case, too, his actions were directed by a murderer-ghost. It turns out that it was. It continues to sit inside him and I guess that he will kill again as soon as he has an opportunity to. I could help this man but I'd need to find him or his family. Even if I did do it, he would still have to do his sentence for many years to come. No-one, after all, will trust him or risk letting him go free and thereby exposing a potential victim to danger.

You'll ask why things happen this way. From my experience I know that there are murderer-ghosts which kill just for killing's sake. They desire blood. A person committing a murder is rarely a murderer in his own right. He is merely a puppet carrying out the murders. This doesn't mean, of course, that such a person should be judged innocent. For as long as he has a ghost or ghosts inside him he will continue to kill. That's what serial killers do. A person who commits murders without any concrete motives is sometimes also a victim, of which he is not aware. The Ghost throws him out of his own body, and after committing a murder, gives it back to him, along with the consequences.

I hear about ejecting people from their bodies quite often along with many less drastic matters. What often happens is that someone I already helped, who has self-awareness and awareness of ghosts, may phone me and complain that they're being ejected out of their bodies by a ghost which won't let them back in. They ask me what they can do. Of course it's quite possible to help them, but how many people in the world are aware of this? Only a handful. What happens most often is that a person who is not aware will do something which is against their own selves or against the law, may go to prison or, at best, in a psychiatric hospital. Often for many years, if not for life.

I have personally come across similar cases to those in the documentary. They have convinced me that I am not mistaken. During one of my trips a woman came up to me in the street and told me who I was and in her first words said: "Mrs Pratnicka, I killed someone but I've served my sentence". This directness took me aback somewhat and I didn't really know how to reply, but she hurriedly went on: "You know, in jail a person has a lot of time to think about things. I knew I would find you here and I came here specially from abroad. I'd like you to help me understand what could have caused me to perform the act of murder. My husband and I never even had any disagreements, let alone arguments or fights. We were messing about with the dog, we were kidding about like little children, and the next thing he was dead. Can you appreciate how much I suffered as a result of that? I couldn't even say goodbye to him, be at his funeral. And all those years of thinking about it. I thought I wouldn't be able to stand it. It was even worse than prison. If they had given me the death sentence I'd have been glad because I'd have been with him again straight away, but as it is my torment was endless". I checked the cause of her action. She was possessed at that time by a ghost which brought about her husband's death. Furthermore, it was inside her still. When we discovered whose ghost it was, she cried out, astonished: "Is it her? She always said she'd take him back from me and that I would regret that he'd chosen me. And she kept her word," she sighed. When I made contact with the ghost it transpired that the perpetrator of the murder was very disappointed by the turn of events. She had no benefit from her actions. She had induced her to murder anticipating that that way she would win back the loved one, that she would keep him at her side. Unfortunately for her, after his death he went straight to the Light, not stopping with her even for a second. She was left with a great sense of guilt inside her and a fear of punishment. I had to perform therapy for both of the ladies, the woman-ghost and the woman who had been innocently sentenced for the murder of her beloved husband. It took a long time for the woman-ghost to forgive herself. When the woman speaking with me forgave her, too, she was happy and left for the other world.

Examining the reasons why ghosts direct people to murder or suicide I come to the conclusion that there are as many reasons as there are cases. Every case can be different. It can, for instance, simply be a case of a desire for vengeance. The ghost may think: "Since I was not allowed to go to the other world at the appropriate time then now, since I am not alive, let others die, too". Another cause can be paying back, retaliation because the ghosts felt themselves to be unloved or the victims of brutality, or were themselves murdered.

The worst reason is killing just for the sake of killing. For some reason the ghost likes it, performing a murder brings it satisfaction, a sense of power. It feels itself to be damned already so one case more or less makes no difference to it. Instead of condemning such a ghost, however, one can always help it, show it to the road to recovery. It will help the ghost and prevent many more disasters.

SUMMONING GHOSTS

People have been trying for centuries, and they continue to try, to make contact with ghosts. They do so for numerous reasons. Some are keen to find out if their near ones who have died are doing well on the other side, if they have stopped suffering, if they perhaps need something. In many cases it's motivated by a concern for the beloved soul which has departed. When we know that it is not suffering and needs nothing, our hearts are made easier. This knowledge allows us to stifle the subconscious fear of what will happen to us when we die. Since the ghost isn't suffering we can hope that we, too, when we die will not suffer. Information about ghosts goes some way to satisfying our curiosity and at the same helps us to overcome our fear of death.

Others contact ghosts wanting to ask about matters which death interrupted and which demand completion. They hope to find out what they should do in order to continue something begun or to make a decision about finishing it off. For death surprises many at the least opportune moments. Not just the living, but the ghost of the dead, too. Many matters the person was involved in get cut off and now rest inert. Those who remain in this life want to put the legacy in some sort of order which it's sometimes impossible for them to do. That's when a desire to contact the recently deceased person may arise. Much will depend on the person's own attitude to their earthly affairs. If, at the moment of death, all earthly matters stopped interesting them, they turn away from us and pass through to the other side of death's curtain. This is the best solution and there isn't an ounce of egoism involved in it. When, however, a ghost is strongly attached to the affairs of this world then it doesn't want to leave it and tries its utmost to make contact with us. It can do this in a number of different ways. It can come to us while we're asleep, knock during the day on various items or move them, influence our thoughts. If we are watchful and are not afraid of it we will find out what it wants to tell us. Many ghosts quite literally stand on their heads to convey something to us but we won't notice it for anything. Maybe because we don't know that this kind of communication is possible. Most likely, however, is that we will be very frightened of the ghost and will refuse to allow its messages into our minds. But the ghost simply doesn't want to go to the other world because of its concern for us. It worries that when it isn't there we won't be able to manage. It had given up on itself and stayed behind but its sacrifice is in truth quite unnecessary because it benefits neither side. The excellent film "Ghost" shows how a ghost might try to contact us. You have probably seen it but I think that you watched it from a different angle. I suggest you see it again. There's an important part in it played by the medium who can be a bridge between us and the dead person's soul. It is with the medium's help that the ghost can convey to us what it needs to tell us. When we decide to accept a medium's help it is essential that we do so directly after a person's death. And our contact with the ghost must end there. We may tell it how much we love it but no matter how much it pains us we must allow it to leave. If it doesn't want to do so, then we must ask it to. This way we are doing the best for both parties - for the dead person's soul and for those who have remained in this life, meaning us. It is very crucial for the ghost because the longer it delays before leaving the harder it is for it to pass through to the Light. We ought to help it to do so in every way we can. For the soul doesn't know that with every moment it is losing its energy, so the time for leaving is limited.

There are also those, and they are many, who seek to contact a ghost expecting they'll find out where the dead person hid their savings, valuables etc. Often a lonely and wealthy person might die. The people close to them imagine that this person must have hidden their life's savings somewhere. That's when the searches begin. It's not unusual for the home of the deceased to be turned upside down right after their death, the walls to be stripped back to the brickwork, the floors ripped up, the yard and the drive dug up. The expected fortune cannot, however, be found even though it was seen just before the death. This question has many facets and I'd like to talk about them. For a human being, death is the end of life here on Earth and the beginning of a new life on the other side of death's curtain. Since it is the end a person ought to finish all their affairs and leave material matters here on Earth. Unfortunately, not everyone can do that. For some people it's so hard to part from their acquisitions that even when they die they want to keep them for themselves. It will depend on the dead person's attitude to the valuables whether or not we will be able to find them after their death. If, along with death, the affairs of this world stop interesting them then we'll find the valuables easily even if they are hidden as deep as possible or in the most unlikely place. Whereas the person who hid their fortune away from the whole world for their own benefit will not allow anyone else to recover it. The ghost will guard it, and ghosts have their own ways of not giving up what is theirs if they decide not to. The seekers of the fortune will, therefore, have great difficulties in finding it if there are ghosts guarding it. The ghosts will give it up only when for some reason they are finished with it. And that can happen only when they mature enough to pass through to the other side and accept that they don't need their fortune for their further journey. Ghosts questioned during spiritualistic séances won't want to say where they have hidden their valuables or money. They will, indeed, lead the seekers off the right track, directing them to the wrong places. But the family won't give up and will go from one clairvoyant to another, from one chiro-mancer to the next. They hope that eventually they will come across someone who will tell them where the fortune is concealed. I, too, am often approached by people who claim that just before someone's death they saw the valuables with their own eyes or the deceased when he or she was hiding them somewhere just before their death. Sometimes the heirs can't even imagine that the person concerned, feeling the approach of death, willed their savings to some cause which they didn't reveal to the family (some charity, the person's own predilection and so on).

Things are a bit different when a person dies a sudden death. It might happen that they hid something important not knowing they were going to die. In such cases it makes sense to look for it and the likelihood that the ghost will want to reveal the place is high. I do hope that knowing this many people will be saved unnecessary delusions and the costs involved in searches which can sometimes last for years.

There is also a small group of people who make contact with ghosts for scientific purposes. These are researchers of the outer worlds who, on the basis of contacts with ghosts, collect proofs that life exists after death. They record conversations with ghosts on audio tapes and sometimes, if they can manage it, on video tapes. They use various methods, e.g. automatic writing, to get in touch with them.

The contacts I've described above have their own justification. There are, however, people who engage in summoning ghosts simply as a game. It's a way of passing the time or spending an evening in the company of friends. Many victims of spiritualist séances come to me. These people don't realize that they're playing with matches in a barn full of straw. When they start their game they don't even imagine what terrible consequences can result from it. It can happen that when they get struck down it is often too late because the "barn" has burned down and the "burnt" ones nurse their wounds for a long time, often till death. It happens to all sorts of people regardless of age or sex or education. I know that children, too, play these games inspired by stories or some film. It can happen that summoning ghosts is introduced to them by some television program, something I've come across personally. I was horrified as I watched it since I know of the harm it will do those viewers who want to try summoning for themselves. The producers of such programs concentrate on only one side of the coin. They try to arouse the greatest possible excitement in their viewers. Maybe they don't take into account the consequences of their broadcast, that is to say the misfortune that imitators will suffer. I'm not asking for sensitive subjects to be ignored. But they have to be done wisely. There can be no surprise that bombs go off if one passes on the recipe for making them. That is not a metaphor. I know from my own practice of many instances where all the participants of a séance, after summoning ghosts, fainted they were so electrified, like they'd been struck by lightning. If things had ended there they'd have been very grateful because they'd only been properly frightened. More often than not, however, it doesn't end there.

In one army unit after the summoning of ghosts half the brigade ended up in the military hospital. Then some of the soldiers were taken to a psychiatric hospital where many of them are still being treated, five years on. In another place, meanwhile, during a lesson of religion a priest was asked about ghosts and was so enthused by the subject that he taught the children to summon them. The consequences of this "game" were similar to those affecting the soldiers. Their results have lasted till today even though all the children have long grown up. Unfortunately, the priest concerned is no longer alive. I'd like very much to know what his motives were. I'd have anticipated more knowledge from a priest, more respect for spiritual phenomena, and most of all more responsibility.

Once knowledge of the astral world and ghosts used to be passed down from generation to generation only to chosen votaries. They were taught how to summon ghosts and, more importantly, how to lead them away. It is very easy to summon ghosts, they are all around us and will come willingly when we call them. If the one we're looking for won't come, there will always be a hundred others willing to take its place. To lead a ghost away is a skill that demands extensive knowledge. Even an experienced medium may not always succeed. A medium, however, knows what to do in such a situation, something which cannot be said of the person who tries it only for a game. Another aspect involved here is a question of respect for ghosts. A medium respects ghosts and ghosts respect a medium. Neither party wants to or will harm the other.

Someone who summons ghosts for a game isn't concerned about their peace so there's no question of respect. That's why a ghost will approach a medium differently than it will a person who's just wanting entertainment. If someone plays games at the ghost's expense then ghosts, too, can harm people by playing games. And we're not talking here about a little lesson but about serious consequences which can last throughout someone's life. I'm not writing this to frighten anyone but just to show the results stemming from an ignorance of the deeper aspects of this game. Judging by the numbers coming to me we're talking here about a quite considerable amount of victims who didn't know what they were doing while they were summoning ghosts. The consequences of such experiments are lamentable regardless of the age of the games' participants.

I've even had parents of children that are a few years old coming to me. When I discover the cause and ask the child about summoning ghosts the parents' reaction is usually the same. More often than not they accuse me of having lost my senses. "My child? You can't know what you're saying, who would he get the idea from, nobody in the family does that sort of thing!" they say, outraged. It turns out, though, that they do get the idea and not just the once. "The little darling", for example, along with its friends, summoned ghosts in the school toilets during the break. For "educational" reasons they might have summoned the ghost of Hitler after a history lesson, or some famous chemist to help them with their tests. They also do it at home, when they're bored. After such games problems often arise with learning, health, concentration and behavior. They become aggressive or quite the reverse. A child that had till now been a live wire suddenly grows apathetic, nothing interests it. The parents and teachers can't figure out how this

sudden change came about. Naturally, they don't have an opportunity to hit upon the possibility that it has something to do with
ghosts. Sometimes these games end in hospital, even psychiatric ones. To a large extent the consequences are dependent on
which ghost has taken control of the child. If the child has been
possessed by a drug addict's ghost, the child will suddenly start
taking an interest in drugs. Despite our most determined efforts
there will be no way of freeing the child from the habit. I'm not
going to analyze all the possibilities here now. It's enough for
me to say that the child may start to steal, curse even if it never
had done before, start fights, drink alcohol, attack its parents
with a knife in its hands to kill them, suddenly fall ill, start to
fear everything, stammer, get allergies etc. Every sudden
change may be a sign that ghosts have hooked up to our child.
The same applies to adults.

I was once at a conference of healers. A small, thin boy
of about fifteen came up to my stall and asked if I would help
him and his girl friend. He claimed they were Satanists who destroyed graves in the night at the cemetery and that he can't
watch his friend suffering, that they are helpless. He looked like
a civilized young boy, well-adjusted and I was about to ask him
if he really knew what he was talking about but he went on:
"You'd have to do it very quickly before those above realize and
strengthen their defenses around her and you won't be able to
manage". I was surprised by the determination with which he
spoke. I agreed to help. At the same moment the boy vanished
only to return a moment later with the girl. She, too, was very
young, she could not have been older than sixteen. She looked
like she'd been taken off the cross. At first glance you might
have thought she was plump. It transpired, though, that she was
swollen all over. She was dressed all in black, in a long skirt
and a blouse buttoned up at her neck. Right from the beginning

she, too, started to ask for help, persuading me that she couldn't cope with it any longer. She started to tell me about orgies she'd taken part in and lots of other improbable things. I couldn't believe in all this, for standing before me were simply children. I was shocked. Lots of people come to me with similar problems so I could recognize immediately the causes of it all and I managed to help the girl quite easily. Her possession was superficial and the ghosts left her quickly, but there are instances where they stay for months or even years. I wondered whether this couple hadn't made up the whole story about Satanists wanting to inspire my pity. Two or three days later they both came to me bringing with them twenty friends. I helped them all. With some it was easier, with others less so, but I managed to cleanse all of them. I asked them how things had come to such a pass. They were all nearly children aged between fifteen and twenty. Once, after school, they started to summon ghosts as a group but they didn't achieve very satisfactory effects. They were missing a real emotional tremor. So they moved to a nearby cemetery and continued the séance there. There they had a plentiful supply of emotions. Everyone experienced them on their own skins. They were very pleased and they promised each other that since it was such a gas they would repeat the séance one more time. When they got home they didn't all feel the same way, but when they said it out loud, the others laughed at them: "Are you chicken? Scared? If you're chicken stay indoors, but we're going," they mocked. After the second and third times, they'd all had enough. Some of them noticed that they'd stopped being themselves. They started to feel pressure to do things they didn't agree with. They were children from so-called good homes, where everything was arranged like clockwork. So a change in personality was immediately apparent to them. Although the children had been very frightened and had had more than enough, something was forcing them into walking to the cemetery, and once there they were no longer themselves. I have described earlier an account of ghosts which, while alive, judged that they would lie in their graves till the Last Judgment. During their lives they had arranged for the place where they would lie, for the appearance of the coffin, for a headstone to be carved etc. When they died they recognized how fearfully they'd been mistaken. They didn't pass through the curtain of death when their time had come and now they didn't know what to do with themselves. Stay in the cemetery? How long for? For all eternity? What they had believed in had turned out to be untrue. Maybe all the other convictions they'd had were also a mistake? At such a time many fall into indescribable despair and fury. They want to destroy what they had built during their lives (namely the headstones) but they don't have the strength to. When by chance a group of children came onto their horizon they could, at last, unload all their fury using them to help. They wanted to destroy, raze to the ground all the headstones so that those who were still living wouldn't allow themselves to be tricked like they had been. When they found themselves in the minds of kids wanting powerful experiences they found it easy to fulfill their desires. That's why sometimes crosses are knocked over with the help of living people, or headstones are torn up, graves are desecrated. Ghosts think only of how they can unload their rage and the possessed kids were not capable of defying them. I write "kids", but this has nothing to do with age. One can run amok at any age if one is possessed by a host of furious ghosts. Besides, the cemeteries are full of all sorts of ghosts just as in life there are all sorts of people. Among them there were some sexual deviants. One of them possessed one of the girls (the one who came to me) and started to rape her. She started to fight, shout, run away. Instantly, other ghosts joined the first one. She fell over some grave. All those present there could see that something was happening to her but they didn't really know what, they stood rooted to the spot. They could see figures approaching her, hooded, like they were faceless. An orgy started, they were all terrified, they didn't know how to help her. After all this she didn't have the strength to go home on her own. The parents notified the police of a crime. Unfortunately, no-one was able to provide a description of the offenders, nor could the girl. To begin with she assumed that she'd been raped by live men, but then she realized that it wasn't finished with when she returned home since the ghosts raped her everywhere, regardless of place or time of day (I refer readers to the chapter on rapes). That's why the kids, not knowing how to release themselves from it, turned to me for help. Before starting to "play" at summoning ghosts none of them even imagined that it could have such fatal consequences. It was supposed to have been a laugh and nothing more just like they'd seen on the television. Shortly before all this there had been a TV program describing step by step how to summon ghosts. They didn't think that it could be dangerous. I have had many more victims of such broadcasts.

Do the people responsible for the emission of such programs believe that it's none of their business what the results of doing it might be? Many do indeed have just such an attitude right up to the moment when the consequences are visited on their children or those close to them.

Please don't imagine that adults are safer when it comes to summoning ghosts. Everyone who does it without the appropriate safeguards is susceptible to possession. The ghosts may not possess them immediately but may remain in the house where the spiritualist séance was carried out. Then a family member, without suspecting anything, may be possessed. It's a bit like cigarette smoke which, though we don't smoke, we inhale. It can happen that the person summoning ghosts may do it just the once and become possessed or may do it several times and not be visited. Only the umpteenth time they may notice that there is something bad happening to them or someone in their circle of friends. Some will then start to look for help, others delude themselves with the hope that it will go away by itself. But it rarely does. At the very beginning the visitation may be almost imperceptible especially if the ghost is of an agreeable disposition, but once the channel has been opened other ghosts can enter till there can be so many of them that a person can't cope. It's like a wasp in the meadow. When there is just one, the likelihood of being stung is not very high. But when we draw one out of its nest we won't be able to get away from it and, in addition, the entire nest may come out, enraged, and then it is far more difficult to deal with them. We won't have anywhere to hide and they will attack us all at once.

As an example of further consequences of summoning ghosts I will now give you another instance. This happened in the circle of very educated, very wealthy people. The husbands successfully ran large business ventures, and their wives were bored at home and helped them only sporadically. The grown-up children had their own lives, business was going very well and the whole circle of friends were frequently bored in the evenings. One of them heard somewhere about summoning ghosts, suggested a game, others picked up on it and the fun was ready to start. None of those gathered there had any preparation for this. They started any old how and learned how to do it step by step. They rejoiced like children when a saucer moved and in time, as they grew more skillful at it, they started to perform all sorts of jokes. First they summoned the ghosts of dead relatives, then they started to throw out any names that came to them of people who had died. When the ghosts answered and the saucer moved they started to ask quite literally about anything that came into their heads. It drew them in so much that they spent every moment of free time doing it. They could see nothing bad in it, on the contrary they were proud that at last their lives had something interesting taking place in it other than work. They regarded the summoning of ghosts as a pleasant way of spending their free time. They were doing it in the wider circle of close friends. When the men were away at work, the ladies played on their own.

During a séance, one of the ladies decided to summon her great- grandmother. When the ghost arrived, she started asking about her future and that of her family. That day the ghost was exceptionally willing to reply. Suddenly, all of them froze. They were terrified by what they had heard. They fell silent and didn't know what to do. The lady who was asking the questions didn't wait for the end of the séance; she leapt up from her chair and ran out like she was mad. She ran into her house, gave a few orders and drove to her husband. Because he had business commitments he had been unable to participate in the séance with his wife. She dragged him out of a meeting crying that they must go save their child immediately because it was in great danger. What parent wouldn't, in such a situation, abandon everything? Now they both drove to save their only son. The couple's "child" was living in digs at the other end of the country and was in the final year of study in two subjects. This was the examination period. The parents came for the boy and took him away as he was. They wouldn't let him do anything crying that he couldn't stay there a moment longer otherwise he'll die. The bemused boy, not knowing what was going on, obediently went with his parents. They put him in the car and drove him back to the other end of the country.

That night I got up at four in the morning because I was getting ready to drive. Outside it was an exceptionally frosty night. I wondered if because of the weather conditions it wouldn't be better to give up the idea of driving the car and to take the train. Suddenly my dogs started to howl, I opened the door to quiet them down but they kept howling. It seemed that there was somebody standing at the gate but despite the shining light I saw nothing in the darkness. I threw something over myself and approached the gate. I was terrified when I saw three figures beyond the gate; they were standing in unnatural poses, like they were frozen. When they saw me they started to shout, telling me to open up instantly because their child's life was at risk. So, in the middle of the night I let in three complete strangers who, in addition, looked very weird. My intuition told me, however, that I was completely safe. The parents started shouting over each other that their child will die, that I have to help them, that the child mustn't be allowed to fall asleep. When I walked into the house I saw before me three people in clothes that were wet through and freezing. I asked them to explain their appearance. They frowned as they pointed at the wet clothes saying that was a trifle. "We drove over a thousand kilometers and we kept pouring water on ourselves so we wouldn't fall asleep. We're not important, though, it's our boy that's the biggest problem. He's had several sleepless nights, as usual before final exams, and he keeps dozing off. Even pouring water over him didn't help, nor did slapping his cheeks, nor even the fear that if he falls asleep he'll die". Now I suddenly understood what this was all about. I took the "child" by his hand and took him to the spare bedroom and put him to bed. He was so terrified that all he asked was: "Do I have to get undressed?". I said he didn't, that he could even lie down in his shoes. Whereupon he fell down like a log. I went down to the parents. When they saw me they started to shout: "What have you done with our child?". I calmly told them that I'd taken him to sleep. I thought that they wanted kill me then. They screamed: "What have you done? Under no circumstances can he be allowed to fall asleep". I asked them who had told them such rubbish. Who can possibly live without sleep? I asked them if they'd let me act in my own way, since they'd come all this way. If they knew better what I should do then why did they bother to come? They fell silent, reconciled. I looked at them with mixed feelings. I needed to get away urgently but I didn't have the heart to leave them in this state though maybe I should have. Maybe that would have taught them some sense. I was mad because an important trip had come to nothing for something so stupid. Their coming to me made no sense whatsoever. But they, of course, didn't know that. If they had phoned I'd have explained everything to them over the phone. I could, however, see their extreme helplessness. I asked myself who can possibly behave so mindlessly that they drive right across the country without making sure that the person they're going to is there. If they'd come a few minutes later I would not have been home. It was like they heard what I was thinking because they both spoke simultaneously and what I heard took me aback. "It doesn't matter that you were going to leave, we even anticipated that. If we hadn't found you at home we'd have looked for you through the radio and television till we'd succeeded. Everything has been arranged, they're just waiting for a sign from us. The police would have brought you back, after all this is a matter of life and death for our only child. The costs are immaterial". I gave a deep sigh and wondered what I was to do with them. The "child" was sleeping peacefully and I was listening to their neurotic accounts. We had to return to the moment of the spiritualist séance, when the ghost of the alleged great-grandmother was responding to the questions about the family's future. She commanded, in a voice that brooked no opposition, to dismantle instantly the company brick by brick to its very foundations, so that no trace of it would remain. For at this moment some terrible family curse was going to be fulfilled, a great danger was threatening them all, and this was the only way of preventing it. As if this wasn't enough, the "great-grandmother" announced that their child would live just as long as it could manage without sleep because when he fell asleep he would never wake again. "That's why we're here!" they shouted, crying. The fate of their child was the most important to them. The fate of their firm they could deal with later.

I didn't know if I should laugh or, along with them, cry. I gave up on what was an important trip and they'd driven all those miles with this piece of nonsense. They were so hysterical that I couldn't get to them to begin with. It lasted a good couple of hours. The "child" woke up well and a bit surprised to find himself not dead. When it was obvious that the boy was all right and there was no danger to him, the lady asked uncertainly: "Maybe the firm, too, can still be saved". I replied that it certainly could, but she denied it nervously. She started to say something chaotically and for a moment we couldn't work out what she was talking about. "And what's wrong with the firm?" we asked virtually simultaneously. It turned out that the husband knew as much about it as I did. Well, to save her family this lady had done exactly what her "great-grandmother" had instructed. The ghost had ordered that the firm be dismantled to the last brick so she had given the necessary instructions. One team was dismantling the firm without their supervision; there were valuable goods and equipment inside the building. They all landed, up to the moment of their return, on the square in front of the company. She sent a second team to fetch all of the son's things. The husband and son found out about all this only in my house. And as we know, they had driven the length of the country for the child and then the next several hundred miles to find themselves at my place. Now, nearly twenty-four hours later, they drove hurriedly home to rescue what was left of the firm. And all this because some ghost had played a joke on them.

You'll be asking: How is all this possible? You'll say that the woman went mad, that something got mixed up in her head. But what about her husband, a man who in everyday life was sure-footed and sensible? She was under the influence of a powerful ghost, but her husband? He hadn't taken part in the séance, so he should have had a sober outlook on the situation. Why does a man who, in everyday life, has to have his feet firmly on the ground in order to deal with various unexpected circumstances so he is not tricked by unfair competitors, trust ghosts so uncritically when their orders refute all common sense and are contrary to any kind of logic? Why did their self-defense mechanism fail them? Hitherto they had been successful because they believed in themselves, trusted their intuition and acted in accordance with it. During the spiritualist séances their inner compass had grown blunt. Since they'd started to believe the ghosts it was like they had surrendered their fate into the ghosts' hands. They did not stop to consider if there was any sense in asking them about everything. Nor did they consider what interest the ghosts had to act for their benefit. After all, they, including the alleged "great-grandmother", had not been alive for a long time. Even if she had been a very wise woman in her life, what could she know about running a contemporary company? In her time women would most often not be involved in business so how would she know how to do it all? People participating in spiritualist séances listen with great reverence to what ghosts have to say to them. They reckon that since they are communications from the other side they must be completely truthful. They believe in the honesty of the communication and in the ghost's good intentions, so they judge that there's no need to verify them. But where does this certainty come from that the ghost we've summoned has a thorough and real knowledge of the subject interesting us? A ghost, spotting how naïve someone is, may for a joke pretend to be any chosen ancestor and play games at the participants' expense just as they are playing at the expense of the ghosts' peace. The fact that it replies to our questions means nothing. It comes quite easily to the ghost for it hears our thoughts and works out more or less what we would like to hear, what reply would most satisfy us. Ghosts don't know the answers to our questions. Only God knows them. If we don't ask Him, we'll never know the truth. To go back to my story, when my guests realized what they had done, they leapt to their feet and ran out to the car. Meanwhile, the inside of the car had completely frozen up thanks to the water they'd used to pour over themselves. Not bothering about the discomfort, they drove home as quickly as possible. I found out later in a phone call that they encountered a very thorough team and though nothing had perished, a large part of the firm's building had been taken down.

I chose this example though I have many others to show how a cunning ghost led people astray even though these people are usually very level-headed. A living person could never manage such a feat. Of course, none of this happened without the people's permission. The ghost must have listened in on many séances because it knew exactly how to act to achieve the apposite result. In addition, it entered the woman and successfully possessed her for many long weeks. Nor did it want to release her. It had no intention of passing through to the other side and it boasted that "it's a long time since I had such excellent fun". At the very beginning ghosts investigate what subconsciously we fear most of all so that, basing themselves on our greatest fears, they can manipulate our activities. They know that what would be an unbearable loss to one person would bring no harm whatever to another. That's why they are capable of steering a situation so perfectly and in many cases they bring about people's ruin, the ruin of relationships with their near ones, the end of great fortunes etc.

This applies, of course, only to those ghosts who have stayed on this side of death's curtain, which have for whatever reason decided not to pass through to the other side. As I've said, contact with the other side makes sense only shortly after someone's death. The condition of success is, of course, that the ghost and we want the same thing equally. But it should be done only in very sporadic cases when we cannot manage in any other way. When more time passes after the death, the soul passes through to the other side of death's curtain and will not want to come at our summons.

Passing through to the Light it leaves all earthly matters far behind and no longer has any reason to contact us. It's not a question of its egoism or indifference. It continues to love and care for us, but in a different way which is diametrically different to our earthly imaginings. On Earth we have grown accustomed to thinking about many matters in a materialistic way. When we cross over to the other side of death's curtain we see everything from a spiritual point of view and that has very little to do with the physical.

To come back to ghosts. The conviction that when a person dies they suddenly have access to all sorts of possibilities that the living haven't must be brought into doubt. It is not true that ghosts know everything because "everything can be seen from up there". If that's what you think then you are in error. A person doesn't change at all after death. A person remains the same with the same faults and virtues, the same fears and emotions, the same limited knowledge and ignorance. And in all this we don't take into account the viciousness of ghosts or replies given just for a joke. For ghosts adore playing with people's naïveté.

ADDICTIONS

It is often the case that people are frightened to look deep into themselves. The whole world shows them the problem they should be confronting, but they seek the solution in flight. A sadness and an emptiness grow inside them which nothing can allay. So they reach for a "gratifier", trying to compensate for this emptiness in some way. This may be alcohol, drugs, medications, sex, gambling, cigarettes, excessive work, watching television, computer games, excessive volubility, constant adjustments to their appearance etc. We don't appreciate that what we're really doing is running away from ourselves, afraid to discover what is the cause of the feeling that keeps coming back to us, asking to be healed. We behave like the proverbial ostriches which hide their heads in the sand when they're afraid in the delusion that they are safe. In the same way, a person who doesn't want to face up to their problem reaches for a "gratifier" thinking that this way they'll run away from the burning problem.

But problems do not solve themselves, indeed they grow at a remarkable rate, coming one on top of another. Other escapees join us in our escape, both living and dead. We could spend a long time wondering which comes first - the chicken or the egg. The same applies to the question did we start to use a "gratifier" first and the ghosts hooked up to us as a consequence, or did the ghosts hook up to and that's why we started to drink, for example.

According to who is the stronger, the ghosts or we, one or other will take control. The results are described below. I'll be writing about alcoholism, but if for that word we substituted drug-addiction, addiction to medicines, sex mania, workaholism, perfectionism, gambling addition etc., then nothing in this chapter would need to change. Nearly all the addictions mentioned here lead to death, but there are people who recover from even the most advanced forms of this terrible disease.

Alcoholism

When someone who was an alcoholic in his life dies then it's very likely that they won't pass through to the other side of death's curtain. There are several reasons why they stay this side. The first and chief reason is the addiction. This will be the motive force of the ghost's activities. Another might be that the ghost will miss the fact of its own death. It may be so blunted by constant drinking, or it may be under the influence of alcohol at the moment of death and so not notice that it has died. Such a ghost, reckoning it is still living, will need the smell of alcohol and will obsessively seek to satisfy its need. It may, of course, stay around bars where alcohol is poured out in gallons. That is what very many ghosts do. Whole herds of them circle round dives, bars, drinks parties, anywhere they might draw into themselves alcoholic fumes. At the same time they have the chance to absorb the energy from the drunk people there. Unfortunately, the partial satisfaction of their habit is not enough for the majority of such ghosts. They would like to participate in the drinking themselves and not just watch it from the sidelines. So they hook up to a drunk person to drink as much as they want and to absorb their energy. Nearly every person who drinks has a ghost hooked up to them. The next day, when they have a hangover, they think that their head aches because of the excess alcohol in their blood. That, too, but even more because of the lack of energy which has been stolen from them by the invisible companions of their libations, namely the ghosts. If you drink more frequently than sporadically then you usually have several, or several dozen, ghosts hooked up to you. From the moment that they're hooked up, you have an increasingly great desire to drink. And, as if by the touch of a magic wand, you get more and more opportunities to drink. Even if you don't fancy a shot of whisky then the ghosts hooked up to you certainly do. They have their ways of persuading you to drink. If a ghost can't manage to persuade you by itself, it comes to an agreement with the ghosts of other drinkers, until good old Joe, also a lover of alcohol with a gang of ghosts attached to him, arrives at the door with a six-pack and invites you for a beer. You wonder how good old Joe suddenly found himself here, how you succumbed and have that drink. You had solemnly promised yourself and your wife that today you would certainly stay sober, yet in the evening you go home drunk.

You didn't even notice that one of the attached ghosts entered your body and now your decision isn't always just your decision. One time it's you who decide what and when you do something, another time someone else, namely the ghost, makes that decision for you. When more ghosts enter (and there can be very many of them, hundreds even) you're most probably not yourself at all. Your character has changed so completely, and your looks have, too, quite often. Hitherto you were always sure of yourself, decisive, you always knew what you wanted, but now you start being more and more lacking in will power, you give way to impulses, you're as changeable as the wind. If you don't take a drink then a tiny part of you still remains in you. Then those around you say: "When he doesn't drink he's a completely different person, but when he takes a drink it's like a devil gets inside him". Yes, but a ghost not a devil has stepped inside and most likely not just one. When you've had a drink you become argumentative, you act crazy and for no reason at all. If you're pushed you'll always find a reason, something like the dinner's too cold, the children are too noisy or whatever. You wake in the morning and you're dreadfully ashamed. More even, most often you can't remember how things came to such a pass because at that time you weren't the master of your body, the ghosts were. You promise yourself that this will never happen again, you want to put it right again, to apologize. You think: "God, how could I have raised my hand to my own wife, I mean I love her so much. What about my kids, whom I love? How will they grow up with me for an example?".

I'll tell you how it works roughly. Let's assume that your wife is a slim, tall blonde. You have always liked this type of woman very much. Naturally, you married your wife not just for her looks but to understand this better let's stick with the external traits. When you'd had a drink a ghost hooked up to you, that of a portly gentleman with tendencies towards violence from the times of Rubens. He, unfortunately, has a liking for plump short brunettes. Whenever you drink you lose control over yourself and unknowingly you give up mastery of your body to this ghost. You come home and what happens now? The ghost sees that some thin stick is floating round his kitchen and he can't bear that type. He didn't look for reasons, that one was more than enough for him. Added to which he could never could bear kids so where did this lot come from? In the morning you wake up and your wife's bruised and your children beaten. You wonder: how could this have happened? You would never raise your hand to anyone, let alone your wife and kids. I mean, you love them so much.

Or it can be that a drunk wife can terrorize the whole family. A drunk wife, though externally she looks the same, is really not your wife at all, but the ghost that has possessed her. I have given these examples for a better comprehension of the problem because these types of incident take place in very many homes. The attached ghost thinks that it's still alive and walking into our lives it gets mad when something isn't the way it was in its life. So it wants to change everything to fit in with its own ideas. It can do this by force, as in the example above, beating your wife and children, or in every other way. The worst of it is that you're not conscious of anything. When the troubles begin that is an indication which should lead us to the right road. These troubles are supposed to help you understand that you're going downhill, to help you get clear of where you're stuck. What seems at first sight to be a misfortune you will, in future, regard as great luck, the thing that helped you clamber up to a higher level of spiritual development. The sooner that happens, the sooner everyone, including you, will benefit. You'll probably ask what kind of troubles I have in mind. Those like when your wife has moved out taking the children with her and now wants a divorce, when your boss at work threatens you with the sack or you've been fired, when your friends no longer want to meet with you, when the family keeps away from you. If that's how things are then you can say you're fortunate, very fortunate indeed. A shock like that gives you the chance to come to your senses, to reflect on the fact that you're acting and thinking in a way you shouldn't be, but above all to realize that something has to be done about it. Something has to change. Now you still have a choice - either lose everything, yourself included, or win everything. If you delay too long it may be too late.

The people who drink but to whom nobody says anything about it are in a sorry situation. Friends and acquaintances consider that it's not appropriate, that it's none of their business. The family can respond in various ways. Some may wait for a miracle in the mistaken hope that everything will change for the better. Others are afraid of starting another row. They refuse to notice that not only does nothing change for the better but that it is getting worse day by day. This can last for many years. No-one will admonish the alcoholic for behaving badly. When he gets drunk again, breaks some law, the whole family gets behind him and tries to cover it up, conceal it. It's like they were all sinking into the morass which he's up to his neck in already. By behaving like this, people close to a drunk are doing themselves and him great harm. Everyone suffers by it. They meant well but everything is turning against them.

Why does this happen? I think that an alcoholic is very strongly pulled towards addiction. It gives him power to manipulate his family, his friends, those around him. Manipulate or, in other words, to resort to all sorts of lies in order to achieve what he so very much wants. They'll tell their children that they must have a drink because the children's mother/father (depending on which one of them is the alcoholic) is unkind to her or him, they'll tell their wives that they're stressed by work and earning the money to look after the family, and their old parents that they have problems with the family and at work. This way they'll always find an excuse for those around him and, above all, for himself. Then they can drink not because they're alcoholics, but because they've got a reason for it. In this way everyone in a family is constantly misled and this often ends with them arguing amongst themselves (because of the alcoholic). Even though they don't condone the drunkenness, nevertheless they do condone it in some way. The alcoholic will achieve a kind of success because instead of being blamed he receives sympathy. He doesn't want to accept that in truth he is cheating himself most of all, that he is on the downward slope from where the road leads in only one direction, namely down. When he appreciates his situation it's often too late to turn back. From my own experience I know that these circumstances can often arise in so-called "good homes", where there is money, education and professional success. That's why you mustn't let yourselves be misled by alcoholics but must take careful note of what is happening in your families. Don't be ashamed to speak out loud about it to all the members of your family. Remember, only you can bring help because an alcoholic, being under the influence of ghosts, will not ask for it.

And you who are drinking to excess, as soon as you sincerely resolve to change something in your life and start to look for help then you will receive it. You won't even realize how much circumstances will start to favor you. All you need to do is make the resolution and the Universe will take care of the rest. If, after a period of sobriety, you happen to return to drinking don't blame yourself and don't be too upset by it. Treat it as a lesson. Now you have the chance to compare what it's like to be sober with what it's like to be drunk. You have the opportunity to observe what happens to you when you've had a drink and compare what you lose and what you gain by it. If you choose sobriety now it will last longer and longer until at last you realize how much better it is not to drink at all. It will be your own free choice, your own mature decision. You'll have won your own life, won yourself.

You'll ask why you have to give up drinking altogether. Could you not continue to drink but exercise more control on the amounts you drink? Many people try to fight against their drunkenness in just this way, but they do not succeed. There are many reasons why that is. I'll just give you the ones associated with ghosts. When you were drinking the ghosts slipped inside you and now the channels are open through which they come in. When you drink even the smallest amount of alcohol you attract them like a magnet. When they smell the odor of alcohol they attack you immediately and possess you. And then you are not master of yourself, you give up control of yourself to someone else. By drinking you give up your body and your mind to the ghosts. Lay people say that an alcoholic is a slave to his habit but in truth he is a slave to the ghosts. When you are sober you have a chance to combat them, to forbid them entry, but when you drink then you don't have this chance. The problem of alcoholism isn't restricted to just adults - sometimes even young people are addicted. More and more men are coming to me asking me to save their alcoholic wives. When one of the parties drinks, be it the husband or the wife, everyone in the house suffers equally and the whole family soon disintegrates.

The most frequent cause of alcoholism is possession by ghosts. Even if someone started to drink for some completely other reason, sooner or later a multitude of ghosts will attach themselves to him. That is the chief reason why it is so hard to stop drinking.

For example, you find yourself at home on your own for

some reason (your husband has gone abroad on business, he is in hospital etc.). You cannot get used to this at all, you feel bad in this solitude, you can't sleep at night, you have never been alone like this for such a long time. You are very unhappy. Your head fills with stupid thoughts more and more often. You ask yourself what your partner is doing now, is he perhaps being unfaithful. Another sleepless night and in the morning you can't get down to anything. To improve your frame of mind you have a small drink of some weak, sweet liquor. You feel better, you calm down, and you have no problems with getting to sleep. Next day you feel rested, relaxed and you remember that that small glass of alcohol helped you to achieve this. So that evening you pour yourself another one. After a few days or weeks just to fall asleep you need to drink two or even more glasses and before you know what's happening you need a bottle of strong liquor just to fall asleep. By then you might well have had ghosts hooked up to you for some time. If there's no way we can manage without drinking then it certainly is down to ghosts. So, as we can see, even if drinking isn't caused directly by possession, then the end result is that it leads to possession.

Sometimes the family or close friends come to me asking me to cleanse an alcoholic. They very often see the huge difference between the state of a drinker when he is cleansed of ghosts and when he is still under their influence. The difference is very obvious to them all. It's not unusual for this state of affairs to be maintained for a long time, often for ever. Unfortunately, it doesn't happen with everyone. After they have been led away, some ghosts return or are replaced by new ones. Returning ghosts are most often those that are emotionally tied to the person concerned. It may be a member of the family or a friend, it doesn't matter how long ago they died but while they were alive they liked a glass from time to time. It doesn't necessarily have to have been a drunk who used to fall about in the street, it may have been an alcoholic who notoriously used to get drunk in secret. There are many more drinkers like that than we imagine. Many of the people we meet on a daily basis have a problem with alcohol and we don't even suspect it. When everyone at home has gone to bed they take out a bottle and empty it, and in the morning they get up to work like nothing happened. These people sometimes realize that what they're doing is senseless and then they look for help. When I lead the ghosts away they are immeasurably grateful and happy. If a person with a drinking habit like that dies and stays on this side of death's curtain then he will want to continue his habit at any price through someone in the family. Only when he fails in this will he look for someone outside the family. If we too have a problem like that then it won't be hard for a familiar ghost to penetrate us. We won't defend ourselves against it as we would against an extraneous one. It will manipulate us through our thoughts which we'll accept as our own because it will seem to us that at that moment we happened to be thinking about the deceased.

Inasmuch as extraneous ghosts do not return to the possessed person after they've been led away, those "familiar" ones will certainly come back. Normally they wouldn't have that opportunity, but we unconsciously draw them, and let them, in ourselves.

When a drinker comes looking for help from me in their own name then they willingly collaborate with me to lead the ghosts away as quickly as possible. Even when the ghosts keep coming back, it's in the drinker's interest to collaborate closely to be rid of them. When I am asked for help on a drinker's behalf by a member of the family who does it in secret from the drinker, a conflict of interests arises. The person wants the alcoholic to stop drinking but the drinker and their ghosts have a different need. But even this solution is a lot better than no solution at all. When I have led the ghosts away, the alcoholic is for a time master of their own self and can decide whether to drink or not. Till now he had drunk out of compulsion, directed to by a ghost, now he has a choice. The problem is that the alcoholic may not be aware that he has a choice because we have kept the whole thing secret from him. It is rare to successfully treat a person who is alcoholic and not aware of the exorcist's help and of the ghosts' existence, as well as their influence on our lives. It can only bring results when the ghost itself wants to leave and is glad to be given the chance. In every other case the alcoholic will draw the ghost back into his or her body. That's why collaboration with the drinker is essential. However, when I ask for it the most frequent response is one of outrage: "Mrs Pratnicka, I will never tell him/her that you helped me. He/she doesn't believe in such nonsense, what are you thinking of, he/she is, despite everything, an intelligent person. Do you want him/her to think of me as a scatter-brain or a lunatic?". Or: "Mrs Pratnicka, I am paying you to do it and I demand that you get results".

I can understand this reaction only in very extreme cases when the person in question is nearly at the very bottom. They are usually drunk, they no longer have contact with reality when sober. At such times it is possible for them to harm the person asking for help on their behalf because for the majority of their ghosts exorcisms are far from convenient. Fear and the ghosts may triumph. But what needs to be taken into account is that the alcoholism itself brings us harm on a daily basis and it could be that the harm issuing from making the addict aware of the exorcisms carried out on their behalf may be no greater than the harm brought by the day by day toleration of the addiction. One has to realize that cleansing of the ghosts may be, for us and for them, the last chance of salvation. Even if the cleansing is only temporary, it will bring us and the alcoholic a little respite.

Nevertheless, I will not be persuaded by the desire to keep the exorcisms a secret just because we are afraid of what a given person will think about us. Either we have a sincere desire to bring unconditional help or we don't. What I find even more amazing is the attitude of people who "pay, demand and don't care how the delinquent is helped". People like that are not aware of one factor. The first and surely most important thing is that the ghost may be someone close to them, a father, mother, grandfather, grandmother, uncle, aunt, neighbor etc. They demand that I "get them out, destroy them!". It is unimportant to them who it is or why they have stayed here. They refuse to accept that a ghost continues to be a living, feeling being, but one that's functioning in a different dimension. The fact that they drank when they were alive may also have been caused by possession by ghosts. When they were alive on earth they had no-one to help them. They continue to believe that theirs an insoluble situation. They could be thrown out, but to where? Won't such insensitive behavior not result in the fact that though our friend is cleansed someone else will be made to suffer instead? Besides which, using therapy is the best time and way to help the ghost. If we know who the ghost was when alive, then knowing its character we can more easily explain to it its situation and help it to solve its problem. When we do this we can ask it to leave and go to God. For we can find the solution to what seems to the ghost to be terrible and hopeless. It's just wanting to do it.

There is also the matter of my recompense. In the past I would most often help people without payment, and in some cases I still do. I did notice, however, that people don't appreciate what they get without payment. They regard "free" as meaning the same as "worthless". That's not all. The more expensive something is, or the harder something is to achieve the more valuable it becomes to them. The value of what they get is many times greater than the value of their payment. What they get from me is sometimes beyond price. Words like "I pay and I demand" are, therefore, out of order. My guess is that the situation of the person saying those words had unbalanced her to such an extent that she didn't really know what she was saying.

A very important aspect is that nobody should be forced to change. What appears to us to be unacceptable may for that person be the most important lesson they need to finish. By acting on their behalf but behind their back, without mentioning anything, we may do that person great harm. That's why I ask for direct collaboration with the interested party.

When someone in our circle of friends starts to drink alcohol we close our eyes to it, judging they have transient problems. We don't realize that alcohol will not only not remove those problems, it will multiply them. In a situation like that, even our concern, an ordinary conversation can bring about a solution to the problem. Unfortunately, we most often do nothing thereby assisting in that person sinking deeper into drunkenness, and with the associated problems. When for example our husband gets drunk and doesn't keep a promise we try to cover it up in some way. If someone complains we reply: "Yes, I understand you, but my husband couldn't finish it because he was sick". We assume that by doing this we'll help him to save face and he'll therefore avoid difficulties. If it happened once then it could be explained away, but it happens more and more often. What makes us do this? Is it a false sense of shame? Do we want to hide the fact that we have a drunkard in the house? Have we asked ourselves where taking sides with a drunk leads to? Why do we take on additional responsibilities more and more often which had previously belonged to our drinking husband, wife, son, daughter, work colleague etc.? Maybe it was a desire to help to begin with, maybe it was pity that he's so hung over, let the poor man rest, he has a headache, he might be sick. But pity was never a good counselor. Added to which, the situation recurs again and again. We didn't even notice how many responsibilities have fallen onto our shoulders. We have become responsible for both of us and we didn't even notice when that responsibility became exclusively ours. To begin with we even liked it. Your husband was grateful and you felt so needed. Behaving like this we pretend, we deceive ourselves that there is nothing dangerous happening to him or to us. With time we stop liking it, we start to object, we start having rows, but when the need arises we help again, we make something up again, anything so long as out "terrible" secret doesn't come out (which everyone probably knows about anyway). Henceforth the drinker stops bothering about anything. Though we kvetch that he drinks he doesn't experience any consequences for his actions. Nor does he bear any consequences at work or among his friends. Thus do we contribute to his addiction. We are jointly guilty because he doesn't have the awareness whereas we, who are sober, do or at least should do. Till now it had seemed to us that we were the victims of our husband's, or wife's, alcoholism but in large measure we have contributed to its arising, we are the silent accomplices of a joint misfortune. To begin with we didn't think we were doing anything wrong. He drank too much, it harmed him, we felt obliged to help. You can help once, even lie. It seemed that it would be just the one time, but it didn't turn out that way. The lie provoked the next lie and we kept driving on until we'd driven into the sands. Truth to say, we cheated not only their boss at work, but ourselves, too, and our drunkard husband or wife. When we realized that we were on a downward slope it could sometimes be too late because in the meantime our spouse had become an addict. He was dragged in by a hunger for alcohol on the one side, and by the ghosts of drunks wanting more and more alcohol on the other. Many of us will ask what should be done in such a situation. As you have certainly realized, right at the very beginning one should never cover up the spouse's weakness nor take their responsibilities onto one's shoulders.

You must tell him straight to his face: "You drink, that's your business. But the consequences of your drinking (dereliction of responsibilities, missing your deadlines) are your business, too, and not mine". We should act the same when it's our son or daughter, or any one of our friends who drinks. Right from the very start we must not tolerate their drinking, even if it's a little. Right from the start it needs to be treated like a developing disease, a future addiction. We must not be guided by false shame and hide their drunkenness from our circle. You'll say you never thought having the odd drink was an addiction. Even now there will be those among you who'll think that it's only a passing indisposition and that when the outside pressures pass then so will the habit. You are very much mistaken. Like every sickness, alcoholism starts by showing symptoms and only later develops more and more until in the end it throws the family onto its knees. When even one person in the family drinks then everyone in it suffers. If you won't think about the drinker, then think of yourselves at least. As time passes it may become increasingly difficult to realize. Our help should consist of not helping at all. That doesn't mean we have to turn away from the drinker completely. We can dedicate our time to conversations, on making a closer and warmer contact with the sick person.

What can be done if alcoholism is at an advanced stage of development? First one has to check that there are no more ghosts. They can be the illness' chief cause. It happens in the majority of, though not all, instances. However, whether or not a ghost leaves depends on the exorcist, on the drinker him or herself, and, of course, on the ghost. Sometimes prolonged therapy needs to be applied to the drinker and to the ghost, too. They have to be taught how to free themselves from one another. Even when they both achieve this they still have a long road ahead of them. The cause why the ghost remained in the astral world needs to be addressed. There can be no talk of complete success until the ghost understands that what is best for it is to pass through to the other side of death's curtain. Cleansing the alcoholic will be of no use if he or she does not comprehend that it is better for them to decide for themselves instead of trusting their fate to ghosts and functioning only as a puppet deprived of its own will. When the drinker has been freed of ghosts one still has to act consistently for a long time afterwards.

The responsibilities that belong to the husband/wife have to be given back to him/her. Even if he/she doesn't perform them one should not do them for him/her. It's better if they suffer the consequences of their own neglect. I'll give an example.

A husband conducted extensive business affairs but, at the same time, was fond of liquor. When he was drunk the wife fixed everything for him. She was professionally active herself and now, more and more often, she was having to do two jobs. When she came home exhausted she often found drinks being served there, and a mixed company taking part. The ladies there didn't conceal their disappointment and made it clear to her that they'd rather she didn't come home at all. Not only did she not hear a kind word from her husband, things often came to blows.

This situation went on for years. Right from the start she helped her husband, judging that that was what was needed at the time. One day she rebelled. Till then, if the phone rang for him when her husband was drunk, she used to invent some clever excuses for him. Now she decided that things would be different regardless of the consequences. She told me that the moment she got rid of her false sense of shame which had been the motive force of her behavior she was ready for anything. Before then she often mentioned that she would sooner die than allow everyone to find out that her husband was a drunk and a libertine. That's why it had been so easy to manipulate her and put more and more responsibilities on her. When the phone rang she said out loud that her husband had broken the promise he gave because he was soused as usual. She did that for the first time in her life. Her husband stood as if he'd been struck by lightning; she thought he was going to hit her, but he ran to the shower from where he came out washed and shaved, and ran out of the house. From that moment on he started to drink in moderation because he was afraid that his wife might by chance say something that would compromise his position. This lady gave back, slowly but effectively, all the duties she'd previously taken onto herself voluntarily. Since then theirs has been a happy marriage. The man hadn't treated his wife with respect because she hadn't respected herself. When she said "enough" she won back not only her husband, but herself, too.

Let us consider what would have happened if the lady hadn't taken such a drastic and courageous step. I am certain that she would have swollen the ranks of the unhappy, abused and even beaten wives and husbands (I mean that: there are very many alcoholic women abusing their husbands). Why did this woman, like so many others, put up with her partner's alcoholism for so many years? When I raise this question the replies are usually very similar. They claim they do so out of love, and yet there has been no love in this relationship for a long time and who knows if there ever was any. Is the sexual drive being confused here with feeling? Has the need to be together, or a mutual attachment stemming from habit been mistaken for love? In such a union the element which caused it to be made is no longer there and yet the union continues to exist. By posing this question consciously I want to provoke people to consider themselves and their situation. What benefits does the party being abused get from this union? If there were no benefits at all, why would he or she put up with it? When we delve deeper into the heart of the problem together we come to specific conclusions. The chief reason turns out to be the fact that what these people subconsciously get from the people around them is what they had previously expected from their marriage. I'm talking about sympathy from those around them, a bit of pity, things which their subconscious equates with a substitute for love. They don't get love from their partner, but they get its substitute from those around them. When they look into themselves, they hear voices: "What a poor thing she is, I'm so sorry for her" and similar things. When some of them realize this they rebel and this gives them the strength to win. Just as the lady I've described did. She decided that she didn't want pity, she wanted love. She resolved that she would start by loving herself and then the world rewarded her with love, as did her husband. Many, however, prefer to remain in the same state and, as a victim, to receive its substitute whereas they could get the real thing - love.

There is just one other problem that needs to be mentioned in this chapter. To help someone who drinks to excess one sometimes has to make very difficult and painful decisions charged with drastic results such as excluding the spouse from the marital home, separation or divorce. The family of the addicted person must at some moment resolve to leave him completely alone and refuse him any help (this applies not only to alcoholics but to gamblers, drug-addicts etc.). There comes a time when one cannot wait any longer in the mistaken hope that the person will change. Constant rescue attempts haven't helped and merely dragged everyone else down deeper and deeper. I know how painful such decisions are but they must be made as soon as possible.

Sometimes it can be very hard for us to accept the fact that someone close to us might die as a result of their addiction. They would die in this way regardless of the efforts we might take to save them. Leaving them to themselves may be the only chance for making them come to their senses and dragging them out of even the most advanced stage of their addiction. Often, those around won't accept the members of such a family. Instead of helping them to stay strong they often persuade them: "Help him, do something to stop him drinking, talk to his friends, pour the alcohol away etc.". Instead of helping they impose on the family a sense of guilt and depress them even further. People suffer but are afraid to take drastic steps for fear of being labeled as monsters who abandon their dear ones in their hour of need. The family of an addicted person needs the full support of those outside. When, for instance, our son starts to drink we must not blame our daughter-in-law, thereby excusing our son, but we should support her. The whole family will benefit from that. Let's give her support, not judgment. At the same time, the members of an addicted person's family must rid themselves of any false sense of shame and must reach out to those around them to receive the necessary support.

A WORD ABOUT BUSINESS

There have been many books written about business but none of them show the influence that ghosts have on it. Many of you will wonder what ghosts can possibly have to do with contemporary companies. They have, and more than many of you might imagine. In the chapter on haunted houses I'll write about situations where a ghost is so tied to its property that it has no intention of leaving it. The same applies to ghosts which conducted business when they were living. It doesn't matter whether it's a one-man business or a multinational firm we're talking about. If a person is strongly attached to their financial concern and devoted all their life to it then after death it is very likely that they won't want to withdraw from it. Here are a few examples.

This was just after the war. Young people weren't all that bothered by the lack of work, housing, or means for living. Many of them married like they wanted to make up for time lost during the war. But it was one thing being just a couple, and quite another when the family started to grow. One of these young fathers, after work at clearing the rubble in the town, spent all his nights in the cellar to supplement his wages and he was making something. He quickly found buyers for the articles he made and the demand was constantly greater than he was able to supply. He gave up his job and set up a tiny workshop in a hurriedly knocked-together shed. He worked alone days and nights until finally came the moment when he had to take on someone to help him. Then another one, and another, until after many years the firm had grown. The owner scarcely knew how to write his own name. To make up for this lack of education his only son was sent to the best schools. He was also groomed to take over his father's firm. For the first few years after the owner's death the company continued to operate by the force he gave it when he was still alive. But the son hadn't traveled round the world and studied just so he could stay in one place. He was every bit as good at the job as his father had been, even better. However, whenever he tried to introduce any kind of improvement he instantly stumbled across some unexpected difficulties. Several years passed after the father's death and there had been literally no improvements introduced into the firm. Yet the demands of the market were forcing the company to introduce innovations. Unfortunately, it wasn't happening in any way. Then it was realized that something was not quite right and I was approached. I ascertained that the father had remained in his empire and continued to direct operations. Though he hadn't possessed any specific person, he nevertheless controlled all the firm's movements from the beyond. The son was so frightened by this that he refused to let anything be changed. All the pleas from the employees and the rest of the family came to nothing. The son honored his father's will and left him his firm. But he didn't crack up and he set up his own company. It started to be very successful. The enterprise that he built up from scratch is vibrant. Shortly afterwards, his father's firm went bankrupt.

Imagine what would happen if a person who conducts a large company is possessed by a ghost which, in its lifetime, had nothing to do with business. You'll ask how that could be possible. A person who is in charge of a serious business must, as they say, have his head screwed on. After all he has to deal on an everyday basis with many unpredictable situations which he has to manage, e.g. not allow himself to be cheated or manipulated by a supplier. Or by a ghost.

I was once approached by a woman who asked me to help her husband, a businessman, who for some time had been making moves that were ruining his enterprise. Furthermore, she could foresee that shortly the family was going to lose the roof over its heads. There were three partners there who were running a large business with associates in many countries. Every one of them had an equal right to make decisions about the firm and in view of their differing qualifications each one of them ran his own part of the business. The business ran splendidly and none of them checked up on the others. One day the partner whom I was supposed to help was driving through the gates of the business in his brand-new car when he thought: "I earn such a lot and I'm sure the caretaker has more children than I do and compared with me he earns a pittance". He made a phone call and the caretaker was given a pay rise. From that day forward he started behaving this way with all the employees. When the partners learned about this they were alarmed, asking him what he was up to because behaving like this he was going to bankrupt the firm. Without reflection he simply left the firm but he didn't change his activities. He gave everything away everywhere completely unconcerned by the fact that his family would shortly have nothing to eat, quite literally. It simply didn't get through to him. When he started poking about in his garage his partners wondered what kind of invention he was trying to conceal from them. It didn't occur to either of them that there was something wrong with him, that his decisions made no sense at all. Even when his wife tried to make them see they suspected her of chicanery aimed at leading them off the scent. When I started cleansing the husband I saw only one ghost, completely unthreatening, which, it seemed to me, could not have such an influence on someone with a personality as strong as his. But it transpired that it did. I started to check who it was and discovered that it was the possessed man's godfather. When I told his wife she replied that when he was a child her husband's father had died and the godfather took his place completely. Unfortunately, when the godfather died her husband was out of the country. The death affected him greatly. He could not rid himself of the feelings of guilt he had for not being there when his godfather was dying or at the funeral. After all, his godfather had invested a lot of care and effort into his upbringing. The wife asked me to help: "Mrs Pratnicka, you don't realize what a good, wise man he is". At the next visit she brought him to me to prove it. He gave the impression of being a schizophrenic, completely absent, he had no idea of what was going on around him. He talked constantly, kept asking about completely disconnected things. His wife asked me to tell him something about his godfather, but nothing got through to him. They returned home and I continued to cleanse him. It lasted about a year, so strong was the attachment between the godson and the godfather. There was no way of separating them. The godfather didn't want to leave because he wanted to go on looking after his godson, and the godson completely unconsciously didn't want to let him go. When they both understood that instead of helping they were harming each other, they parted for ever. When his godfather left, the man came to thank me. I saw a completely different man – intelligent, sharp, self-assured. He told me that if he hadn't been through it himself, he would never have believed that a ghost could change someone's life so much. If it hadn't been for his wife's determination, the firm would have been bankrupt because his partners couldn't manage without him. When he "recovered" his partners immediately suggested he return to the company and everything returned to normal, and in fact it started to develop even better.

Another case. In the market square of a small ancient town was the place's only restaurant. The town was at a crossroads and was visited by very many people. The food there was excellent and people came to it in droves from the neighboring villages. Nobody was bothered by the peeling walls, the old and rickety tables, or the wrecked chairs. The restaurant's owner was an old man and there were many entrepreneurs waiting for the moment when they would be able to take over this, as they called it in the town, little pearl. When he died the authorities sold it to the highest bidders. The new owners refurbished it, stylishly decorated it so it fitted in with the ancient properties around it. They employed cooks and waited for the first customers. People came, looked over the place, admired it, but no-one was willing to put in an order. The same happened over the next few days. The opening was advertised, a new sign put up and nothing. Cars drove past without stopping and the pedestrians kept well away from the restaurant. From time to time some lost customer might arrive, but the new owners hadn't put in all that expense just so the place would stand empty. When they came to me they were on the verge of bankruptcy. Their first words were to ask about a curse put on them by their competitors, about black magic. They couldn't comprehend that in such a busy place nobody stopped and nobody wanted to eat. I checked but I couldn't confirm their suspicions. When I started to look more closely (at a distance, of course, as always) I saw that the restaurant was very busy. It was noisy and full, there was nowhere left to sit. It was only after a while that I understood that the old owner was still running the place, and that the crowd consisted of ghosts. No sensitive person could possibly bear to be there for long. Customers quite simply felt ill-at-ease and decided not to go back. This happens often in bars, but drunks do not sense it. I advised them to look for another place because the one they had was quite effectively taken. Since this was the only restaurant, I argued, then there will be people willing to come even in another spot. The owners, though, were adamant and resolved to wait until something changed. A few years passed and they were in poor health, bitter, without a dime to their name waiting for the bailiffs to come and throw them out. Their debts had completely devoured all their cash. Today they blame God and themselves for not listening to my advice when there was still time to do so.

This is not a unique case. I have been approached about similar cases by the chiefs of various concerns – a photographer, an optician, a confectioner etc. Of course every one of them came from a different town, but the situation was the same as in the account I've given. I was approached by a woman who ran an ophthalmic business on a very busy street in a large town. She claimed that people were walking past her shop as if they didn't see it there. I checked and saw a similar situation to the one with the restaurant. I told her about it. She was terrified, but only because she was scared of ghosts. She instantly started to look for a place which was as attractive as the one she had. It turned out that there was a place free in the next block. She asked if she could move in there. I checked and it turned out she could. The move caused no problems and when she finished with it the customers started to arrive. Her shop, which till then had been empty, is now working at full capacity yet she moved literally only a few meters away.

HAUNTED HOUSES

When we think of haunted houses what comes to mind is an old, abandoned and frightening property which we're scared to approach let alone live in. Such extreme cases of haunting are exceptional. There is a whole gamut of visitations, from the light, completely harmless ones, to the very severe. Some merely make people's lives more difficult, but there are those which make it completely impossible.

How do such phenomena come about? Their cause are ghosts of a specific type. The only aim in life that many people have is to earn as much money as possible, to acquire and maintain the largest possible property. The concept of a large property, or of a fortune, is, of course, relative. What for one person may be a great fortune could, for another, have no value whatsoever. This kind of person may have seen nothing in his life outside the amassing of wealth. He has become so attached to it that he is in no state to leave it while he's alive, nor after his death. He doesn't want to die at all, but since he has to he wonders what he is to do with it. Most of all he would like to take it with him, but how? Maybe he should leave it to someone as an inheritance? Oh, no, he has worked far too hard to get it. Besides, no-one else will look after it in the right way. When he was alive he never thought of himself, never visited anything, never rested, and now he's supposed to leave it all just like that? Never. That would be too great a sacrifice, after all he has paid for that fortune with his soul.

It is of these very people that the Bible says: "It is easier for a camel to pass through the eye of a needle than for a rich man to enter into the kingdom of God". This certainly doesn't mean that God does not love rich people or that He has anything against wealth. There is nothing bad or inappropriate about wealth as long as it hasn't been acquired by dishonest means. Nor is there anything wrong in being rich. What this quotation from the Bible is talking about is not wealth but an attachment to it which detains the soul here on Earth and does not allow it to enter into the kingdom of God. While we are alive we are entitled to make use of our wealth as we wish, but when we set off for the other side we must know how to leave it behind. For how could we enter into that world with a house, a car and our own business? Physical things belong to the physical world and must remain in this world. Unfortunately, not everyone is prepared to accept that. Some people find it so hard to part from their fortunes that they forfeit the happiness that awaits them in "Heaven" for the sake of the surrogate which attachment to their wealth provides. They do not appreciate that the thing they are holding onto so tightly is nothing like as good as what they could have. You could compare these people with someone who lives in a tiny house or a hovel but is too afraid to abandon this property despite the fact the waiting for him is a most magnificent palace.

I'll give you an example. There was a very wealthy businessman who, though his garage contained a Mercedes S and several other fine cars in his firm, constantly had the urge to wash and look after his old, decrepit Trabant. He spent virtually every spare moment in the garage. His family put up with this eccentricity bravely for twenty years. They consoled themselves with the reflection that there are worse addictions in the world. Although he devoted all his free time to this obsession, at least he was at home. Then the Trabant started to disintegrate in some strange way; its owner reacted to this even more strangely. He simply went berserk. Because of this incident, the family found its way to me. When I started to check if there was any connection between car and its owner's sickness, I found that there was, and quite a strong one. Many years previously, before the man started to run his own business, he bought the Trabant unaware of the fact that its previous owner had very nearly caused an accident. This huge stress set off a heart attack and he died at the wheel. The car had been everything in his life, his only possession. After his death he stayed with it, and whenever the opportunity arose (when the businessman had drunk alcohol) he entered the new owner. As a ghost he looked after his property very conscientiously. When I led the ghost away, the man who had been possessed by it awoke as if from a long sleep. He was amazed by the strength of possession and that he hadn't even noticed it. In everyday life he was a serious, wealthy man. He often repeated: "Lucky for me the ghost was so possessive it didn't want to drive the old crate round town, I would never have lived it down".

When someone realizes that they can't take their property with them and when they don't want to leave it to anyone, they resolve to stay with it for ever. Even if they will it to a relative under the pressure of approaching death they will take it back anyway. Let's assume that someone scrimped and saved through most of their life to build a house for their old age. They saved enough money for the materials but didn't take anyone on to help them, building it themselves day by day, putting all their energy into the construction. They had hardly finished the building before they died. The fate of the beneficiaries or of the purchasers is hard indeed when they come to live in the house. They will have to pay a very high price for every brick, for every drop of sweat lost during its construction. For as long as they live there they will know no peace. Only when they move away will they recover their freedom. Every subsequent buyer will be subjected to same the fate.

The living occupants of some of the houses or farms haunted in this way, knew the owner when he was alive. This does not, however, change the situation: their lives are hell on earth.

There is another kind of ghost which visits houses that never belonged to them. These are ghosts who were, in their lives, very grasping in their pursuit of wealth, they were even ready to kill for it. They acquired fortunes in a cruel way. They were guided by the lowest instincts and after their deaths nothing has changed. They are every bit as ruthless and grasping, ready to kill anyone who wants to trespass on their territory. The desire to acquire wealth gave people like that enormous strength, cruelty and fearlessness. It is with the same strength that the ghost guard their treasures, not allowing anyone to get close to them. Let us not assume, however, that there is an enormous treasure hidden behind the doors of every haunted house. The concept of a fortune is very relative. What represents great worth to one person will, to another, be worthless and barely good enough for the garbage tip. So ghosts guard their gains which in their subjective assessment are very valuable. Here's an example.

A ghost who was haunting a particular house had, in its life, been someone who preyed on old ladies. In the majority of cases his booty consisted of the old ladies' pension or the dimes left from them. Those old ladies who weren't particularly attached to money, gave it up to him willingly. Others defended their money to the end and lost everything, including their health and their lives. At the end it turned out he was killing for a couple of pennies. Now, as a ghost, it guards what he looted as if it were the greatest of treasures. It remembers how hard he had had to work to acquire it, going as far as committing murder. The ghost doesn't realize that it is of very little worth. In its view, this is a great treasure. It will be prepared to kill to protect a cheap picture hanging on the wall of the house it is haunting. This house, though it is a hovel, represents something very valuable compared with the sums he looted from the old ladies. A ghost like that won't allow anyone inside, will do anything to smoke the owners out of there. Its greed gives it great strength which other ghosts don't have after their deaths. It is unreconciled, and no arguments can persuade it. That is why some houses stand empty for years. They decline but no-one is able to live in them nor can they knock it down unless the ghost decides to let them.

Another group consists of the ghosts who died suddenly, e.g. in an accident, and aren't aware that they have died. This group is completely different than the previous one in terms of character. They function in the same way they did in their lives. They left home to go to work and in the evening they returned there as ghosts. Between those times a tragic accident took place in which they died on the spot. For them this was a sudden and unforeseen happening which they did not register. So little has changed for them that they guess they're still alive. They leave for work every day, they go shopping, they come back home. They may spend part of the day in the office "working" and another part at home, or at a friend's. If they used to live with someone, parents, a friend, a husband or a wife, then after death they return to their close ones like nothing had happened. The film "Sixth Sense" shows very well what happens to ghosts who died suddenly and don't realize that they're no longer alive. I suggest that anyone who has lost someone close to them in a sudden accident ought to see this film. It shows the dependencies we're talking about very truthfully without exaggerating the fiction.

When they are preparing a funeral the family members aren't at all bothered, indeed they regard it as normal, to hear or sense the ghost of the dead person. Many of them are even pleased that it is visiting them after death. If they knew what it signifies and what consequences it might have they would surely consider how they could best help it and themselves. Many of you will ask: How could they do that? First and foremost by informing the ghost that it is no longer alive. They should light large numbers of candles, do everything to make the house look like a place of mourning from which someone has departed. In the past the remains were kept in the house till the day of the funeral and then the dead person had a chance to view its own body in the coffin, to see the burning candles, the mourners. Nowadays in towns, because of public health issues, this is no longer practiced, and even in the country people are moving away from it. Some houses have days of prayer arranged, but the dead person needs more than that. It is essential that they be informed that they have died. How can one do that? One should speak to the dead person aloud and by name. For example: "Johnny, you are no longer alive, you died in a car accident in these circumstances, on this day, at this time. You died, go towards the Light. Go, don't be afraid, they are already waiting for you there. Go, God loves you very much and is waiting for you, don't be afraid. God had forgiven you all your sins and you must forgive them yourself. We, too, have absolved you of everything. Please forgive us our misdemeanors, too". These words can of course, be modified according to the needs of a given situation. Intuition will prompt us in what we need to say to the dead person. How long should we do this? Till we can be certain that the dead soul has understood and has left. This way we are performing a service for not just the dead person, but for ourselves, too. This ritual should be performed even when the death was of natural causes but we feel intensely that the ghost, for whatever reasons, isn't leaving. In this time we should all also think about a settling of accounts with the dead soul. We have to forgive all the injuries they caused us, and also the fact that they didn't do something they should have done, that they made promises which they didn't keep. At the same time we must forgive ourselves because we may in some way have been at fault with regard to the recently deceased soul.

When for some reason a ghost overlooks the moment of its death then it will live in our house like nothing had happened. For the first few days after the funeral we may even like it, but afterwards it starts to be a problem. When it does, then everything will depend on what kind of person the ghost was in its life. If its nature was tidy, acquiescent, and gentle then we may not experience many physical manifestations of its stay. Though we will feel ill-at-ease, often quite tired, waking in the nights for unknown reasons, we will get accustomed to it in time. When a ghost was an untidy person, taking no notice of others' feelings, then it will also be noisy, bang about, knock things over, move them, make a mess. It will not only be harder

to live in a house like that but we'll start to fall ill, we'll feel lethargic, we'll be unable to see a purpose in what we do, misun-
derstandings will arise for no apparent reason. When we want
to take a nap the ghost will choose that moment to start banging
about. Some ghosts are well aware that they've died and want to
make contact with us. They can do that to try to draw attention
to themselves. Sometimes they may do this for years on end
while we ignore them completely. They become very irritated
then and, after a while, may become very vicious. I refer you to
the chapter entitled: "Troubles with our Children" where I describe the activity of a ghost which, unable to make contact with
its niece, started to get at her by possessing her son. When she
made contact with it, the son didn't raise his hand to her again.

What happens when the whole family dies and the house
stands empty for some time? In the majority of cases the ghosts
immediately come back to it because they don't know they have
died. After a while new occupants move into the house but this
doesn't get through to the ghosts. It's a very difficult moment
for them because they have to confront reality. Till then everything was just like it had been before, they could live in the illusion, but now what about these new people? Where have they
come from? For some ghosts this is the moment of awakening,
but for very many nothing changes. Nor should we be surprised.
You, dear reader, believe that you're alive, you know you are,
but how can you be so sure? You'll say it's because you can see,
hear, feel. That is sufficient proof for you, isn't it? And what
would happen if someone suddenly told you that you're not
alive? You would glance at one another and you'd laugh out
loud in that someone's face. After all, you know perfectly well
that you're alive, so where do these insinuations come from?
There are only a very small number of people who would consider that question at all deeply. But you know and that's

enough for you. It's the same with ghosts. They can see, hear, feel, they can even pinch themselves, they see their own bodies, so which experience will show them that they are no longer alive? When some people (the new occupants) appear in their house they get angry. Some get so angry that they chase the intruders away. Others explain, plead, and when that is unsuccessful they go for a compromise. So then, under one roof, the new and the old occupants, the living and the dead, live together. That's why it's possible to function more or less reasonably in one haunted house while in another house it may be more difficult. It all depends on what the ghosts' attitude was to personal possessions while they were living. If someone was helpful and generous then they won't mind that there's someone living with them. When the ghost was sly, ungenerous in its life, it won't allow others to take advantage of its property.

It can also happen that the people living in a house may not be aware of the existence of the ghosts, and the ghosts may not be aware of the existence of people other than them. That's like two parallel planes existing in the one space, and when they sometimes do cut across each other the ghosts will regard us living people as ghosts, just like we do them. This is shown very vividly in the film "The Others". When you've seen it many of you will start to wonder if perhaps you're not ghosts yourselves which have overlooked the moment of their deaths.

Many people come to me with a variety of problems - diseases, various kinds of misfortunes, suicides, burglaries, and even murders. I start by looking for some starting point, a moment at which everything began. It often turns out to be tied to moving into a new apartment or house. It can happen that a building where more than one person has already died becomes the cause of misfortunes for its new occupants. If we know about it, it's easier to put it right.

In my work I have come across many instances where my clients have moved into a newly-built house, built by themselves, yet things happen in it which are just like the situation mentioned above. It happens that I discover that the cause of their misfortunes is visitation and by many ghosts at that. Then my clients say; "Mrs Pratnicka, when we were building this house people mentioned that there used to be a small cemetery there but it was so long ago that we took no notice".

There are many accounts of visitations stemming from the fact that houses have been built in unsuitable spots. Nowadays there is a trend to build houses quite literally everywhere and anywhere. Sometimes, when I drive past a building site like that and I know what used to be or happened there earlier, it makes my hair stand on end. For I am very well aware what misfortune will meet the people who end up living there. The old wisdom of ensuring before starting to build a house, be it large or small, that the ground is suitable for habitation has almost disappeared. Not only to check the water lines and tectonic plates, but also the history of a given place. For there are places where under no circumstances should any kind of building be erected. In the first place this includes all cemeteries, various kinds of battlefield not just of major battles but even minor skirmishes, places of catastrophes or murders. I draw attention to this because I've noticed that many people have absolutely no idea of the danger which might, in the future, destroy the life of a whole family. Nor do large concerns building multi-occupation houses have any awareness of this. Many large housing estates are constructed in totally unsuitable places. I ask myself if the reason for these decisions is ignorance, thoughtlessness or maybe a soulless desire for profit. It is my opinion that the people with the most to lose, namely the future occupants, should concern themselves with this and that would force the construction firms to change their approach. If every one of the occupants checked to see that their apartment is suitable for habitation the builders would have to take the consequences of their short-sighted attitude. Houses built in unsuitable places would stand empty and then the firms would think twice about building them any old where. It would motivate them to check assiduously the terrain of future construction and thereby our children would have a better future. When this is not talked about the lives of many families become complicated for reasons unknown to them.

A woman came to me asking for help for her daughter Margaret who, during the day, functioned quite normally but at night experienced appalling stomach aches. This situation had lasted several years. She complained that the pain created a very realistic sensation that her insides were pouring out of her onto the outside so that when the pain passed she started to look for them all around herself. When she ascertained that her stomach was whole she could not believe it. Exhausted, she fell asleep. When she woke up she remembered literally nothing of what had gone on before. At the beginning the neighbors asked what had happened to make her suffer so much. She wondered with amazement what they were talking about. Then she realized. She was examined by many doctors but none of them found any cause for such a great pain. Psychiatrists, too, examined her and found nothing. They did not solve her problem. Her screams would often reverberate round the block. Some of them found it such a torture that they moved out just so as not to hear what was going on the other side of the wall. For a couple of years there was nobody who could help her. When I was approached I assumed it was the activity of a ghost which was suffering a great deal. I was not wrong. I discovered in Margaret the ghost of a young woman who, while fighting during the uprising, had been shot in the stomach and died alone suffering terribly for many days. About sixty years had passed since the war, despite that, however, the ghost was still in a state of terrible shock and suffered torments every night. To take it out of this state of shock I needed Margaret's help. I asked her mother to let me talk to Margaret, but she wouldn't agree thinking that her daughter wouldn't cope with such knowledge. So I had to struggle with this problem on my own. Whenever I managed to get through to the ghost even for a short while, Margaret had a quiet night, and even several nights in a row. After a while, though, things went back to the way they had been before. After they had had a bit of peace, the recurrence of the pain was even harder to cope with both for Margaret and her neighbors. Reaching a ghost which is in a state of shock is not at all easy, indeed it verges on the miraculous. Imagine that there is a person in a state of shock next to you. You try to quieten them, explain something to them, but they don't react at all to your efforts, they don't even hear that you're speaking. The case dragged on for about half a year and I wanted to give it up when the mother decided herself to let me contact her daughter. From then on the matter progressed much more quickly and after I healed the ghost, Margaret had no more pain. What do you think the cause of the visitation was? It transpired that the apartment block had been built on a plot where the partisans had fought many skirmishes and where many people had been shot.

If we move into a house built on the ground of a former cemetery, battlefield, place of execution of hostages, crime or catastrophe, then we expose ourselves to having to live through the most extreme of human experiences, the suicides of people close to us and maybe even our own. That is the very thing we seek to avoid when we build or move into a new home. Even an apartment needs to be checked to ascertain if the previous owner died and, if he did, whether or not he has passed through to the other side.

When things are awry in the family, everyone's always ill, always arguing, they have suicidal thoughts, they drink, then, looking to be rescued, they often come to me. I then cleanse the family once, then a second time and then again. Whenever the ghosts don't depart, or if new ones keep appearing, I ask myself what could be the reason for it. Why is the whole family possessed? I ask many questions and when I receive more and more fresh replies which don't satisfy me I ask more and more questions. In many cases the cause are water lines running beneath the building, or tectonic faults. Ghosts draw energy from them so there is usually a larger number of them there. In houses like this people suffer from numerous diseases and even die one after another. There are frequent suicides. A symptom of it may be alcoholism throughout the family, arguments, or various kinds of trouble.

A man came to me asking for help for his mother. He claimed his mother was close to death. I saw, however, that this man was in urgent need of help for himself, too. He came from quite a poor family where the father worked and the mother looked after a large group of children. The money which the father earned was entirely swallowed up by the construction of a house. Until it was completed, the whole family lived, over a period of several years, at the grandparents', in very trying conditions. During the move to the new house the man, who was nearly an adult now, found work in a county town and shortly afterwards got married. He was not, however, contented by the fact that at least his life had panned out successfully. He had a great feeling of guilt. He kept thinking about his family. His mother suffered from many illnesses at once and she was taken to hospital, close to death. That's when he turned to me for help.

I cleansed the mother of ghosts and she started to recover her health at a fast rate. It gave the son much food for thought and he asked me to check the whole family. I also checked the house and saw in it large numbers of ghosts. When I told him about it, he confessed that that had been the reason why he, his wife and their children didn't want to move there. They felt very bad there. His parents and siblings had given him an ultimatum: either he returns to them or they will disown him. There was almost nowhere in his parents' house which was free of the radiation of water lines, apart from a small store-room and bits of a corridor. The house had been built on a confluence of lines which formed a small underwater marsh. It was lucky that his mother, during her stay in hospital, had had a taste of life without illnesses, had seen what it was like to have a peaceful night's rest and she resolved to go on living in just this way. When she found out from her son what the cause of the illnesses had been she demanded that the store-room be redecorated immediately. The parents moved their whole lives to this healthy part of the house and they both started to return to health. The children, together with their families, however, continued to live on the water lines and didn't for a moment consider changing. Moreover, they believed that the whole question of water lines was veritable nonsense and that their brother was messing up their parents' heads unnecessarily by talking about it.

This multi-family house, built with such effort and devotion by the whole family, is totally unsuitable for habitation. And nothing can fix that. No radiation shields, no remedies can help. No remedial methods exist that will allow normal life to return to this place. The only solution is to move to another place. All that family's work and money have been wasted.

Many people recover their peace, health and harmony when they rebuild their homes. The best solution, however, is to check the ground before starting to build. A large number of people have to move their bedding to a spot free from water lines every night since they cannot rebuild their home. There are those who have been helped from a radiesthesist. Unfortunately they are living in ignorance, exposed to the consequences of constant radiation. When I draw their attention to the powerful radiation in the building they reply: "Yes, we know about it, Mrs Pratnicka. A few years ago we asked a radiesthesist to come and he said the same thing. He set something up at the time so at least we're safe as far as that's concerned". They do not realize, however, that the shield set up has long since stopped helping them, and is, furthermore, very likely an additional source of radiation. Unfortunately, anti-radiation shields are not able to protect the occupants from illnesses or misfortunes. Many radiesthesists live in buildings beneath which water lines can be found. Unable to find help from anywhere else, they look for anti-radiation shields which would release them from their problem. Some repellents are better, some worse. But they are always effective for only a specific length of time. Radiesthetists would like to be rid of the trouble caused by water lines once and for all and they look for anti-radiation devices that would have a permanent effect. The demand is great and there are products appearing on the market which have in their name the words: "Permanent anti-radiation protection". This promise is, however, very far from the truth. An anti-radiation device is like a dam which collects the water. And however large it may be and however good the materials it's made of, the reservoir will, after a time, fill up. For it to collect more, the water that is already in the reservoir needs to be let out. However, one needs to know where and when that can be done. One can also build another dam and then another, but some time even those reservoirs will be filled. Let me tell you about an incident that will bring this question home to you.

There was a man who lived with his family in a small house on a very small plot. He had inherited the house from his family. Unfortunately, it had been built on a great water line. The owner was an engineer. He took an interest in radiesthesis for his own needs. Any anti-radiation devices installed in his house either didn't work or worked for a short time only. He was critical of their fallibility and resolved to construct a device that would solve the problem once and for all. His own constructions, however, were also effective only for a short time. He was determined and hoped that he would manage to invent a device that would meet his family's expectations as well as those of others in a similar situation to his own. At last he managed to invent a new kind of shield. He boasted about it all over the place, and as usual he started to test it on himself. He had the right conditions for it, because there was a huge water line running under his bed. When he had laid down the anti-radiation shields under his bed he finally started to sleep peacefully. He was well pleased with this. His colleagues persuaded him to go into large-scale production of the anti-radiation shields. He put it off, however, because a longed-for holiday break was approaching. He went on holiday with his family. When he returned home he found his house looking like it had been bombed. His bed was one storey higher then before, in the attic, and was completely in pieces. Luckily, at the time of the explosion none of the family was home. The neighbors didn't notice anything either because they weren't home during the holiday period. It's frightening to think what would have happened if the whole family hadn't gone away on holiday or if the production of the anti-radiation shield had been started on an industrial scale.

I am writing about this because there is no such thing as

an anti-radiation device that is effective for ever. That's why the positioning of a house must be considered very carefully before building begins. If there is no other way then it is essential that the bedrooms at least are in spots that are free from radiation. If we live in a house like that then the best solution is to leave it completely. The financial losses that we suffer doing so will be far less than the loss of our health if we don't.

OTHER ACTIVITIES OF GHOSTS

Ghosts can also exert an indirect influence on us. For example, we may live in a block where the people above us walk about all night long in heavy, steel-capped boots, or tap on radiators, or open and close squeaking doors, flush or pour out water, switch on a noisy vacuum cleaner, washing machine, radio or similar. All night long we haven't closed our eyes and in the morning we have to get up and go to work, to school or to university. You think to yourself: "This is such an important day and I look like a scarecrow, my eyes are swollen, I have a splitting headache, I can't concentrate on anything. The children have a test, and there's an important delegation coming to see my husband - how's he going to manage? The whole family's day is ruined". We threaten to have a talk about it to the people from upstairs, downstairs, next door or wherever. We wonder what's happened to them, they were always so nice. When this is repeated every night or every other night you crack and have a terrible row with the neighbors, you write a letter of complaint to the management, you call the police, it sometimes degenerates into a fist-fight. You are outraged and you're right to be. But the neighbors you can't even look at now, whom you torment through the police, the management, are just as outraged by your behavior. Added to which they haven't the slightest clue what's got into you, what's made you act like a lunatic. Not surprising since you haven't explained to them that it's all about the sounds coming from their apartment. How could they know that when there is no banging in their home, they have complete peace there and sleep through each night serenely?

You, in turn, are so certain that it's the neighbors who are annoying you that it doesn't enter your head to talk to them calmly, to consider together if what's tormenting you may not be something other than you suppose it to be.

Many neighboring households are in conflict with each other in just this way. The disputes between them can last for many years. This can be dealt with from the very beginning if we only know what phenomenon it is that is at issue. Its manifestation consists of hearing noises on one side of the wall which sound like they're coming from the other side, whereas on the other side of the wall, in the neighbor's apartment, everything is as quiet as can be. If these sounds reached both apartments, then the neighbor being criticized would work out what your complaint is about and would probably criticize you for causing the noise.

You'll ask: how is this possible? As I have written earlier, after death so little changes that many ghosts don't notice that they are no longer alive. So they come back home as normal, to their relatives, and try to function normally. Since a ghost has made itself at home with us it means it wants to make contact with us, wants to tell us something, to apologize, explain. When we don't allow it into our consciousness and cover our ears so as not to hear, then the ghost tries even harder to get through to us, till eventually the situation becomes absurd. Life will be easier for us if we think with sympathy that this is our deceased husband, mother or whoever making the noise because they badly want to tell us something, than if we constantly feel ourselves to be the victims of our neighbors' activities. Two very good films on this subject have been made recently - "The Others" and "Ghost". Both are worth seeing by all those who feel they have this kind of problem. I do hope that after seeing these films many readers will rid themselves of unnecessary fear and hear out their dead near ones so they can finish all their affairs and pass through to the other world in peace. Unfortunately, there are only a few really good films which deal not only with the subject of death and the other world but also show in a credible, serious way what happens to souls after a sudden, unexpected death. It pains me to state that the majority of films on this subject are based on fiction and through their fantastical implications serve only to lead viewers into error.

Other phenomena of a similar nature occur in some apartments - you get up in the morning and your door is smeared with something, sometimes in a very specific way. For instance, it wouldn't have been possible to reach certain places normally because the doors or windows were locked and no-one could have smeared them from the inside. You wonder which of your neighbors was insolent enough to have done this to you. So you buy some appropriate stuff and smear his door. He thinks you've gone crazy and you think he has. In some families, wars like that last for years. People lose their health, their good names, peace of mind and the responsibility is down to our uninvited tenants, namely ghosts. After they have been led away all such troubles vanish.

Many people keep changing their place of residence or force their "tiresome neighbors" to move, but as luck would have it the new ones create a similar noise. This lasts until we check if this is all happening because of ghosts. When we know it is, then it's easier for us to cope with it. For then we can ask an exorcist to help or ask the ghosts to pass through to the other world.

Sometimes what happens is that a certain spot in the home emits a strong odor. We blame the builders, the plasterers or the painters. We strip the plaster, rip up the floorboards but we can't find the cause of the unpleasant smell. Even the most thoroughgoing refurbishment isn't able to remove it permanently, after a while it returns again. Some people start to suspect their close or distant acquaintances of using black magic. I have been brought cases which are hard to credit. Most often though it's down to the activity of a very powerful vicious ghost. The stronger the ghost, the stronger the smell. After it has been led away, everything returns to normal. A warning! If you have a problem like this, it is essential to take great care of all the members of the household, give each other a lot of mutual support and warmth, because ghosts like this often drive the people they possess to suicide.

I wouldn't want to frighten anyone, but it's often only after someone's suicide that we recall that this strange smell or odor really was present around them constantly. If we had reacted appropriately then most likely the tragedy could have been avoided.

There are always situations where various multicolored stains, painted inscriptions, appear on objects in our home or on our clothes, stains you'll not see in any shop. Unfortunately, no stain remover is able to shift them. The furniture is thrown away and exchanged for new, only for the stains to reappear in exactly the same places as before. Once again, suspicions arise about the use of black magic or voodoo, but the cause is the same as in the examples already cited.

Another phenomenon is theft and the moving of objects. By force of habit you leave some object in a specific place where it always stayed in peace. Now things start to get lost or you find them in some other place or in a changed state. You wonder who could have done this to you. Suspicions arise, inquiries, unpleasant situations. It might have been the neighbor when she popped in to borrow salt, or friends when they were visiting. In such cases we have several suspects but it can happen that we had no visits and still the thing gets lost. This pattern can be repeated simultaneously at home, at our son's school, our husband's workplace etc. It can happen that we find the stolen piece e.g. in our work-mate's locker. We have the thief, but he swears by everything he holds holy that he didn't take it, has no idea how it ended up where it did. You complain that now you can't trust anyone because even your best friends are stealing from you. You hold it against him that not only did he steal but he hasn't the courage to own up to it. There are many homes where this sort of things leads to terrible rows. The person who suffered the theft is furious, and the members of the family unjustly accused of the theft are furious, too. Sometimes the things turns up a couple of days later somewhere completely different. We accuse the person of having put it there himself and forgotten about it. He himself starts to wonder if he is in his right mind or if it's just his memory that is starting to go. Often, the perpetrators of such thefts are ghosts. Some of them are able to carry things from one place to another, and sometimes they can dematerialize them and carry them out of the home.

Once I was phoned by an old man asking me for help. After fifty years of a perfect marriage his wife started suspecting him of theft. "Mrs Pratnicka, I can't cope with this much longer," he moaned. "Can you explain what's happening?" I checked and said that indeed I could. I saw the ghost-thief and the way he did it. I asked the wife to come to the phone and explained the whole thing to her. She didn't want to believe me and even suspected me of plotting with her husband, but she agreed to keep a check on the ghost-thief. One Sunday their home was visited by their children and grandchildren, and there was a whole lot of them. At one moment someone noticed a huge fifty-liter demijohn of wine rising into the air and moving across the yard to the shed, like it was being carried by an invisible hand. The family members started to nudge one another, one of them screamed with terror. At this moment the demijohn fell and shattered into pieces. They lost the wine but regained their wished-for peace of mind. Nothing vanished from their home again.

Why do ghosts do this? Equally when they bang, paint, move or take away - the reasons are many. Most often the ghost uses this as a way of demonstrating its presence. Doing it, it wants to say: "Look at me, Katy, it's me, your Chris" or "I am still alive and I want to show you that by doing this". If Katy interprets this in the right way, everything's fine. If the ghost continues to try contacting us that means that it wants something more. Maybe the resolution of some matter. It has probably tried many times in many ways to draw attention to itself but we are most often deaf to its attempts. When the vanishing objects belong to various members of the family that means the ghost is resorting to such tricks because it badly wants to make contact with any member of the family. It will do so for as long as it takes to achieve its aim which may seem to us to be very prosaic but is very significant to the ghost. Sometimes the thing that is lost is something which might remind you of the dead person or something which, for the ghost, was some kind of symbol when it was alive. As a rule, though, we don't associate the objects with such things. Sometimes the ghost wants to sow confusion by its activities so that eventually someone will realize that it is doing them. Only in rare cases does a ghost do this viciously, to settle accounts with the living.

It sometimes happens that a thieving ghost was, when alive, a thief and retains that trait in its nature. It steals for the sake of stealing. Sometimes it will take the objects outside but after a thorough search we find them hidden in the corners of the house or nearby. These things may be dematerialized or be found in pieces in various places. For instance, a piece of a thing may be here, and another piece there, or we may find pieces from various things all joined together like a mosaic.

Summing up, then: it has to be stated that this banging, scraping, painting, moving or hiding objects kind of ghost is usually someone close to us who has died and using this method wants to remind us of him or herself or of something important to them.

If we are aware of this then instead of being afraid, looking for spitefulness, getting agitated because someone is disturbing our peace, we will ask ourselves what it is the ghost is trying to tell us. Most usually, though, the motive force of our reaction is fear. It can be so strong that it stops us living in the homes where the unexplained phenomena occur. We then try to shelter from them. But the moment comes when we have to return and then everything starts afresh. I ask such people who are often on the verge of nervous collapse why they are so afraid of ghosts. Did they also fear their e.g. granny or husband so much when they were alive? Of course, in the majority of cases the answer is no. Does their fear stem from the fact that they saw their rigid corpses in the coffin? Did your mother or grandmother harm you when they were alive? You'll almost certainly say no. In that case why, after their deaths, don't we even want to know what they have to say to us? Is the fact that they are now invisible a reason to fear them and to close yourself off from them? You'll say that you're shutting yourself off because you don't know if those noises are in fact your mother or husband. Someone else will say that they are so afraid of ghosts that they don't want to see or hear them. That way we create a vicious circle since the more we shut ourselves off the more insistent the ghost becomes until at some moment it gets into a rage. What would you do if people kept turning away from you and pretending that they didn't hear you? I think you would do exactly the same that ghosts do. I refer you to the chapter on "Troubles with our Children".

THEFTS

Hitherto I've been describing what happens when it is the ghosts themselves that commit thefts. It's usually the case that we don't have the opportunity to observe them in action. It can happen, though, that they function as vibrations which are very close to the vibrations of our world and then they can be seen and heard. This doesn't, of course, apply to mediums who are able to see, hear or sense ghosts whenever they want.

I'd like to look at the problem of theft from another side. People who stole when they were alive do not rid themselves of their predispositions after their deaths. I'm talking here only about ghosts suspended between Heaven and Earth and not about ghosts which have passed through to the other side of death's curtain. Such ghosts, when they have hooked up to a person, will try to persuade them to commit thefts. They will think how they can acquire something, suggesting to the possessed person's mind all the advantages to be had from the crime and it can happen that they are successful. We often hear people who have committed some misdemeanor say: "The devil must have tempted me". In some sense they are close to the truth, it's just that instead of the devil it's the ghost of a former thief at work here. For consolation I can tell you that ghosts will only influence those people who haven't yet done their lesson on theft. If, for instance, we have come to this world to learn honesty then during our lives we will often come across thefts, chicanery and manipulation. At the level of the soul we can decide to steal something in order to see what it's like to experience the consequences of such an act, starting from shame if we're caught red-handed all the way to a prison sentence. Another time we will be the ones who are robbed and we'll see for ourselves what it's like to go through the results of such an act, e.g. in the form of deprivations. One person may do this once and no more, while another cannot learn even after a hundred lessons.

What can happen is that in previous incarnations we were thieves more than once, stealing whatever we could get our hands on, and in this incarnation it is we who are robbed. A person who hasn't yet done the lesson of honesty is an easy prey for ghosts. Anyone is able to induce him, even a child, just having the opportunity is enough to make him steal. A person who has done their lesson in honesty fully cannot be persuaded even by a ghost which has hooked up to them. A person like that is immune to its suggestions. The ghost, seeing it won't achieve anything here, will seek out another victim.

When the ghost is on the outside of a person and merely persuades them then the person has a choice - either to succumb to the persuasion or to resist it. The case is different, however, when the ghost of a thief penetrates the body of the possessed person or takes control of their mind. The person then becomes a puppet, and has little chance of resisting the ghost. Then the ghost can commit blatant robberies but if it is caught it's the person who has to answer for them. Then everyone's surprised that a person who "comes from such a decent family has become a black sheep bringing shame to everyone" or "he was such a decent young man, it's incredible how he's gone to the bad". All reprimands, prison sentences or other kinds of punishment are in vain. The punishment is meted out to the human being John for the activity of the ghost of Frank. No matter how hard he tries, John will have no influence on matters. It can happen that a person's body becomes dominated by a ghost whereupon he loses self-awareness. One moment he may possess a small degree of awareness, and the next - none at all. He experiences torments when he finds out he has done wrong, he is punished for it, and he doesn't even know when and how he did it.

The life of a person possessed by a thief-ghost can develop in various ways. They may steal just once and then never again submit to the ghost because their conscience warns them to be constantly on their guard. Then again they may steal smaller or larger things for which they have no need. This applies to people of all professions, of various levels of wealth. Sometimes they have no material needs at all. It's then trumpeted by everyone and it's very humiliating for the people concerned. For instance, a university professor is repeatedly caught shop-lifting in a supermarket. How low must he feel being conscious of the fact that all his students know about it and he cannot control it? We call this kleptomania. When a person like that is cleansed of ghosts then the impulse guiding him leaves instantly.

JEALOUSY

Jealousy in itself is neither good nor bad. It is an emotion like any other. It is only we who give it meaning. We can be jealous of everything - a house, a car, better earnings, position, fame, a girl, love, children. I could go on. Several of you will ask: "What good can there be in jealousy?" When we envy someone something, e.g. a magnificent house, it can become an excellent motivator for us to get to live in a house like that. You might say that you'll never be able to earn enough for a house like that, or if you do it'll only be when you're old and you don't need it. If you think this way then jealousy is a bad emotion because it unempowers you, takes away your strength, clouds your capabilities. When jealousy is a constructive emotion it provides a whole range of possibilities. You might, for instance, find a house whose owner might rent it to you and then in time will sell it. You might manage to negotiate it so your rent counts towards paying off the debt so that with every passing month you are more and more close to being the owner of the desired property. You might look after a beautiful house whose owners have gone abroad, or whose owner is staying with relatives. Whichever way it works, jealousy can act as a motivating force to try for such a house, or an even better one, or it can be the cause of a frustration that lasts till the end of your life. As we can see, every emotion can be either constructive or destructive for us.

One can be envious constantly and of everything or merely in specific situations. Jealousy can affect each one of us - men, women, the old, the young or even children.

For example, you were envious of something but only from time to time. You didn't attach too much weight to it because you judged that it's completely normal, that everyone experiences it. Even when you were attacked for being envious you didn't change anything in your life because you considered that you were okay with it and it didn't get in your way. You met an interesting girl, you've been dating her for a time, and you're constantly thinking: "God, she's magnificent, everyone thinks she's great, my friends can't keep their eyes off her, how could she choose me? There's nothing special about me. I can't get it into my head that she could fall in love with me, after all I am a very ordinary kind of guy". When you think like this you start worrying that you might lose her, you think: "I must keep an eye on her otherwise someone else will get off with her". You can't see that since she chose you above all those other boys it proves that to her you are worth something more than you think. Earlier you were and now you start becoming more and more jealous. Now you think that you really do have something to be jealous about. You ask yourself day and night how you can keep her. You're afraid that the very thing that attracted her to you might now start being of interest to your friends. You say to yourself: "She's so carefree, so naïve, she could easily be seduced", and your jealousy grows. You can't eat, sleep, or work. It seems to you that your girl has given you cause for jealousy because she looked at someone, or smiled. Seeing the changes in your behavior someone might say: "Guy, are you sure you're okay?" You've noticed that something's wrong yourself, but you think: "I've fallen in love and that's why I'm a bit off color". You haven't realized that first one and then several other ghosts of jealous men have hooked up to you. In normal circumstances these ghosts wouldn't have had any chance of hooking onto you but you have carried jealousy in your heart earlier and that's why it was hard for you to notice the encroaching changes. This apparently tiny flaw has attracted ghosts with a similar flaw. It's like you might have called for help and that help had come in keeping with the principle that "birds of a feather flock together". It could even be that to begin with your increased jealousy gave you strength or suggestions in your contacts with your beloved. To begin with you didn't notice any changes in yourself, then you laid the blame for everything onto being in love. Now you follow her every step and it doesn't matter if she has done nothing or if she really is playing you false. You know that she has the potential to betray you and that is enough for you. Even if a random passer-by stops to ask her for directions, you see in him a potential rival.

I've given as an example a boy's jealousy of a girl, but gender plays no role in this. There are the same number of jealous women as there are jealous men. In some cultures jealousy is considered a positive thing, a proof that the other side loves even if a little too strongly. You may delude yourself into thinking that when love's flames diminish everything will return to normal. Time passes and jealousy, instead of dying out grows in strength so much that the other party can scarcely breathe. If

this happens at the start of the relationship, the person on the receiving end may find enough determination to leave. It's different when jealousy becomes a problem for someone who has
been in a relationship a very long time, when children have
come, or even grandchildren and great grandchildren. Till then
they could be a truly harmonious, loving couple, have a shared
house, a family, friends and acquaintances. Then a real drama,
or even something horrific, can envelope both parties. For they
are both equally hurt by such a situation, they are both victims
of jealousy. What in the first moment seemed to be an ally has
now become a curse.

When someone is possessed by many jealous ghosts
people say they're possessed by jealousy. They have no self-
awareness, no awareness of their actions, they behave like ro-
bots whom the ghosts tell: "Now do this, now do that". It is always doing something bereft of feeling. It appears that it is
done in the name of love, but it has nothing at all to do with
love. A person possessed by jealousy is very rarely aware of
their state. They don't experience even a moment's peace. They
spy, check, search through pockets, drawers, shirt-collars, look
for hairs on coats. They look for proofs of betrayal everywhere,
they see betrayal everywhere, in every person, too, in every action, in every male or female colleague at work, in every client,
in every passer-by. A person like that believes that the whole
world has entered a conspiracy against them. Those that might
have been able to help are considered enemies. It would seem to
them that they have proofs of betrayal even if the "betraying"
person is shut in alone at home, has no access to the telephone,
has a high wall shutting them off from the street and the neighbors.

A person suspected of betrayal feels like someone in a
cul-de-sac from which there is no way out. What used to be a

proof of love has become a curse. Often a jealous person is so sick that she is ready to kill the person she loved, that person's supposed lover, people assisting in the betrayal and herself, too. Sometimes we hear in the media of cases where a husband kills his wife, or the wife kills her husband, then kills the children and him or herself.

There is often nothing the person suspected of betrayal can do; all assurances of love, explanations and proofs of innocence are useless. The person would feel more free in prison. He can't stay but can't leave, either. Stay and live like this for how long? Stay in the hope that eventually something will change? He may delude himself: "She must love me very much if she behaves in a way which is on the edge of being ludicrous". Often the person suspected of betrayal is very attached to his/her partner and puts up with it all patiently. Sometimes they are tied by the children, the property and sometimes they simply have nowhere to go. Sometimes their situation becomes so impossible that they have to abandon everything they have and resolve to leave. Sometimes they have to hide from their jealous partner till the end of their lives. He wants to hunt her down, observe her, and bring her back by force to his home. However many times she may run away and organize her life, she will be hunted down and dragged back to her prison.

When a person like that dies you can imagine what they might persuade the person they possess to do. The ghost will reproduce the situation of its own life and the moment of its death. That's why cleansing and the breaking of this vicious circle is so important. After cleansing the person may not remember that they created so much trouble, may become pleasant, loving, forgiving. The person often has a great sense of guilt, is ashamed of what they did to their partner and those around them. They try very hard to make up for the time lost and to put everything right. Unfortunately, sometimes nothing remains to be put right.

Once an elderly couple came to see me. They had been together for nearly fifty years. Till then theirs had been a very harmonious marriage, but recently the husband had started to be jealous about everything. To begin with this was amusing, but when his rivals started to be his grand-daughter's friends, or passers-by in the street, his obsession became unbearable. He suffered terribly while she laughed: "Oh, you old fool, what could these young things possibly want to do with me since I already have one foot on the other side?". But nothing could persuade him, he knew what he knew and that was the end of it. After the ghosts left everything returned to normal, and he remembers nothing of that period. As you can see, jealousy can strike at any age.

The same applies to meanness. Ghosts hook up to our trait and we don't even notice when our innate trait takes on gigantic proportions. We turn from being careful with our money into a terrible miser. Even when we lack for nothing we are possessed by a mania for saving. We constantly have before our eyes a vision of poverty, privation, and we will do anything to prevent it happening. Even in the wealthiest of households starvation rations of food are served, restrictions verging on the absurd are introduced. Severe punishments are meted out for losing, smashing, destroying, dirtying anything. The reason is the same as above. When the ghosts are led away the person who is cutting back on everything suddenly becomes completely normal.

HOW TO HELP THEM, HOW TO HELP YOURSELF

If we lead a ghost away several times and it doesn't want to go then the most probable reason is that it isn't aware that it has died. One of the ways of reminding it of the fact is to show it its grave. Many of you will say that since the death of the person you keep going to their grave. That's true, but since it seems to the ghost that it is still alive, it may not associate that grave with its own death.)It sees that you are going to the grave "for someone" but it has no awareness that this is "its" grave. That's why we have to show it this in a special way, like we might explain something for the first time to a small child, speaking out loud: "See here, Johnny (address it by its name, using the same name as you used during its life), you are no longer alive, you are lying in this grave. This is your gravestone with your name on it, see," (read out loud what is written on it, e.g.: "John Smith, you died on such and such a day, then and there". Inspect the grave slowly from every side. Be warned! The ghost's reactions can be various. I'll give examples below to show that they can sometimes be dangerous. That's why when you go to a cemetery for this purpose remember never to do it on your own. Ask someone for help and, naturally, warn that person why you are going there. If it's you accompanying someone else then be prepared for all kinds of sensation. It is rare for them not to happen. As a rule the ghost in the haunted person doesn't want to look at its grave at all even if, till then, visiting the cemetery had not been a problem for it. The person may start to laugh hysterically, want to demolish the grave, faint, cry, scream that it's all untrue etc. If this happens try to calm them down and re-peat the activity of looking at the grave and the headstone till you sense the certainty that the ghost has taken in the informa-tion. Most often it happens more or less the way I describe in the examples below.

There was a man who, because of a ghost which pos-sessed him, lost everything - his health, his wife, his house, his business. When all methods of trying to free himself from it proved fruitless, he set off to the cemetery with great determina-tion but alone. He must have dismissed my advice or maybe he didn't have anyone he could take with him. Maybe he was sim-ply embarrassed to confess his problems to anyone. After he'd started to look at the grave in the way I've described he suddenly leapt to his feet and started to run away. He remembers that there was no way he could control himself, he just ran and ran till there was no more strength in his legs. There is a gap in his memory of what happened next. He lost consciousness. When he recovered, he saw himself with both arms wound tightly round the pillar of the cemetery entrance, shaking with fear. All around him was a crowd of rubber-necks. A lot of time must have elapsed between the first and second moment of memory because at that time of year not many people visited the ceme-

tery yet a large crowd had gathered around him. Despite persuasion he was unable to let go of the pillar and return home on
his own. An acquaintance of his helped him, but he couldn't recall how he got home. From that moment on there was no way
he could function normally. The only way to rid himself of his
fear would be to return to the cemetery, but he didn't have the
courage to make the decision. He repeated his attempt only after a couple of weeks, having been persuaded by friends and acquaintances, strong, well-built guys who were able to restrain
him should he panic. Once again he started to show the ghost its
grave and he felt it leaving him.

Another man started to run away, running blindly over
the graves, breaking both legs and arms. He lay like that for half
a day before a visitor to the cemetery found him. While he was
lying there in pain he understood that it wasn't he who had been
afraid but the ghost which had possessed him, and that is very
different. As soon as they put the plaster of Paris on he had
himself taken to the cemetery once again and showing the ghost
its grave demanded that it leave him for ever, which indeed did
happen.

A woman who was seriously ill with cancer fell into a
rage when she discovered whose ghost it was that had hooked
up to her and caused the illness. Even though she was a poor
motorist she borrowed a car from a colleague and drove to the
other end of the country to the grave of the dead person's ghost.
Her poor motoring skills, her sickness and the distance tired her
greatly. She reached the place exhausted and instead of resting,
breathless, she rushed to the grave and threw out at it all of her
pain, resentment, and everything which she had kept inside for
so many years, not sparing the ghost plenty of name-calling.
"Mrs Pratnicka, it's just as well I didn't demolish the grave. I
was so furious I was ready to start kicking it," she said. At a

certain moment she sensed that the ghost was leaving her and she was overwhelmed by great gratitude. She suddenly felt very light, as if she'd had a great weight taken off her shoulders. Delighted, she returned home. After her return she started to be tormented by terrible pangs of guilt which she couldn't cope with at all. They were, of course, associated with her behavior at her friend's grave. She couldn't forgive herself for the things she had said and done there. Her illness intensified and she already had one foot on the other side. Nevertheless she was conscious of the fact that if she died without forgiving herself then most likely she wouldn't pass through to the other side of death's curtain and would in the future be the cause of someone else's possession. She was prepared to die but before then she needed to resolve whether or not to forgive herself. When she did so with all her heart the illness started to recede and she returned to full health.

The people described above were aware of the cause of their possession. But what can be done when the possessed person isn't ready to understand what is happening to them or why? Unfortunately, there are far more such cases than the ones I've presented. If a family member or a friend knows who the ghost is then they must do exactly the same but the person concerned has to be made aware of what they are going to see. First of all one must be prepared and not allow the ghost to panic. If it does panic, then the person needs to be calmed down and, if possible, the whole procedure needs to be started afresh. At the graveside a conversation should start with reminiscences, as if we were telling a little child about the ghost. How it died, when, in what circumstances, and slowly showing the grave and the headstone with the inscription. All this has to be shown precisely to the possessed person so they can see it with their own eyes. A lot also depends on the ghost. If it comprehends that it is no longer alive, it may want to leave and then it will be easier for the exorcist to lead it away. A ghost is often a relative or a friend. We knew them well and we can find the best way to get through to them ourselves.

As you can see, the above behavior confirms the fact that ghosts are completely unaware of the fact that they're not alive. They usually leave immediately as soon as they comprehend the fact. It can happen that a ghost will leave initially, but after a while will come back. Usually the underlying reason for this is some deeper cause, an unfinished piece of business, anger, hurt. There is no other way out of this than to forgive everything and everyone. This has to be done equally for the ghost's and for the person's sake. If the possessed person is not able to do it himself, then try to do it in his name. If there is a lot of resentment or anger within you, then take some loose sheets of paper and write a letter in which you pour out everything that's bothering you. Don't hold back, even if it means using bad language. Write as long as it takes for your resentment to be poured out onto the paper and you ascertain that you have actually said everything. Maybe you'll see that you no longer have anything against the dead person. You may even be able to forgive them. If, after a couple of days, something makes itself heard again, repeat the procedure till you sense that there is no more anger in you nor anything which might demand forgiveness. Meanwhile you will most likely discover that the ghost is no longer beside you because, released, it has left for the other world. The piles of sheets with reproaches or apologies you can burn over the grave or in the garden, and give them to God.

EXORCISMS

I have often wondered why so many people turn to me to ask me for exorcism and not directly to a priest. After all, it's part of their duties. It turns out that nearly all of my patients have previously sought for help from the church. Many traveled from parish to parish in vain. Some even went all the way to the Vatican, also in vain. The priests' reactions to this kind of request are varied. Some order the petitioners to pray and repent their sins, others believe that the patient's state is payment for their sinful lives, others again direct them to a psychiatrist. Only a very few assessed that what was really needed was exorcism but added instantly that exorcisms were not performed in their parish. These people were more likely to meet with indifference to their problems than with any kind of help. There are those among my patients on whom exorcisms were performed either once or several times. Unfortunately, they did not always help, or they helped only for a short time.

The answer to the questions which had taxed me came during an exorcists' conference. It turned out that there were only five of them in the whole of Poland. If these five exorcists were to look after the people of just one town I know from my own experience that they would have their hands full. And since there are only five of them in the whole of the country it is no wonder that people have no chance of getting to see them. Nor does everyone know where to find them because unfortunately in their parishes there is no-one who could let them know. The same is true, unfortunately, in other countries. Even Italy, or the Vatican itself, is not in a much better situation.

I couldn't understand why this should be so. I found out that in churches of other persuasions one can receive an exorcism without any problems. Since that is so, why do the priests of the Catholic Church not want to perform it, why don't they want to help? Where does their passivity towards so many people in need of help stem from? I have directed these questions to the priests themselves. In my conversations with them I argued that Jesus was the greatest exorcist and therefore his priests have assumed that role as continuators of his teachings. They should do what he once started. I regard it as a betrayal of Christ that they teach what he taught but do not do as he did. Furthermore, their passivity contradicts Jesus' teaching. In St Mark's gospel we read: "And these signs shall follow them that believe: In my name shall they cast out devils" (Mark 16, v.17). Jesus gave this power not only to the apostles and disciples, but to all people who believe in Him. The promise of this power is still valid today and every human being can make use of it. And because of his vocation, the priest more than anyone. I can understand that a possessed person won't make use of it, being unable to do so under the influence of a ghost, but why do the priests not do it? Since God gave us the power to free ourselves from the ghosts possessing us it must mean that He didn't want us to suffer or to regard possession as a punishment for our sins. Yet unfortunately that is the way many priests explain the causes of the possession experienced by the people coming to them.

Since the priests were unable to explain these matters directly, I looked for an answer in the history of the Church. I discovered the reason why priests were unable to meet the demands that are placed on them. I hope this will bring understanding to all those who needed their help and, at the same time, will mollify the bitterness stemming from the fact that they did not receive it, accusing the priests and the Church of ill will.

From the times of Jesus every Christian could be an exorcist. In the middle of the third century, however, at the time that it was starting up, the Church limited these powers and started to bring in various formulae all the way through to the ordination of exorcists. From then on it wasn't permitted for a believer to perform exorcisms. Those could be done only by an appropriate person, chosen and ordained by the Church. These restrictions became more and more severe until in the 16th century at the Council of Trent the Church banned completely the carrying out of any exorcisms, even by priests. This ban was in force for nearly three centuries.

It was only in 1886 that Pope Leo XIII overturned this ban. He was possessed by evil ghosts as he was saying Holy Mass. He composed a prayer about cleansing, distributed it to the bishops all over the world and instructed that it be said after every mass. He also wrote a special exorcism which he ordered his bishops and priests to say in their dioceses. In just one moment they were obliged to do something about which none of them had the faintest idea. There were no books left from the times when exorcism was performed and permitted, nor any descriptions of exorcisms written by priests. Even if such things had existed, they had most probably been destroyed. So all knowledge of exorcism was forgotten. The only thing the Church possessed was a ritual dating from 1614. It's like an instruction manual for those exorcising, but it was written for the needs and conditions of those times - the times of the Inquisition, heresy, stockpiles and tortures. Transferring it to the contemporary world gives scant help and, consequently, has scant results. Its greatest shortcoming is that a person is often exorcised over a period of many years. Nevertheless, this knowledge is better than none. Apart from this ritual, there are in existence only two other documents about exorcism - from the 9th and 10th centuries. That is all the priest-exorcist has to draw on for any kind of knowledge. It should be passed on from the master to the apprentice, but the masters of exorcism have all died out during the previous three centuries.

And so it was that the priests, knowing nothing about exorcisms, not learning about them in seminaries, suddenly, from one day to the next, were obliged to carry them out. It's one thing to speak the words of a formula because the superior commands it, and another thing entirely to perform an exorcism because one believes in its power and efficacy. It's like the difference between night and day. One has the power to change things, the other does not. It's a bit like giving someone an instruction manual and ordering them, e.g. to operate on an appendix or to build a high-rise block. The results will be like in a lottery, good one time, bad another.

Whether or not a priest will become an exorcist at all let alone a good one depends in large measure on the ghost which has possessed a person. If it wanted to leave after the first session then the priest scored a success and acquired faith in his abilities to do it. With every successful case it became easier for him even if he suffered a setback. A priest who fails at the first step will soon lose his enthusiasm. He may even want very much to become an exorcist and to help people but when he constantly fails he loses faith in what he's doing for ever. Discouragement may also be the result of a conviction that he is fighting against something powerful which he will never overcome. It may not even occur to him that it was only the way in which he carried out the exorcism that was unsuccessful. Either way, a defeat brings about a lack of faith in what he is doing. Often horror starts to creep in, too. The ghosts not only refuse to leave but they also try to frighten the priest more and more. That's why many priests give it up, and many others watching them don't even start on exorcism. Many priests are frightened of the devil, his vengeance, and they also fear possessed people. In such cases it is easier to ascribe mental diseases to every symptom and to send the patient off to a hospital just to have at least one case taken off one's hands. But these instances do not diminish, there are more and more of them.

Every year I receive several invitations to appear on television programs. Usually I decline because I don't like the way in which the subject of ghosts is to be presented. If I were to agree to take part it would bring more harm than benefit. Even little children know that ghosts exist. Showing the problems associated with ghosts in a light manner, which is the requirement for a short television program, brings harm. Contrary to appearances the subject matter is serious, wide-ranging and showing only a small fragment of it will not illuminate this complex matter but arouse spurious sensationalism. The latest proposal was unusual because I was invited to appear in a program in which exorcist priests were also going to take part. As I always do I asked what the guiding thought of the program was going to be and I was told that the priests want to prove on the basis of their case histories that possession is a mental illness. The producer, wanting to reassure me, told me that I wouldn't have to say very much. My job, as a secular exorcist, was to confirm this thesis. I replied that she had come to the wrong person because I think the very opposite. I advised her to ask, instead of me, some psychiatric doctors who, after all, know all about mental illnesses. She must have misunderstood me the first time. So I explained that it is possession itself which causes mental illnesses. Possession comes first and is followed by mental illness. Another important cause of these illnesses, if ghosts have no part in them, are mental injuries of all kinds. The producer started to ask me many questions. I declared that the best proof would be my patients who had been diagnosed as mentally ill by many priests (including those from the Vatican) and psychiatrists and are now completely well. I was asked for their addresses and telephone numbers. I received my patients' permission and passed them on to the producer. A few days before the program I was called with apologies that the program would not now be made because the priests who were going to take part in it had withdrawn, claiming that for the moment they were too preoccupied with their commitments. I was pleased by this turn of events because this program would not have brought any good. It would have confirmed the people possessed by ghosts in their conviction that they have no chance of a cure other than through many years, or life-long, treatment with psychotropic drugs, and yet that is not so. What helped these priests to adjust their convictions were conversations with my patients. Maybe it will also help other priests.

If knowledge about exorcisms had been passed down from one generation to the next, then beside the votary priest there would be another priest - the master who would have many years' experience of exorcisms. He would have taught the novice, encouraged him, but above all would have cleansed him when he was possessed during the instruction. In the history of the Church there were only a few who felt the need to practice exorcism. Hundreds of people begging for help came to their door. There were, however, so few of them that they collapsed with exhaustion wanting to help them all. They had nowhere they could find models so they acted by trial and error. Many of them fell victim to possession. Another priest wasn't at such case always able to help. Often he was unable to do so, and seeing his colleague's fate was afraid for his own safety. These exorcists were like lone sailors left to themselves and often ridiculed for their work.

All exorcists were ordained by their bishops. Many priests refused ordination because performing exorcisms frightened them. Many were forced to perform this role and often considered this "promotion" to be a punishment. Besides which, performing an exorcism under compulsion without the vocation meant the attempt was doomed in advance to be unsatisfactory. In 1972 Pope Paul VI abolished the ordination of exorcists. Now every priest can decide for himself whether or not he wishes to become an exorcist. The problem is that not only does nobody teach it in any seminary, the subject is never even mentioned. Hence many priests regard exorcism as a superstition, some relic dug up from the past, and therefore of no use to anyone.

A possessed person rarely gets help because priests help only when the possessed person blasphemes against the Church or against God. They ascribe the possession not to the ghosts of dead people, but to the devil, or Satan. This attitude changes radically when one of the priests or someone from the priest's family succumbs to possession. During cleansing, when the ghost leaves and then comes back, they notice that it is not a devil that has possessed them but, for example, their own mother or father who are dead. It would be difficult to ascribe satanic traits to the dead parents since, when they were alive, they were good, devout, honest, loving people. Then the priest opens his eyes wide with amazement and ascertains that in truth there is something which till that moment he had denied. Naturally, priests always start by looking for help within the Church, but they, too, don't always get it. Then some of them come to me. To begin with nearly every one of them conceals the fact that they are priests, but when they receive relief from their suffering they confess: "Mrs Pratnicka, you have probably already guessed that I am a priest. I felt awkward about telling you at the beginning. I apologize and thank you very much for your help". However, it's much more often the case that I provide help in an indirect manner, when I am asked to do so by a nun, another priest, a member of the family, or quite simply a parishioner from the church. Usually it will be someone whom I have helped previously. They don't always tell me straight off that it's about a priest, they simply give me the personal details.

A certain widow, the mother of sixteen children, long before her death stopped going to church. They lived in solitude in the fields, a long way from the main road. While the husband was still alive he would take the whole company on a cart to the church every Sunday. After his death the elder children went their way to the towns to look for work, some to study, and the younger ones who stayed at home were unable to harness the horse to the cart. None of the people living nearby took any interest in the fate of the numerous family even though the mother's health was deteriorating. She died of cancer, surrounded by her younger children. A mass of people came to the funeral. The preparations for the funeral were begun but for some unknown reason the priest wasn't keen on the burial. The mourners started to mutter amongst themselves that if the deceased had been rich then the priest would have come of his own volition and taken an interest in the funeral, but since she was as poor as a church mouse he was delaying the preparations. The day of the funeral arrived. It was the custom in that parish to accompany the coffin on the way to the church where the funeral service was conducted in the presence of the mourners. When the funeral cortège reached the church it found the doors locked (even though the priest had been informed about the time of the ceremony). All the local people were petrified with fear because they knew what was about to happen. The mourners who had come from further afield, on the other hand, hurriedly started to look for the priest. They stood outside the church for about an hour before he was found and they demanded that he bury the dead woman and open the church door. It was inconceivable to the mourners who had come from town that the priest might not want to conduct the requiem mass. They started to insist that he should not only bury the deceased but that he should, as was the custom there, conduct the service. The priest refused. When he was asked for his reasons, he replied: "This is a splendid opportunity for me to call my faithful parishioners to order. If I gave way now then from the next Sunday on I would have nobody at Mass. This way I'll summon everyone to attendance at church. Otherwise I would need to take a whip and force the faithful to come". No amount of excusing her by reference to her severe illness, to the distance, to the number and ages of her children helped. After a couple of hours' beseeching, the priest graciously agreed to participating in the funeral and the burial of the woman in the cemetery. But, to the mourners' distress, he would not allow anyone inside the church. The situation was such that only the priest had access to God and salvation which he would not give to those participating in the funeral. The faithful of that parish had been able to understand earlier stands like this when the person in question was some drunkard, or someone who was living in sin, or who had an illegitimate child or a lover. But in this case they judged the priest's behavior as being grossly exaggerated and they rebelled. The more harsh he was, the more they turned away from him. So, after this incident, the church was usually empty. Then I was asked to help. It transpired that the priest was under the sway of a large number of ghosts. Among them were some whom he had previously refused to bury and now they were very troublesome. But the majority of them were his close family. His and his whole family's faulty thinking meant that none of them wanted to depart from this world. I started to cleanse the priest, but the ghosts kept coming back. After some time the priest himself came to me, asking to be cleansed. With his collaboration I found it much easier and eventually the ghosts left him for good. When they had left, his behavior towards the faithful changed radically. He started to behave very differently, too, towards the dying. He understood that his attitude will decide whether a dying soul will go to God or stay on this side and will, in the future, be the cause of someone's possession. From that time on he was always present at the side of the dying, not only in the last moments of their lives but often for a long time before. I have also noticed the same change in behavior with other priests I have cleansed. Every one of them could henceforth give help himself, but when he couldn't manage then he knew where he should send his patient.

Many priests have wondered where I got my knowledge of ghosts since they had not been taught it even in theology. It's because I have always helped people when I was asked to and my intention was to assuage people's suffering. I didn't begin my activity by cleansing people of ghosts. It was only after years of helping people that I came across a case of possession and I knew nothing about the subject. Though I helped them successfully then, I saw "something" without being aware that that "something" was ghosts. This was, for me, a great discovery which I studied diligently. After I had helped several people, in some strange way I was given more and more cases of possession. I started to study it closely and every case brought greater understanding. After many years of study I reached the conclusions which I am describing in this book. It consists of years of observing the state of people when they are possessed and immediately afterward, when the people have recovered and return to normal. The states during which the ghosts leave and then return teach me a lot. What teaches me the most, though, are the ghosts themselves.

I have often asked myself why I look at the problem of ghosts so very differently from the way priests do. Is my view of the matter mistaken? I have reached the conclusion that my experience and the experience of exorcist priests was acquired in completely different ways. Our views are different because I didn't do it under compulsion. Nor did I have to think that exorcism was a battle with the devil. I was not given a strict formula telling me that the problem is a devil and, consequently, I have to act in such and such a way, say this, ask about that. Just as well, otherwise I too might have been terrified by it. Since I didn't have all the baggage that hindered the priests I looked for the tools to help me understand ghosts. I observed, examined, checked, asked about everything I wanted to know at a given moment. I wasn't scared of what I was doing. My faith in God gives me the certainty that nothing bad will happen to me while I am doing what I am doing. I'm writing about this because through my many years of work I have noticed things which aren't even taken into account by priests and by the Church. The prevailing dogmas, formulas etc. simply do not permit it. I have noticed that what the Church calls Satan is nothing other than the ghost of some person who has died and which for some reason has not passed through to the other side of death's curtain (I name the reasons I have observed to explain this in the chapter "When they remain"). My observations are confirmed by all the priests who were possessed and whom I subsequently cleansed. They had thought the devil had possessed them but in reality it was someone close to them who had died and who was afraid to pass over to the other side because they had understood something awry or felt themselves to be unworthy. Some of the perturbed ghosts are priests. They, like many others in their situation, guessed that for some reason they could not let themselves pass through to the other side. The fact that a ghost has remained since it was very afraid of punishment, felt itself unworthy or misunderstood the teachings of the Church does not make it a devil. Many people turned to me because they were very afraid of demonic possession. What always transpired was that it was the ghost of an exceptionally angry person. It felt it had been cheated by the Church, by its religion, by God, because it had believed in something which, after death, proved to be untrue. It was equally furious with itself, so furious that it was capable of killing someone. Nor should such a ghost surprise us. In everyday life we constantly meet living people who blame God for all their misfortunes. Condemning them will not bring any benefit. But it can be very harmful. The priests condemn the ghosts, accusing them of demonism, curse them and chase them off. But where is such a ghost to go? It is already in a situation where it doesn't know what to do with itself. It is lonely and lost. How much longer does it have to put up with this? Jesus forgave his tormentors when He was still on the cross. Why should we human beings not forgive a ghost which has erred? When I start to help them they are afraid and they resist. When I explain everything to them, and thereby help to heal their problem, they are no longer mad at God. They were hating ghosts because they feared Him. They imagined God to be vengeful and punitive. They learned this kind of thinking from their parents, their environment. Wanting to keep a child well disciplined people often say: "If you're not well-behaved then God will punish you". When a child involuntarily does something wrong it is terrified not only that it will be punished by its parents but (which is even worse) by God, too. Embedding this program has consequences right to the end of a person's life and even after death. When a ghost has it explained that God is Love, that He loves it, and that all the ghost needs to do now is to forgive God and itself, and the ghost understands that, then at that moment it experiences love and departs. Often all the other ghosts which happened to be nearby also depart. They have taken advantage of my lesson, are full of gratitude and love, because they now know that God has forgiven them too. When a lost ghost isn't helped during exorcism in just this way, or when it is chased out of the possessed person, then perhaps the person concerned may be released from their suffering but the ghost will either return to them or it will go into someone else. The problem with that is that now it will be even more mad then before at everything and will be even more troublesome. It is all the same to the ghost what will happen to it now. There is no future for it. Since it is damned anyway, it's all the same to it however much evil it does and to whomever. It certainly didn't expect help and might not know that such help exists. It has suffered an injustice and evil gives rise to an even greater evil. It's the slippery slope that leads to a greater and greater abyss. That, among others, is why church exorcism take so long (the norm is two to three years).

I am certain that my observations would be confirmed by priest exorcists. Some of them are afraid even to think about it because if they admitted it was true it would bring down their knowledge and at least a part of their belief system. Besides which we still wouldn't have anyone to share this knowledge with. What they are supposed to believe has been set down by the Councils of Leon and Florence: "There are no good spirits other than angels, as there are no evil spirits other than devils. The souls of the dead go either to heaven or to hell or to purgatory. The dead who appear during spiritualistic séances or the souls of the dead present in living creatures in order to torment them are evil ghosts". In my view evil ghosts are not devils or satans, but "ghosts of evil" like hatred, jealousy, enmity, feeling of hurt, desire for revenge, bad will. Those are the devils tormenting people. It is with them that we have to come to terms inside us and not to succumb to them.

Religions explain the presence of evil in the world by the presence of Satan as a spiritual entity. That way we personify the devil giving him a personality. Satan is not an identity and does not have a personality. It is a force that comes out of our negative thoughts, actions and speech. It exists everywhere. If we create hatred, if we are accompanied by vengeful, insistent, destructive thoughts aimed against others, when we are jealous, desirous of revenge, when we are inimically disposed, feel unfairly treated, ill-will, then we create around ourselves negative currents. They join up with similar energy currents from other people and thus they accumulate. This constantly flowing energy intensifies creating a great, terrifying force. It is something that everyone can feel when they are near it, or when they come into permanent contact with an environment that's full of hatred and dark, oppressive power. This bad energy brings about in the person who creates it sicknesses and accidents. When it succumbs to the process of accumulation which stems from a large number of people then it becomes the cause of catastrophes. When the energy emanates from a whole society it becomes so intense that it causes cataclysms or wars.

From our positive thoughts, actions and words also comes an enormous force which may neutralize this negative force. Nature always tends to want to establish equilibrium and harmony.

Very many people are of the opinion, and this includes some priests I have met, that Satan is an invisible entity with a great power to do things, its strength being sometimes greater even than God's. And if God isn't always able to cope with it then what chance have me, mere people. It is the priests who created the idea of Satan. Its purpose was to keep the society of the time disciplined, and it was successful in that. People were then still at the stage of development where explanations would have had little effect. Mankind, however, has progressed in its spiritual development and what once was good now has the opposite effect. When we think of the devil as a creature (or person) then though people fear it the fear is not constructive, merely paralyzing, disarming. It brings more harm than benefits. Instead of leading to understanding, it leads to giving up, and it sows fear among many priests. That is one of the reasons why there are so few exorcists in the world willing to help people. They are panic-stricken about Satan. When they understand the idea of the devil correctly then the time needed for exorcisms will shorten markedly, needless suffering experienced by the possessed person and the ghost alike will end, as it will for the exorcist priest. If the devil really did exist then God could not be God Almighty. He would rule over just a part of the Universe and Satan would rule over the other part.

But the devil exists only in our minds. Whatever is to be

found there will be manifested outside. One can't say that evil is either inside or outside us. When it is real to us then it is inside and outside. There is no way that one can separate it. Depending on what our leading thoughts, actions and words are so will our reality be. It is our perception of the world that governs our reaction to our surroundings. That's why two people finding themselves in the same enclosed space may react completely differently to the situation. One of them may be morbidly unhappy and the other may see nothing but joy. Everything depends on our conception which drives our perception. It is that which ensures that inside us there is either good, or God, or evil, or "Satan". If we think good thoughts, speak well and perform good deeds then there is no need for us to fear the devil because we'll always be safe in God's hands.

Many people find it impossible to believe that a good God could have created evil, too. That's why they find it easier to believe in the existence of the devil and to ascribe to him the creation of evil in the world. Nevertheless it was God who created good and evil. Even though God can do "evil", He has chosen to do only "good" since He has unlimited power. Even if "good" assumes the form which could be interpreted as "evil" then it is still "good" and comprises part of the Divine Plan. God's Project. God knows what to preserve, what to take away, what to mend and what to destroy. Even if He destroys something He will create it again in contrast to some people who, when they have broken something, are unable to recreate it. It is hard for us to see the "good" in "evil" at the moment in which it is happening. That comes from a lack of understanding, only and exclusively that. It's only when we look at the thing we interpreted as being "evil" from time's perspective do we comprehend the total meaning of the appearance of that "evil". "Evil" is a kind of shock, the consequence of errors that we have committed. When we experience the effects of our errors we are shocked and we realize that what we once did was not appropriate. We don't have to persist in our errors. Even if we commit them a hundred times it doesn't mean we have to continue to do so. From the time we become aware of this and we start to think, speak and do what is good then, in the future, we will avoid "evil". The appearance of that which we interpret as "evil" is our lesson, something we had to learn. When we understand that we will also notice that it is our errors that are the causes of our suffering and our misfortune, and not the devil or Satan. We will see that in reality everything in this world is for us a good, even "evil". We will also see that we are the creators of every event that happens in our lives. If we do not understand the lesson, in other words if we don't draw from our experience of "evil" the appropriate meaning which God has given us for the growth of our souls, then another opportunity will come along. If we understand it this time then there will be no more "evil" happening to us. I am not the only who thinks this way. In the Bible, too, it is written: "I form the light, and create darkness: I make peace, and create evil: I the Lord do all these things" (Isaiah, 45, v.7).

As you can see, God created all opposing pairs like, for instance, white and black, hot and cold, long and short, healthy and sick, as also good and evil, just so that every human being can fully experience everything. If everyone was happy then how would they know that what they are experiencing is indeed happiness? How would they recognize it? If only good existed then you would not find out that what you are going through at this moment is indeed good and not something else. You would not experience joy if sorrow didn't exist, you wouldn't know what health was if there was no sickness. You would not know what safety was if you were never in any danger. By analogy, you wouldn't know what good was if there was no evil. So it is that good is nothing other than the diametrically opposite pole of good. On the line between good and evil there are very many shades of good and evil, depending on the direction in which we are moving.

I believe there is only one great scale. At one end is Love and at the opposite end fear (and all its derivatives, like hatred, desire for revenge, envy, jealousy, feeling of guilt etc.). When we are moving towards Love we feel well, we are happy, healthy, safe, we have all we need to fulfill our lives. Love is limitless, never ends, is the Love of God without beginning or end. When we go in the direction of fear then we feel worse and worse, we start to suffer, fall ill, feel insecure and unsafe, unloved, unhealthy, cold, restrained, deprived of means to live. The closer we get to the pole of hatred (fear) the more we feel a lack of everything. The thing we feel the greatest lack of is Love. Love has created us and we are Love. We desire it, therefore, more than anything else in the world. It's like on a bitterly cold night we wanted to get warm by moving away from the burning fire. But there is no need to be afraid. God is constantly watching over us and when we move too far away He reminds us that we are going down the wrong road. First, He will remind us of Himself gently. That's when we get a feeling that we're not going the right way. If we don't listen to this, He will make us feel it more strongly. If we continue to resist we will sense it even more intensely. We might even notice some phenomenon - the further we move away from God, the greater the fear that we experience, the fear of what will become of us, the fear that there is never enough of anything. That's when we feel that everything we need has to be fought for. That's when our self-hatred intensifies, our hatred of God, of the whole world. We feel like we were in a dead-end where the more we desire something, the further the object of it moves away. We haven't noticed that it's we who are moving away from God. That's when it seems to us that we are in the clutches of Satan.

When people use this force in a wise, creative, harmonious way then they call it God, Allah, Brahma, Buddha, Love, health, good, happiness, riches, peace, freedom, fulfillment. When we use this same force in a harmful way, injuring ourselves or others, then we will call it the devil, Satan, fear, misery, suffering, deprivation, limitation. Every force in Nature can be exploited in two ways. Fire can cook our dinner for us or it can burn us, or even burn down our home. Water can quench our thirst, give life to plants, but it can drown us, destroy fields. It is not water or fire that are evil, but the way we approach them. That's why it's my view that the theological devil is an invention of the Church.

Many of you will say that the devil is mentioned many times in the Bible. That's true, but the Bible, like other Holy Books, was written in the language of those times and the meaning of the words used in it isn't always the same as it is in the contemporary world. The Greek word to describe the devil *is diabolos* - creating barriers. Stretching back as far as we can into antiquity, secret knowledge was concentrated in the hands of the priests. They guarded it like it was the most precious treasure and they passed it down from mouth to mouth, from generation to generation, in the strictest secrecy. The entire contents of this knowledge was encoded through the use of allegory and symbols. This made certain that it wouldn't pass into unauthorized hands. Oral accounts and the explanations of the master ensured that its deep contents would not be lost. When the alphabet was invented (about a thousand years before the birth of Jesus), the stories that had been passed down from mouth to mouth by the elders started to be written down on parchment scrolls. The priests were unable to contain this avalanche and they started to censor everything that was written down. The Bible received its name in honor of the town Byblos where the alphabet was invented. The New Testament was written down in the same way long after the death of Jesus. None of the evangelists describing his life knew Him personally. The writing of it was finished nearly three hundred years after His death. Throughout the period when the New Testament came into being, the priests censored and selected its contents. Nevertheless not everything that was written found its way into the final document since several churches had already sprung up out of Jesus' teachings. Within each one of them, the priests decided which elements of Jesus' history could be told and in what way. Even many centuries after the first books had been written down, the Church's Great Council was prescribing again which truths and doctrines could be contained in the official Bible - and which disclosures would be "premature" or "unhelpful".

Besides which, the Church has often declared its faith in something which was later discredited when it turned out to be false, e.g. that the Sun moves round the Earth, or that the Earth is flat etc. Subsequent discoveries overturned the significance of those that existed previously. Is it not the case also that in the matter of the devil and of the possession of people by ghosts that the Church is in error?

Summing up, since the times of Jesus every human being who believed in God could perform exorcisms for themselves and for their nearest and dearest. They did it effectively and no-one needed to help them do it. Later this was forbidden and people were commanded to turn exclusively to priests. Then they, too, were forbidden to do it. Fear of punishment excised very effectively the knowledge of exorcism from people's memories. Contemporary man turns to priests for exorcism.

They for the most part are unable to help. So, over a period of centuries, people have gone round in a huge circle. Unable to get help from priests, contemporary man is forced to help himself, just as in Jesus' time, and to use the power that God gives to every believer. Those who are interested in studying this subject should refer to, among others, the works of Father Gabriele Amorth, who is an exorcist in the diocese of Rome and the president of the Association of Exorcists. In his books he writes about people who have come to him and who had unsuccessfully sought help over many years. He asks this question: "And how many are there who will not receive this help?". And he himself gives this reply: "Very many, and that's because there are very few priests who want or know how to do it".

CONCLUSION

I hope that the majority of readers have understood my purpose and that they have now resolved what to do with themselves after their deaths. I also hope that I have at least in part softened your fear of death but above all that I have made you conscious of the fact that one should not detain those who have died but allow them to depart in peace.

Those who by dint of their profession meet with death on an everyday basis have a great part to play here. These are the people who work in hospices, retirement homes, hospitals and of course priests. Your duty is not only to ensure that a person dies with dignity but also that they are not afraid to pass through to the other side and that they do not swell the ranks of wandering ghosts.

Many people ask me this question: "Mrs Pratnicka, how can it be? Everything was done the way it should have been. When our... (here the names change) died, the priest gave the last rites, a normal funeral followed, there was a Mass. Why then did the ghost not leave? What was amiss in it all?". I think I have given a satisfactory and exhaustive reply to that question.

If we forgive everything and everyone (but above all ourselves) then, having the knowledge we now possess, death will not take us by surprise. Without any encumbrances, fully conscious and trustingly we will direct ourselves towards the Light, into the hands of a loving God. I wish everyone that with all my heart.

HELP

Dear reader, if you are in a situation where you cannot cope you may turn to me and ask me to help at the following address:

Wanda Pratnicka
P.O. Box 257
81-963 Gdynia 1
Poland
E-mail: office@TheExorcisms.com
Web: www.TheExorcisms.com

You may also phone my office at:

New phone numbers: 15
US: 631 402 1254
UK: 0 2081 900 405 12

In case you are calling from the <u>United Kingdom</u> you can dial:

0 207 078 7562

If you are calling from the <u>United States</u> your phone number is:

858 964 4685

I will need to have the following information:

1) Forename and surname
2) Date of birth
3) Place of permanent stay
4) Symptoms of the problem

For the help to be effective I will most often need to have the details of all the people residing in the house/apartment because in the majority of cases the whole family is in need of help. Consultation by telephone or email and to ascertain if a problem is connected with possession by ghosts or has some other cause is free of charge.

If the subject of this book has aroused your interest then I will be happy to hear your opinion of it.

BOOK ORDERING

You can order this book at the following address:

Wanda Pratnicka
P.O. Box 257
81-963 Gdynia
Poland
e-mail: order@TheExorcisms.com,
or use our ordering page at
www.TheExorcisms.com , or
phone us at: + 48 58 555 9815, or
fax us at: + 48 58 550 6812

DONATIONS

Dear Reader! I receive hundreds of letters confirming how essential the knowledge contained in this book was to its readers, how it changed their lives, how it helped them look at life from a completely different perspective. Oftentimes readers emphasize that this book should be read by everyone, that it should find a place in just about every home. I am of the same opinion. There are so many people who find themselves in such dire financial straits that they cannot afford to buy books at all. Some of them have the courage to ask for help, others do not. Naturally, I help everyone, using all the means available to me.

My patients are people from all over the world. Having such a panoramic overview and knowing that the problems described in this book affect the majority of people, I would like to disseminate this knowledge among the very poorest people whose need for it is often the greatest. My ambition is to submit a free copy of the book you are holding in your hands to every library in the world. Unfortunately my financial means do not permit me to fulfill this ambition. That's why, dear reader, I'm asking for your help in this initiative. If you agree with me and would like to give financial support to this undertaking then I would ask you to contact me at the following address:

Wanda Pratnicka
P.O. Box 257
81- 963 Gdynia 1
Poland
Email: donation@TheExorcisms.com

You may also make direct payment into my bank account (marked "Donation"):

Account holder: Centrum, Wanda Pratnicka
Bank: Citibank Handlowy
Bank's address: ul. Senatorska 16, 00-923 Warszawa
Account number: PL58 1030 0019 0109 8530 0002 8082
Swift code: CITIPLPX

Thank you.

Wanda Pratnicka